MW00586838

THE VANISHING AT SMOKESTACK HOLLOW

ALSO BY JAKE ANDERSON

Gone at Midnight: The Mysterious Death of Elisa Lam

The Vanishing at Smokestack Hollow

A MISSING FAMILY, A DESPERATE PLAN,
AN UNSOLVED MYSTERY

JAKE ANDERSON

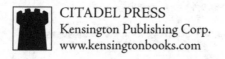

CITADEL PRESS
Kensington Publishing Corp.
www.kensingtonbooks.com

CITADEL PRESS BOOKS are published by

Kensington Publishing Corp.
900 Third Avenue
New York, NY 10022

Copyright © 2024 by Jake Anderson

All rights reserved. No part of this book may be reproduced in any form or by any means without the prior written consent of the publisher, excepting brief quotes used in reviews.

All Kensington titles, imprints, and distributed lines are available at special quantity discounts for bulk purchases for sales promotions, premiums, fund-raising, educational, or institutional use. Special book excerpts or customized printings can also be created to fit specific needs. For details, write or phone the office of the Kensington sales manager: Kensington Publishing Corp., 900 Third Avenue, New York, NY 10022, attn Sales Department; phone 1-800-221-2647.

CITADEL PRESS and the Citadel logo are Reg. U.S. Pat. & TM Off.

10 9 8 7 6 5 4 3 2 1

First Citadel hardcover printing: October 2024

Printed in the United States of America

ISBN: 978-0-8065-4247-8

ISBN: 978-0-8065-4249-2 (e-book)

Library of Congress Control Number: 2024936525

For Laura, love o' my life, and Madyson, the indigo child

https://www.okproperty.com

LAND FOR SALE, ACREAGE AVAILABLE, OFF-GRID | OK PROPERTY

There's land for sale on Panola Mountain, OK, including secluded mountain acreage, cheap off-grid property with cabins and tiny houses. Legacy land in Latimer County, great for hunting wildlife, the perfect property for a dream home awaits . . .

———————

https://www.soonersellers.com

BUY CHEAP LAND, SECLUDED MOUNTAIN PLOTS | SOONER SELLERS

Find land for sale in Panola, OK including cheap property, secluded homes, and undisturbed land . . . A once in a lifetime opportunity to own this gorgeous 12.1 acre off grid, legacy land, true food foraging paradise. The perfect property for freedom, modular living . . .

———————

https://www.modularliving.com

SHIPPING CONTAINER HOMES & STORAGE | LIVING OFF GRID

Modular living rejects the daily grind, the rat race. Living independently and minimally off the grid allows you to realize your destiny. Unplug from the chaos and uncover the real way to live life on your own terms. Disconnect and Discover your true freedom today!

———————

https://www.evangelicalwiki.com

HOW TO CAST OUT DEMONS, SPIRITUAL WARFARE | EVANGELICAL . . .

"Lord, you know the demons that oppress me. I renounce any form of the occult in my life and the life of my ancestors." Deliverance warriors, fight spiritual sickness and holy assault. Demon manifestations may include coughing, yawning, tears, vomiting, screaming, & speaking in tongue, as well as financial despair, addiction, mental illness, & physical decay . . .

Contents

Prologue

IN SOUTHEAST OKLAHOMA, THE FLOODPLAINS and oil fields of Ironhead Country merge with the lake shoreline, meandering 800 miles in the shape of a gnarled shuriken. Under its spindly northwest arm, the reservoir cradles the sleepy terminus town of Eufaula.

Highway 9 bypasses the Canadian River junction and exits onto Honeysuckle Road, which cuts through a swampy scrubland of pin oaks, willows, and cottonwoods. Turtles nap on the denuded roots of cypress trees, and every so often they tumble and *plop* into the water, sending ripples to the shore. At sunset, mosquitoes and fireflies hover against indigo sky, and bullbats plummet into a blood-red horizon.

The first evening breeze breaks the summer heat, stirring a timeless rhapsody of chirping crickets, buzzing cicadas, burping frogs, and the whistling birdsong of geese and whip-poor-wills.

Honeysuckle dead-ends just downwind from the town's solid waste transfer station, where on a June evening in 2009, the McIntosh County Fairgrounds hosted two separate gatherings.

The first, a large riotous crowd of cowboys, rodeo staffers, and spectators, flocked to and packed the Eufaula Round-Up Club for a night of bull-riding, mutton-busting, and steer-wrestling. Hints of manure and popcorn, along with the auctioneering prattle of the announcer, carried to the perimeter of the grounds where the second, much smaller, more pensive group formed a line and disappeared into a squat white event compound.

Flanked by two church elders, a portly bespectacled pastor stood at the head of the gathering and allowed everyone to get settled on the rectangular bales of hay comprising the makeshift pew. Behind him, a banner read:

Muskogee Seventh-day Adventist Church
"Proclaiming The Three Angels' Messages"

He asked about their doubts and fears and then, introducing the Book of Daniel, reviewed scripture and literature from the Adventist org.

Before Jesus's Second Coming, He is investigating the entire earth, everyone who has ever lived, every choice every human being has made...

As he scanned the faces of the congregants, Alonso took notice of a gaunt couple in their late thirties or early forties who, accompanied by their young daughter, observed from the back shadows. The dyadic intensity of their gaze momentarily caused the pastor to double-back and lock eyes.

... God wants it to be clear to us, and to the watching universe, that not one person will experience a fate they did not choose.

AFTER THE SERVICE, Brandon and Reeves collected sign-up forms and answered questions. As Pastor Alonso shuffled around, chatting with the prospective parishioners, he noticed the couple—both skinny as rails—waiting to move up in a line to talk to Brandon.

Lazing between and around their waists was a cherubic little girl with bleached blond hair.

There was something about the couple and their girl that caught the pastor's attention. He couldn't pinpoint what it was— a feeling of unease.

When they reached the front of the line, Brandon had to lean in to hear them over the din of cross talk. The couple took turns speaking—the man into his left ear and the woman into his right.

After a few exchanges, the church elder glanced up, seemingly caught off guard by something that was said.

As he moved closer to eavesdrop, Pastor Alonso caught bits and pieces from the woman, whose wavy, auburn hair concealed her eyes as she spoke. She said something about a dark presence, an oppressive force in their home.

The man gave an animated description of seeing "three or four of 'em" on their "roof at three in the morning."

Usually a pillar of forbearance, the elder looked increasingly uncomfortable with the conversation. The pastor moved even closer.

The child, who had become restless, slid playfully into her mom's arms and began to softly sing.

"Sometimes they... appear as children ..." the woman said, running her hand through the girl's blanched hair. "... Stormy speaks to them—she's my little indigo child."

PART I

The Mountain

"The woods are lovely, dark and deep,
But I have promises to keep,
And miles to go before I sleep"
—ROBERT FROST, "STOPPING BY WOODS
ON A SNOWY EVENING"

CHAPTER 1

Footprints

For the Latimer County Sheriff's Department, the night-mare began late in the evening on October 17, 2009. Sheriff Israel Beauchamp, who was burning the midnight oil as per usual, took a break to bull-jive with the handful of deputies still on duty.

That's when the call came in.

A deer hunter from Red Oak reported an abandoned truck left in a clearing on Panola Mountain.

Probably a theft or a dead alternator, Beauchamp thought.

He dispatched one of his deputies to check it out.

Nestled within the densely wooded Sans Bois Mountains, Panola and its closest neighbor Red Oak originated as remote outpost camps for railroad workers in the 1850s. Neither town was developed with access points in mind. Navigating to a discrete location is difficult even with precise directions and the aid of daylight.

By night, forget it.

No officer really wanted to traipse alone into the untamed wilds in the middle of the night. Earlier that year in May, Sasquatch hunters in the nearby Kiamichi Mountains made headlines when they reported footprints measuring fifteen inches long and five inches wide. The local history is rich with folklore about a tall, reddish-brown creature with big eyes who is said to make birdlike noises that mimic the whip-poor-will and the owl.

Deputies faced more tangible threats, of course, in stumbling upon a meth lab cook with nothing to lose. But cryptozoological mysteries are a tradition in these parts—a veritable tourist industry for some towns—and the stories cascade down to each successive generation of children.

At the base of the mountain, Deputy Ferguson met the deer hunter who called in and followed his truck up into the dark abyss.

"You'd've never found it otherwise," the man told him.

After weeks of rain, muddy debris and disgorged thicket formed a thick blanket of earthy gruel over the slopes. Ferguson ascended the roads carefully, hugging a seemingly endless succession of tight switchbacks in a spiraling orbit up and around the cliffs. With little moonlight and a thick mist descending, he could see only the wispy spectral patterns illuminated by his low beams.

Eight miles later, his guide pointed him down a narrow, pitch-black path, then turned around and left. His red taillights gradually disappeared.

Ferguson took a dirt-access road that was more like a mudflow and entered a clearing.

Flipping on his cruiser's high beams afforded a slightly enhanced glimpse of the extent of his isolation. This was what people meant when they said the "middle of nowhere."

As he stepped out of the cruiser, his eyes caught something ahead, a faint prismatic gleam like pixie dust or pixelation puncturing the blackness. The deputy pointed his flashlight into the gloom and saw rear retroreflectors: about thirty yards down the road, banked against the bluff near the clearing's unmarked egress, sat the abandoned truck—a white utility pickup, just as the deer hunter reported.

Pausing, he shined his light up at the rock face of the bluff overlooking him, and then back to the clearing, where he caught something else in the near distance, the garbled frame of a junkyard vehicle covered in graffiti and occult symbols.

Ferguson proceeded on foot, watching as his once shiny, county-issued loafers were covered in mud.

When he turned his light back to the truck, now only twenty yards away, the deputy thought he saw movement in the rear window—a stirring so slight and ephemeral it might have been a perceptual artifact or his eyes adjusting to the dark.

He focused squarely on the window for ten seconds…

When the movement did not repeat, he cautiously approached the rear of the truck. Projecting the white fluorescent beam of the flashlight into the cabin with one hand and cupping the other over his eyes, he leaned in close enough that the tip of his nose touched the glass.

At first, there was nothing. Then the deputy heard a bleating sound—a guttural moaning—as something eclipsed his light.

For a timeless moment, a feral glowing eye stared through him.

WHILE HIS DEPUTY was reporting to the scene, Beauchamp received a second call from the Red Oak man, who had returned from the mountain to clarify his initial report: he'd notified a nearby landowner about the location of the abandoned truck and this man remembered seeing a family of three—two adults and a child—with the vehicle a week earlier.

Beauchamp thanked him and then answered the call from Ferguson.

What the deputy said changed Beauchamp's calculus. The situation appeared to be more complicated than he originally thought.

The sheriff left one deputy to tend to the fort and told the other three to follow him to Panola Mountain. On the way, he had his deputy back at the office run the license plate number of the truck.

Beauchamp led his small caravan off Highway 2 into Wilburton and onto a backroad, ascending into the high sticks of the Red Oak area. When the troop reached the clearing on Panola Mountain, they inspected the partially shattered cabin window.

Ferguson sat on the ground, hunched over. The deputy held in his arms a small, emaciated dog, which licked his face, weakly.

When Ferguson called and told him there was a dog in the truck, there wasn't much of a choice but to authorize breaking the window. Beauchamp was reluctant to enter a locked vehicle without probable cause. But the deer hunter said the truck had last been seen there with the family a week earlier. If the dog had been trapped inside this whole time with no food or water—which, by her behavior, appeared to be the case—it was a miracle she was still breathing.

Beauchamp opened the cabin door of the truck and shined his flashlight inside. There was nibbled feces on the seat and a cooler with a tiny bit of dirty water at the bottom.

At around 11:00 p.m., Colton Mangum's phone rang. It was a Saturday night, and the high school linebacker was spending the night at his buddy's house. A call from the McIntosh County Sheriff's Office was about the last thing he expected.

"You Bobby Jamison's boy?" the sheriff asked.

"Yessir," Colton replied. "He's my stepfather."

The sheriff told him that a truck registered to Bobby had been found abandoned.

"Do you have their home number?"

Colton gave him Bobby's number, as well as his mother Sherilyn's number and the landline. The call abruptly ended, and Colton sat there, wondering what his family had gotten into now.

A short while later, the sheriff called back and asked Colton if he would try calling his mom and stepdad. He did, got nothing, and told the sheriff as much.

"We're going to send a deputy to check their home. Is their primary residence still off Texanna in Eufaula?"

"Yessir."

"Is that where you live, too, son?"

"No sir, not anymore," Colton replied with a lump in his throat.

The deputy heard only the sound of crunching gravel as he drove through the darkness of a flat backcountry copse, arriving at a remote vista of houses overlooking Eufaula Lake.

The neighborhood was part of a small community in a secluded town, where folks generally frowned upon midnight
welfare checks by the police, a fact that did not escape the deputy
as he pulled within view of the Jamison home and stopped. A
plume of dust rose into the glare of his low beams.

Framed against the black expanse of sky and water, the scene
unexpectedly lit up as several lights in the house were on, shining
through drawn curtains.

The deputy approached the front door and knocked several
times, then waited, listening for footsteps.

He knocked again, louder this time, and rang the doorbell.
Nothing.

Despite the electricity surging through its rooms and hallways,
the place appeared devoid of human life, a conclusion he radioed
back to the McIntosh County Sheriff.

On his way out, the deputy briefly glanced around the property, looking for any obvious signs of suspicious activity. At the
corner of the yard touching the dust road, the contours of a dark
object took form, visible only as a large geometric shape looming
in the empty night.

He approached, stopping a few feet from a large moving container. Swirling black lines came into view, obscured by the
blinding sheen of incandescent light reflecting off metallic alloy.

Someone had tagged the side of the container with spray paint.
He read one of the bulkier messages slowly, as though it were an
ancient cave painting, tracing each character with his flashlight as
he traveled the length of the pod:

> 3 CATS KILLED TO DATE BUY [sic] PEOPLE IN THIS
> AREA ... WITCHES DON'T LIKE THERE [sic] BLACK
> CAT KILLED

The Last-Known Point

The clearing on Panola Mountain was a well pad, one of the few
spaces in the area not ensconced in thick vegetation. Like the rest of

the mountain, it was accessible only by a narrow, unpaved oil and gas access road, a relic of Oklahoma's twentieth-century petroleum boom.

The truck had come to a stop near the end of the clearing, nose-down on a slight incline with three-foot rivets of sludgy ground soil enclosing both the driver's and passenger's sides.

Not an ideal place to stop and stretch one's legs.

There was nothing on the ground around the vehicle. The tires had air. There were no footprints, no signs of damage, broken glass, or blood in the immediate area. There was no evidence that any kind of struggle had taken place, nor was there any indication of a maintenance issue with the vehicle.

Officers took inventory of the truck's interior. They found bill-folds, a purse, jackets, a map, a GPS device, and a couple of cell phones, all splayed in a pile. The IDs in the billfolds belonged to Bobby Jamison, to whom the license plate was registered, and Sherilyn Jamison.

Records showed the two had a six-year-old daughter named Madyson, and objects in the vehicle, including a life-sized Barbie doll, indicated the presence of a child.

Clues

The scene suggested the family had meant to return to their truck but, for whatever reason, didn't. The most immediate logical ex-planation available was that they had stopped to travel by foot and gotten lost.

Using the family's cell phones and GPS device, deputies recon-structed their last logged movements. The data drew Beauchamp and company about 100–200 yards north through trees and vege-tation so thick they couldn't see more than a few feet ahead. As deputies called out to the Jamisons, their visibility was limited to awkward glimpses of colleagues crashing through the wet foliage and fumbling with their flashlights.

The small troop reached a hill and began to ascend it. Halfway up, they saw footprints—small ones, the unmistakable impressions of a child's shoes—that tapered off quickly, dead-ending at the rocky plateau at the top of the bluff.

LATER IN THE early morning hours, deputies found an image on one of the family's cell phones. It showed a young girl, presumably Bobby and Sherilyn's daughter Madyson, standing alone. The scenery around her—boulders, trees, maroon and green leaves, and pine needles—resembled the bluff at the top of the hill where they spotted the footprints.

In the picture, the little girl's bleached blond hair flowed down over her shoulders. She wore a light-colored T-shirt and blue-jean trousers. Her eyes peered into the distance, mouth open, exposing her missing front baby teeth. Her arms were crossed in a kind of anxious self-hug, with her right hand grasping her left elbow and her left hand holding her right bicep.

She was either standing or mid-step, in what appeared to be a candid picture—unposed, unplanned ... and unnerving.

AS THE FIRST inkling of dawn touched the overcast mountain, Beauchamp stood alone, assessing the truck from a new angle on the clearing.

Something was off.

A shadowy figure silhouetted against the sky approached him from the direction of the truck, where the deputies' activity had intensified.

"Sheriff, I think you need to see this."

"What is it?"

Beauchamp followed him back over to the truck.

"We found something underneath the floor compartment ... there is a substantial amount of money in this vehicle, sir."

As he parted the silent gathering of deputies, a shrill, cold wind picked up around them like the atonal swell from an orchestra pit. It stopped as suddenly as it started, and a stillness descended.

Beauchamp's eyes lowered to the surface of the back seat, where stacks of cash spilled out of a bank bag.

CHAPTER 2

The Search

As the morning of Saturday, October 18, 2009, broke over the mountain, Latimer County deputies got their first daylight glimpse of the truck and the clearing on which it had been abandoned. The cold rain persisted, and more fog rolled in, smearing the tree line into a spectral blur.

Upon seeing the money, which amounted to approximately 32,000 dollars, Beauchamp ordered everybody to step back to prevent contamination. He had the area taped off as a potential crime scene.

"In the backwoods of southeast Oklahoma," Beauchamp later remarked, "when a sheriff finds that much money, his mind automatically goes to drugs."

He found it very unlikely that the adult Jamisons would have voluntarily walked away from their vehicle when it contained this kind of money—not to mention their dog—but there were no signs of a struggle or foul play, which typically leaves behind physical clues or trace evidence.

The police eventually confirmed that up to a week or more may have elapsed between the time that the Jamisons were last seen and when the truck was reported. Plenty of time to clean up

THE SEARCH   15

any incriminating artifacts. But, if the Jamisons had been the target of a crime, why did the perpetrator leave behind their truck? And the loot?

Beauchamp began reaching out to family members of the Jamisons, delivering the kind of cryptic news one hopes to never receive from a law enforcement officer.

He also contacted the Latimer County Emergency Management, which enlisted the help of all the local fire and forestry departments, as well as Emergency Medical Services (EMS). As word spread that a family was missing, searchers and law enforcement officers from other agencies and counties began arriving, as did local residents, some of whom showed up on four-wheelers and ATVs.

What the volunteers lacked in formal search and rescue experience, they made up for with their familiarity with the area. This was important because, in addition to the chilly temperatures, heavy rain, and poor visibility, searchers faced a vast, treacherous, and labyrinthine terrain.

Several K9 teams arrived, both live scent tracking and human remains detection (HRD). The tracking dogs were given items from the Jamisons' truck to help them establish a scent. The HRD, or cadaver dogs, searched for the scent of human decomposition.

The first dog to get a hit led his handler on a mad dash through the rainy, uneven forest. Several more dogs lit out in other directions, sniffing and yipping.

Their paths eventually converged in one location.

The Aspiring Marshal

On his one day off, Reade Hogan received an early morning call from a Latimer County deputy requesting his assistance on Panola Mountain. They needed as many trained investigators as they could get, as well as his truck's flare unit.

Reade lived just southeast of Tulsa, in Tahlequah, about two and a half hours away from the mountain. He made it in just over an hour, blaring his emergency sirens and whatever hard metal he could find on the radio.

As soon as he reached the base of Panola and started his ascent, it became clear how challenging a search operation here would be from a logistical standpoint. The only thruway was a single one-lane access road covered in thick mud. Without his Tahoe's four-wheel drive, there's no way he would have made it to the top.

When he reached the clearing, he saw a number of other vehicles and about fifty people already on-site.

One of them, Sheriff Beauchamp, walked in his direction.

"Sheriff," Reade said, nodding.

"Get to work," Beauchamp responded without stopping.

The situation, Reade learned after asking around, was grim. If the Jamisons were out there alive—a big *if*, considering how long they had been missing—they faced the risk of dehydration and starvation.

Perhaps even more urgently, the longer they were exposed to wet, cold conditions, the greater the chance of hypothermia. According to the Centers for Disease Control and Prevention (CDC), hypothermia is responsible for an average of 1,301 deaths per year in the United States, based on data from 2011 to 2015. Even in non-freezing temperatures, hypothermia can incapacitate a healthy person in short order, especially in rainy conditions.

Lost Person Behavior

Compounding the direness of the situation was the child, Madyson. It made one hope, however naïvely, that the Jamisons had found refuge in a cave and built a fire. But this was a cinematic image of survivalism that experienced searchers say rarely plays out in reality. When lost in the raw elemental forces of nature, most people struggle to carry out even the most basic steps that could optimize their chances of rescue.

This is due to what is colloquially known as "woodshock."

Unlike the grids of our cities and districts, the forest wilderness lacks any defined paths, edges, or nodes. Like a fog or whiteout, this miasma untethers us from spatial reality, scrambling our cognitive maps. The realization of being lost activates an evolutionary trigger that makes it nearly impossible to stay calm or still. Primal recall, fueled by what search and rescue expert Robert Koester calls a "full-flown fight-or-flight catecholamine dump," mandates that we move.

Being lost in the woods, even for a few moments, conjures a physiological flashback to one of our most ancient collective traumas—when prehistoric humans were hunted by animal predators. The trigger deprives us of the ability to reason or recognize spatial cues, so we're lost and moving without any sense of direction, getting more lost with each passing moment. The best thing to do in this situation is to simply stop and stay in one place. But as the panic accelerates, and the urge to extricate oneself from the wilderness intensifies, lost people often make their situation worse by trying to cover more ground.

Eventually, as their blind arcs incrementally bend, lost persons begin to unwittingly travel in circles. This little piece of search and rescue folklore has been borne out in studies. Researcher Jan Souman took volunteers to Germany's Bienwald forest and the Sahara Desert and used GPS devices to track their efforts to walk straight. The results confirmed that without access to spatial signifiers or external cues, such as cloudy days or moonless nights, people can't travel on foot too much more than 100 meters from their starting point no matter how long they walk, because they're moving in circles. This inherent tendency to arc is the result of an accumulation of many small orientational and navigational misjudgments.

Fortunately, thanks to the effort of search and rescue teams, the vast majority, over ninety percent of lost and missing people, are found. But it's a time-sensitive enterprise if ever there was one. Data from the International Search & Rescue Incident Database (ISRID) shows that lost persons who aren't found within the first twenty-four hours have a twenty-five percent fatality rate. After fifty-one hours—just over two days—only one percent of lost persons are found alive.

The Jamisons were on day ten. And searchers knew little to nothing about their condition. Were they mobile? Were they trapped or incapacitated? Were they responsive? Injured or sick? Despondent or experiencing mental illness?

It's not impossible for a lost party to be rescued after such a prolonged period of time, but it's rare.

Scent Work

Reade ventured off the clearing into the forest to test his Tahoe's flare rig. He quickly learned that the terrain made off-road driving impossible. He would have needed a tank to scale some of the boulders—a flying tank to traverse the ravines. The lighting rig was a bust, too. The mountain's dense foliage absorbed photons like a coal trap; the flare's pyrotechnic luminance offered little more than disco-ball shimmers of fuchsia on the understory.

But he was still determined to help.

Reade worked for the United Keetoowah Band tribal agency, doing mostly data and DNA collection. The tribe had a cross-agreement with the US Marshals Service, and once a week, he got to go into the field and observe cases being worked on by marshals. Every two weeks, he assisted them as they checked in with parolees.

There was a clear pipeline between his job and the US Marshals, and if he played his hand right, that was a career path that was available to him. This day, he realized, represented an opportunity to both help people and prove his investigative mettle to state law enforcement officials. At the very least, it beat data entry and compliance rituals with convicted sex offenders.

Reade assisted a K9 tracking team that consisted of Betsy and her golden retriever, Hazel. Betsy was a short, heavyset woman with wise, expressive eyes and over twenty years of experience in search and rescue. Hazel was five, still a puppy at heart but a seasoned pro at tracking.

They started at the truck, the family's last-known point, and strafed laterally along the bluff wall until they were traveling uphill and north from the well pad. Reade watched Hazel in amazement as Betsy gave a mini-TED talk about canine scent work.

Every minute, she explained, a living human body sheds approximately 40,000 microscopic particles, called raft particles. We leave a constant trail of them everywhere we go. About half of them fall to the ground and concentrate there, while the other half stay in the air. The canine nose can track both through footprint-to-footprint on the ground or by air scenting. Among a trillion particles of air, a competent tracking dog can detect human concentrations as low as three. In 1994, police in Salt Lake City were searching for a girl who had been abducted into a car and driven off; a rottweiler got on her trail and air-scented for forty miles, leading police to the child.

The use of dogs' olfactory powers has a long history that extends back to ancient times. There are stories of seventeenth-century Swiss monks who needed dogs to find the snow-covered path back to their monasteries. During the late nineteenth century and early twentieth century, several countries trained "medical dogs" to locate wounded soldiers or ferry supplies, messages, and ammunition. During the Spanish War, "ambulance bloodhounds" sometimes sat in the trenches with soldiers. The US military sent around 30,000 dogs to assist in World War I (with ninety percent not returning home), and 200,000 for the Second World War, during which the idea of rubble searchers, or "disaster dogs," took form. Pearl Harbor inspired Dogs for Defense and the first formal conscription of "sentry" hounds into the wartime effort.

Some fifty years later, Oklahoma was the site of a horrifying historical event that popularized the idea of search and rescue dogs in the minds of Americans. The 1995 bombing of the Alfred P. Murrah Federal Building in Oklahoma City killed 168 people and wounded 680 others, many of whom were buried under mounds of rubble. K9 teams helped with the rescue effort, locating some survivors but many, many more who were dead. Finding so many lifeless bodies took such a toll on the dogs' morale that handlers staged survivors for them to find to lift their spirits.

Incredibly, at the time, there were only fifteen FEMA-certified disaster search dog teams in the entire country. After the OKC bombing, the training and deployment of search and rescue canines proliferated. Six years later, on 9/11, some 300 K9 teams were deployed just in the preliminary waves of first responders.

Reade watched Hazel stop and lift her big regal head solemnly into the air, nose quivering and moist, then drop it back down to the ground, huffing and snorting, for another round of reconnaissance.

Hazel led Betsy and Reade to the hill where the Jamisons were believed to have spent time. On the way up, they saw the child-sized footprints noted by the first deputies at the scene. He looked closer to study the impression and its dimensions.

Why only the one set? Reade wondered. *Where were the parents' footprints?*

They followed Hazel's lead to the top of the hill, where the scent seemed to terminate. Hazel ran around the perimeter searching for it, but she seemed agitated.

"It's okay, baby," Betsy said, giving her a treat. "Good girl!"

After a break, they pushed on.

Hazel would periodically get excited and go into tracking mode, as though locked onto a scent, only to stop in bewilderment. This happened multiple times throughout the day. Betsy said that in all her years doing search and rescue, she'd never seen such strange tracking conditions. The scent seemed to be everywhere and nowhere at once, as though someone had taken a vial of the family's raft particles and sprinkled them indiscriminately across miles of mountain terrain just to confuse the dogs.

But a week of persistent rainfall could have diluted much of the scent information. Most of the particles left behind by the Jamisons during their time on the mountain were now part of the Earth's hydrologic cycle.

"How accurate is Hazel when it comes to tracking?" Reade asked.

Betsy cited the higher-end estimates of up to ninety-six percent, depending on the conditions and environment, but there is

no exact answer. The question of cadaver dogs' accuracy was debated in court during one of "the most heavily reported missing
person case[s] in modern history." During an inquiry into the
2003 disappearance of four-year-old Madeleine McCann, investigators stated that cadaver dogs had identified the victim's "smell
of death" on a Cuddle Cat toy and her mother's clothes. But without the girl's body, they couldn't rule out a false positive.

The attorneys for Madeleine's beleaguered parents argued in
court that cadaver dogs have a success rate of only twenty-two to
thirty-eight percent. The prosecution pegged the number at more
like sixty to sixty-nine percent.

Ultimately, the accuracy of a cadaver dog depends on the specific chemicals emitted by a person's decomposing remains, which
themselves depend on a confluence of factors unique to each
case—the amount of time a body has been exposed, environmen-
tal conditions like temperature and humidity, and even the
victim's diet.

Researchers have to date identified about 452 unique compounds and esters (organic compounds) released by the human
body as it decomposes, but only eight of those are specific to humans (and pigs), and only five esters are specific to just humans.

The molecules putrescine and cadaverine have long been cited
as the signature components of our so-called human "death scent,"
but more recent research has shown that these two chemicals
aren't always present during decomposition. In fact, some of the
gasses released during the first and last stages have been described
as producing "pleasant" aromas. In the earliest phase of decomposition, the body excretes hexanal and butanol, which have been
compared to the smells of "freshly mown grass" and "leaf litter and
forest floors," respectively. During the first postmortem days,
these gasses also blend with hexadecanoic acid, which is commonly described as an aroma similar to "old people's homes."

Roughly a week after death, the human body starts producing
the putrid smells one commonly associates with rotting corpses.
This is the bloat stage, when gut bacteria produce a large volume
of gasses like dimethyl disulphide, trisulphide, and indole, adding

strong notes of garlic, rotting cabbage, and fecal matter. After that, active decay commences; marked by legions of squirming maggots that eat through the corpse's intestines, this stage unleashes 2-methylbutanoic acid, trimethylamine, and butyric acid, which induce scents likened to "cheesy feet," spoiled fish, and vomit.

Later in the decomposition process, large quantities of phenol, which is said to smell like "sweet, burning rubber," and finally, the earthy, "woody" notes of skeletonization, join the palette.

All of this is to say that cadaver dogs must differentiate the faint aromatic scent of human decomposition from the billion other organic scents contained in the wilderness. Fortunately, dogs have a secret weapon, a special vomeronasal tripwire called Jacobson's organ, a secondary olfactory system designed specifically for chemical communication. These nerve cells respond to a range of substances that often have no odor at all, allowing dogs to recognize and follow "undetectable" odors.

"The Jacobson's organ," Reade repeated.

Betsy winked and, with a grin on her face, said, "It's also why they like sniffing each other's butts."

The Cistern

Eventually, Hazel locked onto a hit that lured them deep into the woods. When she finally indicated they had reached the source, Reade and Betsy looked up and saw that they were not alone. Their path had intersected with several other canine search teams.

They stood before a water tank, a roughly ten-foot metal cylinder that rose like a monolith out of the forest groundcover. Besides the clearing and the hill, this was the only repeated hit of the day. The dogs kept returning to it.

Beauchamp arrived and arranged for the tank to be inspected. Everyone was cold, wet, and exhausted; now they braced for the very real possibility of finding bodies.

When the hatch opened, the inside of the cistern was dark. Flashlights exposed nothing floating on the surface. They slowly drained the water, which joined the rain in making a small swamp around the tank. Once again, they looked inside with flashlights. Nothing.

A heart-stopping false alarm—and a time-consuming one.

Somebody had started a mini-bonfire at center camp so that searchers could warm themselves from the bone-chilling cold. Reade went and held his hands close to the flames as they whipped and crackled against the starry night.

The young deputy only assisted in the search for that one day. And toward the early evening, he became too frustrated to continue.

Reade eventually left the mountain, driving back to Tahlequah in silence—no music or sirens this time. He thought about the lost girl—Madyson. Her footprints, her face in the picture.

Then he thought about his encounter on the mountain. He wouldn't say anything about it publicly for over a decade, but Reade had an experience on Panola that afternoon that would haunt him.

The Letter

The elements continued their assault, with temperatures remaining unseasonably low and frigid rain pelting the land. Sheriff Beauchamp couldn't remember a colder October. His friend, Deputy Adam Woodruff, who had arrived on day two with an abscessed tooth, felt like he was freezing to death.

On the third day of searching, it rained so hard that the sole access road—a circuitous tendril connecting the base of the mountain to the clearing—washed out, marooning a number of volunteers and personnel whose vehicles became stranded. Beauchamp had to call county services to come out with several metric tons of gravel and reconstruct the flooded zones with makeshift causeways.

Police, fire, and highway patrol crews, along with a gaggle of volunteers, continued searching all day Saturday and Sunday when six more dog teams joined the effort. Still, searchers found nothing.

On Monday, Beauchamp temporarily suspended the search, though small teams of locals familiar with the terrain continued looking for the missing family.

Under the headline "Authorities seek clues in search for family," *The Oklahoman* released one of the first newspaper articles about the case on October 22nd, reporting that authorities planned another full-scale search for the upcoming Friday. In the meantime, agents from the FBI and the Oklahoma State Bureau of Investigation (OSBI) began assisting the sheriff's office in interviewing family members and friends.

Beauchamp spent seventy-two consecutive hours searching before going home to grab a nap. He would practically live on the mountain for the next two weeks without finding any substantive leads on the condition or location of the family.

By the 24th, he was still not ready to publicly call it a "recovery," holding out hope the Jamison family was still alive. He owed that much faith to Madyson.

After discovering the money, deputies continued their inspection of the truck's interior, hoping to find more clues. And they did. Tucked away in one of the vehicle's messy nooks and crannies, they discovered a small heap of filled-out notebook pages.

Beauchamp later described it as a "hate letter" from Sherilyn to Bobby—eleven handwritten pages of resentment, frustration, and marital discord.

They also found empty prescription painkiller bottles.

The investigative side of the search intensified as privately, and soon publicly, Beauchamp and other law enforcement officials began to question their assumptions about the case. The biggest revelation came when members of the Jamison family were interviewed and said that Sherilyn owned a .22 pistol that she kept on or near her at all times.

CHAPTER 3

Hunting Season

Latimer County conducted another large-scale grid search in early November, using 100 new searchers, helicopters, drones, and a fixed-wing plane equipped with heat-seeking radar. Texas EquuSearch, a search and rescue organization, sent private investigators who inspected the terrain on horseback. The National Center for Missing and Exploited Children also assisted, meeting with Undersheriff Matt Bohn on the mountain.

Searchers looked for clothing, disturbed ground, and any creeks or waterways.

One volunteer said, "The tracking aspect of it is pretty much out the window. What you'll wind up doing is grid searches or stuff like this, looking for clues."

In search and rescue (SAR) operations, the grid search is a widely used method to search for lost persons in vast wilderness areas. It is a systematic approach that involves dividing the search area into smaller, manageable sections or grids, and then searching each grid in a coordinated and organized manner. This is particularly useful in complex search areas, such as the mountain wilderness of Panola, where the search area is large and difficult to navigate.

Sheriff Beauchamp, Undersheriff Bohn, Deputy Woodruff, and hundreds of search volunteers spent countless hours within arm's length of each other, moving in lines through the woods and wheeling around rugged features like a giant human drawing compass.

Eventually, the grueling physicality and exposure took a toll, and searchers began dropping out, sometimes collapsing. Because of the cold temperatures, when the first casualty hit, Beauchamp assumed it was due to hypothermia, frostbite, or possibly dehydration, but it was actually heat exhaustion. As the numbers climbed, he tried to organize a triage system so that searchers who needed rest or medical care were taken back down the mountain.

But as before, bottlenecks clogged every artery of the operation. Mud produced by rainfall, combined with the uneven terrain and smothering wreaths of tangled undergrowth, made ground transportation slow-going and difficult. Even the horses got gummed up and spooked. SAR and volunteers, already overwhelmed by the size and topography of the area, had to compromise their lines, abandoning inch-by-inch coverage.

The layers of slop complicated even the most basic and essential requirements for a search operation: site access and mobility. Dumping gravel onto the road was a workable stopgap measure until the rain stopped.

But the rain didn't stop.

"We've already had to have people towed out," Beauchamp told a reporter. "We've had people slide off the side. The conditions on the road are getting worse, and they're just going to get worse as more people come up here." When asked if the chances for good news were becoming slimmer, he answered, "It would be safe to assume that, yes."

The effort by air was no better off. Strong winds made navigation harder for helicopter pilots, who were already frustrated by the dense vegetation. The forested regions of the Sans Bois Mountains contain triple-canopy foliage—three distinct tiers of vegetation, which, combined with the mist, considerably reduced the helicopter pilot's overhead ground visibility. Hundreds of searchers moved in lines below but could hardly be seen, much less tracked.

Beauchamp tapped his connections to get some remote-control drones, which were significantly harder to come by in 2009. They deployed these first-generation drones to specific grids of the mountain to obtain photos and check for bodies, disturbed ground, and other clues. During one stretch, Beauchamp and Woodruff did drone reconnaissance for twenty hours straight.

But they didn't find anything related to the Jamisons.

When darkness fell in the evening, the black expanse felt positively existential. At midnight, Beauchamp was on the mountain, staring up at the sky as a helicopter did a pass. It was in the near distance, not more than 100 yards away, yet it seemed like it was in a different universe.

He imagined if, in a miracle, the pilot caught a glimpse of something in a tiny pocket of the darkness below, jumped on the radio, and excitedly announced, "Sheriff, I think I found something!"

"All right, where is it?"

Hard pause.

How would they even explain a location in the undifferentiated sea of blackness? Geographical coordinates and physical proximity felt meaningless here.

FURTHER COMPOUNDING THEIR difficulties was the approach of black-powder hunting season, which would begin in a few days. Oklahoma's popular nine-day muzzleloader harvest would draw over 100,000 traditionalist hunters wielding primitive firearms and ammo, ranging from flintlock rifles with Pyrodex pellets and sabot bullets to in-line muzzleloaders.

"That will just about make it too risky to be out there searching after that," Bohn told reporters.

Beauchamp echoed this, saying, "This is probably the last day we're going to do this for a while."

But the next day and week, searchers re-entered the woods donning bright orange vests, continuing to check off grids of land from the thousands of acres around them.

Again, they found nothing.

On the day before Halloween, nearly two weeks after the dis-covery of the Jamisons' abandoned truck, Sheriff Beauchamp issued a press release stating that his office would be scaling back on-the-ground search efforts.

"We have had more than three hundred and thirty volunteers and trained SAR personnel searching a ten-square mile area try-ing to find the Jamison family or clues of where they may lead in the direction that the family may have traveled . . ." Beauchamp stated, adding, "As I said before, I won't personally stop searching, even if it takes the remainder of my three years in office."

Though it wasn't explicitly stated, this presumably meant the authorities had given up on finding the Jamisons alive. As is the case in missing-person investigations, after a certain amount of time passes, heat imaging devices are no longer deployed, and searchers no longer bring live scent-tracking dogs.

The search for the Jamisons hadn't stopped. Both the OSBI and FBI were still assisting. But the case had shifted more into an investigative phase. There was nothing even close to a coherent narrative to explain the three missing family members. Some in-vestigators believed they had most likely gotten lost and died from injury or hypothermia; others believed they had been mur-dered in some kind of a drug deal gone bad.

More than a few investigators, including Beauchamp, considered the possibility that the family wasn't lost—that their disappear-ance was an intentional act, that they didn't want to be found.

Beauchamp also considered the possibility of a murder-suicide, though it was hard to imagine how their bodies had just vanished from the mountain. Killers can hide the bodies of their victims, but they can't hide their own, the sheriff later said.

The range of wildly divergent theories frustrated him.

"Normally, you can go through an investigation, and one by one, start to eliminate certain scenarios," Beauchamp said. "We haven't been able to do that in this case. With this family, every-thing seems possible."

But the way the truck was left had always felt off.

"It didn't look like to me that they got out and walked, it just looked like they got out and that was it," Beauchamp said to News on 6-TV. "They didn't take their coats—it was kind of cold that day—they didn't take their cell phones, of course they didn't take their dog, [either]."

It looked like the Jamisons had been approached, or even intercepted by, another vehicle and compelled to stop.

Early on, the question that tripped him up was: why would the perpetrators have left behind such a large amount of money? But there was a plausible answer to this. The cash was found underneath one of the seats in the Jamisons' truck; it could have easily been missed by an inattentive criminal, especially one who is cowed by a barking dog.

Perhaps the bigger question was: why had the Jamisons come to the mountain with 32,000 dollars in the first place?

CHAPTER 4

Three Cats Killed

IN EARLY NOVEMBER 2009, WORD began to travel throughout
the region that a family was missing in the mountains. The
McIntosh County Democrat ran two stories in its "Spotlight Crime
of the Week" feature:

> McIntosh County Sheriff's Office is conducting an in-
> vestigation into cows being shot and killed in the
> Central High area of McIntosh County. Since January
> of 2009, over 20 cows have been shot.

The next paragraph down read:

> McIntosh County Crime Stoppers are also offering up
> to $1,000 cash reward for information in the disappear-
> ance of the Jamison family . . . residents of Sandy Bass
> Bay #3 in McIntosh County.

When the missing posters for the Jamisons went out, residents
of Latimer County and McIntosh County saw the last image of
Madyson taken on the mountain. Now that it was blown up and

printed on paper, the details were a bit fuzzier, stretched, and washed out. The missing posters had been taped or stapled to telephone poles, business storefronts, and inside their places of employment.

Mrs. Sherilyn Graham of Quinton saw one in her office lobby. Gazing mournfully at Madyson, she imagined her child missing. When her eyes drifted over and saw that the missing woman had her first name, she felt a chill down her spine.

Madyson's two front teeth were missing, a visual hallmark for six-year-old children. Six is a big year in a child's growth: they start to develop a sense of body image; they begin to understand cause and effect relationships; they learn to differentiate between reality and imagination, between the past and the present; six-year-olds start thinking about the feelings of others and developing empathy for them. It is also the age at which children begin to grasp the finality of death.

The thought of ultimate horror befalling a child of that or any age made her feel sick. But Mrs. Graham had no clue at this time how the falling dominoes would lead her to intersect with the child in the picture. If she had, the nausea would have been overwhelming.

THERE WERE MANY opinions and interpretations of the meaning of Madyson's picture. Some believed the image was harmless— the same face children make all the time when they're feeling fussy or want something. Even if the look on her face was interpreted as being upset, this could be explained by any of the countless things kids get upset about.

For others, though, particularly those who knew the child, Madyson's expression and the way she held herself were deeply unsettling.

When family friend Niki Shenold first laid eyes on the picture, she broke down. She saw a frightened child who didn't know what to do. And she wondered who was behind the camera taking the picture—she didn't think it was Bobby or Sherilyn.

Niki spoke with Bobby's mother Starlet Jamison about the picture, and she agreed.

"Madyson is looking away from the camera," Starlet said, "she looks unhappy, and she has her arms crossed. She loved having her picture taken, and if that had been Bobby or Sherilyn behind the camera, she would not have looked like that."

Starlet was in a state of shock. Her granddaughter was her best friend, a special child—the greatest gift that ever graced her and her son's life.

The situation didn't make sense to her, particularly the suggestion that Bobby and Sherilyn had just walked off into the woods. There was no way that they would have left the dog, Maisy, in the truck, as she and Madyson were inseparable, Starlet said to media outlets. The dog went everywhere she did.

Starlet knew Bobby and Sherilyn would never let anything happen to their girl unless an event beyond their control took place on the mountain.

"It doesn't make sense that my son would just get up and walk away," she said. "They must have seen something they weren't supposed to see."

Sherilyn's mother, Connie Kokotan, believed this, too. From the moment she heard they were missing, Connie felt in her heart that her daughter had been murdered.

"There's no way they just wandered off and got lost," she told reporters. "What I truly believe is that they went up there, saw something they shouldn't, and were murdered by someone."

The way their truck was left looked to her like someone had forced them to stop.

"Everyone round here knows there are lots of evil people up in those mountains. . . . It's so isolated; I'm scared to go up there."

One of the most commonly repeated murder theories was that the Jamisons inadvertently stumbled upon or witnessed something—presumably a drug deal or illicit activity—that they weren't supposed to see. Southeast Oklahoma was in the middle of a methamphetamine epidemic at this time, and the secluded Sans Bois Mountains was a notorious destination for mobile meth labs and drug deals.

"There are lots of them up there," Starlet said. "It is well known. Maybe they stumbled across one of them when they were there and someone came after them?"

Starlet stood to lose her only child and her only grandchild; Connie had already lost one daughter and now feared losing the other. Niki was devastated and also irritated because it seemed like investigators were chomping at the bit to call the case drug-related and/or a murder-suicide, especially after they learned that Sherilyn owned a gun and had been diagnosed with bipolar disorder.

On a more logistical level, the notion of Bobby hiking miles into the rugged wilderness on foot didn't make sense to his closest family and friends, because they knew how difficult this would have been for him physically. He had suffered for years with chronic, debilitating back pain and frequently had trouble just standing and walking around the house. How would he have traversed miles of mountain terrain?

Eufaula Lake

The Jamisons lived on the far side of an isolated neighborhood called Sandy Bass Bay, a thinly forested hinterland of janky gravel roads that end in an arc of waterfront properties overlooking Eufaula Lake.

Nicknamed "the gentle giant," the reservoir is Oklahoma's largest capacity body of water, touching four counties and spanning over 105,000 surface acres. Beautiful, temperate, and filled with crappie, white bass, catfish, striper, walleye, and others, the lake is a top choice in the area among tournament anglers and casual fishers, as well as vacationers looking for marinas, houseboats, pontoon boats, ski boats, and paddleboats. Hunters flock to the lake's surrounding natural wetlands and floodplains for their 31,000 acres of public hunting land with ample populations of whitetail deer, wild turkeys, and cottontail rabbits.

The lake, which draws thousands of local and out-of-state tourists every year, is the heart and soul of Eufaula, as well as its primary source of economic revenue.

The Jamisons' home looked right out over the main attraction. On a sunny, warm day when the water and sky seem to merge into a celestial sphere, it's easy to see why a young family would choose this environment to put their roots down.

WHEN THE FBI conducted a search of the Jamison property, few details were released through the local papers about what they found inside the house. Agents confiscated one of the Jamisons' computers and Sherilyn's notebook. The content found in their search history and writings, as well as materials in both the truck and house, backed up statements by family and friends who said that Bobby and Sherilyn had been looking into buying land and likely drove to Panola Mountain to inspect a plot of acreage.

Local news articles reported that agents found a book on witchcraft inside the home, as well as a copy of *The Satanic Bible*. Other articles reported that there were notes found around the house addressed to Satan.

Thematically, this aligned with what was the most widely reported discovery from the search, which occurred outside near the perimeter of the property where the Jamisons owned a large moving container. Pictures from the scene showed a weathered maroon pod with the size and dimensions of a small bus, whose surface contained spray-painted messages.

The largest and longest message, tagged in black across the street-facing side panel, read:

> 3 CATS KILLED TO DATE BUY [*sic*] PEOPLE IN THIS AREA . . . WITCHES DON'T LIKE THERE [*sic*] BLACK CAT KILLED

Additional inscriptions, found on the door panels, said:

+ "God loves you"

+ "Only God can judge"
+ "We know who you are, may God Bless your soul,"
  and
+ "Gossip is a sin."

Sherilyn once told Niki, "If you have a problem with people, make them think you're crazy; the crazier they think you are, the more they'll leave you alone."

She knew their neighbors thought she was weird and leaned into it. When they took a walk past the house, Sherilyn would invite them in "for some witch's brew."

This tactical trolling intensified when one of their neighbors complained that the Jamisons' cats were getting into their shop boats. An argument ensued and, shortly thereafter, the family's cats started mysteriously dying. One died in the middle of the night; Sherilyn and Colton discovered her in the morning, lying motionless on the back porch.

The Jamisons, especially Sherilyn, believed the neighbors were poisoning the cats, but because they couldn't prove it (pet toxicology reports are expensive), Sherilyn retaliated by invoking spells against them and spray-painting intimidating messages on their street-facing moving container.

The Footage

Investigators found the moving pod less interesting for its graffiti and more for what Bobby's mother Starlet said was affixed to its exterior: a security camera system.

After agents confiscated the equipment, they found footage of Bobby and Sherilyn from the day they left their home for Panola Mountain. It was low-quality, blurry, and pixelated, but it provided two angles of the family's side yard and driveway, which contained several parked vehicles, including a car, a boat, and the white utility truck that would later be abandoned on the mountain.

Only a few minutes of still frames from this footage were publicly released, but Sheriff Beauchamp described the full video in several interviews. Most of it, he said, was Bobby and Sherilyn carrying bags and items from the house and packing them into the truck. This occurred dozens of times in succession: the two traversed the yard and driveway, loaded something into the truck, and returned back to the house.

It became apparent to Beauchamp that there was something off about Bobby and Sherilyn. They looked gaunt and thin—really thin. Based on family pictures, he knew both of the Jamison adults were skinny. But there's skinny and then there's emaciation.

Even more strange for Beauchamp was the way they were moving and behaving. Bobby and Sherilyn walked almost as if they were sleepwalking or in a trance. Over the course of dozens of trips back and forth between the house and truck, the couple didn't appear to speak a word to each other or interact at all.

At times, one of them took an item already packed into the truck and returned it back to the house, only to later carry it back out and return it again to the truck. This happened repeatedly—silently and seemingly arbitrarily undoing and redoing each others' work. At a few different points, they each stopped for long periods to stare absently into nothing.

Baffled and a bit creeped out by the behavior, Beauchamp had a psychologist take a look at the footage. Her analysis was, simply, "Drugs," probably methamphetamine.

This had already crossed the sheriff's mind, of course. During an interview, he admitted, "We automatically assume here in southeastern Oklahoma that if you're on a drug, it's methamphetamine, because we have such a problem with it."

The presence of the 32,000 dollars in the truck had been the first red flag. But the lack of any evidence supporting illicit drug use or possession had pushed back. Now, in the minds of Beauchamp and others, the security footage raised another red flag.

Would Bobby's pain pills cause such behavior? Starlet told them the pills "did make him woozy." But would prescription opioids, even at a high dosage, cause two people—one of whom hadn't even been prescribed the meds—to spend hours in a silent trance of packing and unpacking a car?

Once again, a promising piece of evidence had failed to answer any of the major questions. The case was maddening—none of the leads led anywhere.

When Starlet told investigators about the security cameras, however, she divulged something interesting. The installation of the cameras, she said, was her idea, a measure by which Bobby might protect his family from the one man they jointly feared: her soon-to-be ex-husband and Bobby's father, Bobby Dean Jamison.

PART II

The Plan

Unlike the randomness generated by a system with many variables, chaos has its own pattern, a peculiar kind of order. This pattern is known whimsically as a strange attractor, because the chaotic system seems to be strangely attracted to an ideal behavior.

—GARY TAUBES, *DISCOVER*, MAY 1989

AT FIRST LIGHT, THE LADY on the Mountain renewed her search. The land was still dark under the canopy, but a web of glowing crimson lineaments outlined the crown shyness.

She recalled a proverb from her youth: "A red sky at night is a shepherd's delight! A red sky in the morning is a shepherd's warning."

It was just her now. Everyone else had given up.

As she flipped on her headlamp, a spooked coyote bolted through the foliage; in the sliver of a moment that she could track its movement, the animal appeared to be clutching a human hand in its maw.

She knew it wasn't real, but she had trouble discerning reality from her anxiety. The constant hectoring and uncertainty had taken a toll.

They got lost, she told herself every few minutes. *We don't murder people up here.*

But the die was cast.

Every day she went to the sheriff's office, praying for a break in the case. But it never came. So every day, she went right back to the mountain and continued searching.

She wasn't cut out for this kind of thing. She was just a Realtor, a caretaker.

She took a break to visit D.C., who had just finished laying some fresh foundation.

"I swear to ya, Peggy—hand on the good book—I never seen 'em going back down."

Later, as she scanned the nearby ridges with her binoculars, the sun began to set, casting an eerie orange glow over the landscape. The trees looked like twisted fingers reaching toward the sky.

Her best chance of finding the family at this point, she realized with a grim sigh, was to follow the buzzards.

A FEW MILES away, Mr. and Mrs. Graham and their extended family observed a time-honored tradition, kicking off the 2009 muzzleloader season with a deer camp. They'd been coming to this spot on the mountain for a decade and knew it like their own backyard.

The Grahams told jokes, swapped Sasquatch stories, and sipped beverages. When it came time to scout deer stand locations, Tim jokingly bickered with the cousins about which county they were technically in.

It was a cold, wet November morning, and not a single thing was out of place in Smokestack Hollow.

CHAPTER 5

How It Started,
How It's Going

Niki was driving her daughter to school when she got the call. She could barely process what the voice on the other end was telling her.

Afterward, she must have looked like she had spoken to a ghost.

"What is it, Mommy?" her daughter Ronnie asked.

Niki was lost for several moments before she could manage a coherent response. "Nothing, honey," she said, smiling. "Just something for work."

After she dropped Ronnie off at school, she collapsed into her seat and took deep breaths. Surely, this is a misunderstanding. *They just went on one of their off-grid adventures,* she told herself. *It's just part of their episodic disappearing act. People are overreacting.*

Over the next couple of days, however, as details of the situation trickled in from Starlet and others, a slow-moving panic attack began to engulf her. The truck abandoned with Maisy inside didn't make any sense. She tried to come up with explanations—elaborate happy-ending scenarios that she imagined laughing about with Sherilyn one day. But the cognitive dissonance made her head hurt. There was simply no logical narrative in which it made sense. There was no way Bobby and Sherilyn

41

would have left the dog behind and disappeared into the woods with Madyson.

By day three, when an FBI agent in Muskogee, Oklahoma, called her, Niki was sitting on her old vintage couch, lost in thought, remembering how it all started.

Feng Shui

She met Sherilyn in Oklahoma City in 1998, only a few years removed from the horror of what was then considered the deadliest terrorist attack on United States soil. In the aftermath of the bombing, Oklahomans experienced a time of unprecedented solidarity and state unity. The following years saw local divorce rates decline while childbirth soared.

Niki was bartending at a small pub called Hot Shots at the time. One day, during a particularly dead happy-hour shift, she stood behind the bar, slouched against the counter, reading a book on feng shui.

Attuned to the feel of being watched, a kind of tingling spider-sense, Niki glanced up from the page to see a crop of wavy auburn hair framing two wild, benevolent eyes. Seated on the stool closest to the door, the watchful woman rested her head horizontally on her arm, which lay draped across the bar. Her face was blushed to nearly the color of her hair, and in the cave-like din of the tavern—lit only by a few ornamental sconces and the lambent glow of the jukebox's LED panels—her eyes seemed to emit warmth and luminance.

"So, how's your chi?" she asked with a slightly sarcastic "valley girl" inflection.

Niki smiled, tapping the cover of her book, and moved in her direction. They had a couple of drinks together and talked about feng shui. They were both drawn to the idea of cosmic energy flowing through one's home in a symbiotic balance between an individual and her environment.

Also, no television in the bedroom, as the positive ions might drain your life force.

"That's what husbands are for," Sherilyn quipped.

"I'm Niki, by the way, Niki Shenold," she said, laughing.

"Sherilyn Mangum."

Sherilyn began coming in regularly to drink and chat with Niki during the slow shifts. After only a few cumulative hours together, their connection was so electric, one might have thought they'd been friends for years. It was one of those rare times in life when you hit it off with someone and instantly know you were cut from the same cloth, part of the same unnamed tribe of souls migrating together through the cosmos.

One day, Sherilyn came in and invited her to go bowling later that evening with her and her then-husband Billy. They were in a league and needed an extra team member.

Niki's main memory from that night wasn't bowling. Near the end of the night, they discovered a 1970s-style vintage couch that someone had abandoned by the back exit. Sherilyn gasped with a twinkle in her eyes and then hunted down the manager to ask if they were getting rid of it. He looked over at the piece of furniture—a ratty, godforsaken heirloom with worn upholstery, frayed fabric, and no arms—and nodded hesitantly like a deer in headlights, a response he replicated when Sherilyn asked if she could take it.

Thrilled with her find, she pulled her truck to the back. When Billy refused to help load the couch, Sherilyn once again found herself needing a walk-on teammate, and, again, Niki filled the slot. She and Sherilyn successfully hoisted the couch onto the truck.

They were about to leave when Billy, the father of Sherilyn's son Colton, decided to exert an executive authority he believed he had the power to invoke. No couch, he said, putting his foot down.

They both burst into hysterics again. Niki let her store the couch at her place.

She found in Sherilyn someone who was aggressively authentic and self-sufficient. Starting as early as junior high, she had filled the role of parent figure for her siblings and, to some degree, her own mother. Overwhelmed by the responsibility, she got married at sixteen as a way to escape.

Niki, who had cared for her younger brother while her mother worked and partied, identified with Sherilyn's childhood. Both of their fathers left the picture early; both ran away from home to become teen brides.

"My sister Marla was the closest thing to a parent I had," Sherilyn said to Niki one day.

It was the first she'd heard of her sister.

"More like my best friend. But we raised each other."

"Were Bobby and Sherilyn having marriage issues, relationship issues?" the FBI agent asked.

Niki blinked, broken from her reverie. To her surprise, she had started to smile as she recalled the golden years. The smile collapsed instantaneously upon the agent's question.

"You know, did they fight? Was one or both of 'em stepping out?" The man's voice adopted an artificially benign inflection.

"Things got bad the last coupla years . . . last few times I saw them, they were fighting and yelling. Sherilyn said they were gettin' divorced, but she said that a lot."

"Did the fights get physical?"

"Not that I saw. But I hadn't talked to Sherilyn in months."

"Oh yeah?" The agent absorbed what he could from a case that had stumped local, state, and federal investigators. "And when was that, the last time you talked to her?"

Niki felt a nausea course through her. Of all the questions he would ask her, this was the worst. And in her mind, she leapt a decade, from the golden years to the dark ages.

The Last Visit

Niki's morning had started, simply enough, with Ronnie waking up sick.

She lay in bed with her and started making a list for the unavoidable Walgreens run. Cold medicine, cough syrup, lozenges, soup, snacks, and treats, were the first entries. There would be more. Few things test the mettle of a parent more than a sick toddler.

As she went to the kitchen to make chicken soup, she looked out the window and saw a car speedily pulling up in front of her house and coming to a dramatic halt. Niki didn't at first recognize the woman who got out of the driver's side; her movements were so harried, her body language so frazzled and angry that the spectacle of it must have stunned whatever part of her brain was responsible for facial recognition.

The driver opened the back passenger seat, and a child emerged. Niki recognized her adorable cheeks instantly. Madyson lifted Maisy out of the back seat and, with the Matryoshka doll-like extraction complete, Sherilyn rushed them to Niki's front door.

Niki answered the door as they arrived. Sherilyn was holding a brown attaché in one hand and Madyson's hand in the other. She looked pale and weak—the deadened countenance of someone who spends all day in bed but never gets a good night's sleep.

"I'm leaving Bobby," she said, dispassionately.

Niki had heard many iterations of this before. Her friends' fights had evolved into their own form of communication, an ever-present current of hostility lying below the surface, capable of consuming them whole at any moment.

Niki saw the sadness and fear in Madyson's eyes. She smiled at her, and the child eagerly grinned back, flushed cheeks and love momentarily returning to her cherubic face.

Sherilyn stormed past her as far into the room as she could. "I just came from Star's with my half of the money—we're done, it's over. I may need to crash here."

Niki looked at Madyson again, but this time, neither was smiling. Sherilyn, realizing the silence that had passed, stopped and looked back. Niki's arms were crossed, nervously, each hand on the opposite bicep.

"You're the only friend I have right now," Sherilyn stated.

Niki looked at the woman before her and remembered the friend she'd met a decade earlier.

How had so much changed?

CHAPTER 6

The Accident

Aᶠᵗᵉʳ ᵗʰᵉ ᶜᵃˡˡ ᶠʳᵒᵐ ᵗʰᵉ sheriff, Colton didn't hear anything for days. Then, between forty-eight and seventy-two hours after the search began, he was contacted by the FBI, which was assisting the Latimer County Sheriff's Department in the investigation. He agreed to visit Panola Mountain for an on-site interview.

Seated in the makeshift incident command center on the clearing, the young man could see that efforts to find his family were being coordinated all around him. Bobby's white truck loomed in the distance.

Referencing laptop computers, photos, and journals owned by Bobby and Sherilyn, agents questioned Colton about his mother and stepfather, as well as his life in the Jamison house.

Colton had lived with Sherilyn and Bobby for most of his life. Shortly before their disappearance, however, Colton moved out to live with his biological father.

"Why was that?" the agent asked him. "Why did you move out?"

"I wasn't getting along with my mom and . . . you know, it kinda just felt like it was time," Colton responded.

"Why weren't you getting along?"

Colton thought for a moment and then said: "We were fighting a lot."

"Were they fighting, too—Bobby and Sherilyn?"

"Yeah, all the time. Every day."

But it hadn't always been like this.

WHEN THEY FIRST moved to Eufaula in 2004, Colton remembered a period of time in which things were normal, good even. Bobby and Sherilyn married in Hot Springs, Arkansas, and secured a mortgage loan for their "dream home," a two-story house on the shore of Eufaula Lake. The house was a gut job, but they were excited about renovating it.

The Jamison tribe was starting a new life by the water, and for a time, they made an effort to socialize. They had family and friends over to stay every other month or so and hung out on the back porch, soaking in the sun and scenic beauty of the lake.

Colton only saw his real father about twice a year, so he considered Bobby his dad. After fighting off two bouts of testicular cancer, Bobby was told he most likely couldn't reproduce. Colton was the only child he would ever have, and he wanted him to feel loved.

Colton learned everything he needed from Bobby, who was a natural outdoorsman and could navigate the lake in the dark. He took Colton out in the boat and taught him to fish; he took him out to the woods and taught him to hunt. Bobby taught Colton the principles he knew best: patience and problem-solving. He never had a cross word for his son. Never snapped, never yelled.

Colton loved his mom, too. Sherilyn was attentive and loving, made great meals from scratch, and cleaned the house even while working hard as a hairdresser. There was a little bit of weirdness going on, but all things considered, Colton believed his family was pretty prototypical, at least for a couple of years.

But of the two freak accidents that set off destabilizing chain reactions in the Jamisons' lives, one had already been set into motion.

The Miracle Child

Before she became a nurse, Chrissie Palmore had worked as a hair-stylist with Sherilyn for two or three years in Oklahoma City. Chrissie remembered when Sherilyn first met Bobby, because she came to work at the salon the next day and told her all about it. She had fallen for him almost immediately.

Sherilyn got a different feeling from Bobby than the other guys. He was quiet and gentle. He listened more than he spoke— a rare quality, especially in men. They met at a bar while drinking and had what was ostensibly a one-night stand.

"Did you use protection?" Chrissie asked in a faux-motherly voice.

"No, he's sterile. Can't have kids," Sherilyn responded.

A week later, when Sherilyn found out she was pregnant, Chrissie helped her with her morning sickness.

After that, Bobby started coming into the salon and bringing Sherilyn flowers while she worked. The two might have been caught off guard by the universe's sudden trajectory change, but neither seemed unhappy about the pregnancy.

Quite the opposite, they were elated. Madyson, the miracle child, had bucked all the prognostications of Western doctors, who had told Bobby he wouldn't be able to have children. She was destined to be special.

A couple of months later, Chrissie found out she was pregnant, too, and Sherilyn and her joked about whether there was something in the water at the salon.

After Sherilyn had Madyson, Chrissie had her baby a few months later. The two helped each other and looked after each other's children in the salon while they worked. The twin-crucibles of motherhood and the working-class hustle bonded them like soldiers at war.

The Injury

A few months after Madyson was born, they were at the salon working when a tremendous crashing sound came from the street behind the salon. Sherilyn, who knew Bobby was on his way from his father's tree farm, immediately ran for the back exit.

Bobby had been t-boned by an oncoming car after taking a blind curve. A second vehicle smashed him from the other side.

Chrissie covered Sherilyn's shift while she took him to the hospital.

Bobby suffered a serious spine injury from the accident that left him with chronic back pain. There were days he couldn't get out of bed or walk up the stairs.

He received a small settlement from the accident, but for a new father with a mortgage, bills, and countless future expenses to pay, it was a life-changing setback.

Bobby was prescribed opioid painkillers for the injury, and they often made him woozy.

SOMETIMES COLTON COULDN'T help but overhear his parents' arguments, during which it became clear that the injury was affecting Bobby and Sherilyn's relationship in many ways. Bobby's inability to work made both the family's breadwinners reliant on disability insurance, further eroding their already tenuous financial situation. The injury also affected Bobby's ability to be physically intimate, which frustrated Sherilyn.

If there's something worse for a young teenage boy than hearing his parents fighting, it's hearing them fighting about the quality of their sex life.

The cumulative effects of the situation sent the normally even-keeled Bobby into a significant depression. He and Sherilyn—and, by proxy, Colton and Madyson—became more isolated. They stopped having people over and rarely left the house. Even the dog wasn't let out. If the family did venture from their home, it was to disappear on trips that no one else knew about.

In her "hate letter," Sherilyn would later blame Bobby for turning the family into "hermits."

But Bobby wasn't the only member of the household to become reclusive due to a freakish twist of fate.

The Bee

In 2006, Sherilyn's sister Marla visited the Jamisons for a weekend at the lake. Like Sherilyn, who had worked hard as a hairstylist, her sister Marla pursued a career in cosmetology, working for Glamour Shots for many years before retiring to be a stay-at-home mother.

For most of their lives, Sherilyn and Marla had been as close as sisters could be. During this visit, however, conflict arose. It was the kind of conflict born of a needful love, endemic to siblings who raised each other, who once knew each other better than they knew themselves.

Verbal bickering ensued and, before long, they were in a bad fight. Marla packed up and left early, returning to Ohio.

The two didn't speak to each other for a while. They were both stubborn, and the longer they waited, the more awkward and bitter the silence became. Like most people, they assumed they had a surplus of time.

But they were wrong.

In mid-September of 2007, Sherilyn received a phone call from a family member who told her a story that was so unbelievable that the conversation unfurled like a nightmarish prank.

One day earlier, she was told, Marla went to a cookout party with her friends in Ohio. At some point in the night, she stepped out onto the deck to check the grill. Marla paused to sip her beer and felt a sharp stinging pain on her tongue. As she pulled the can away from her mouth, a bee flew off to die.

By the time her friends found her lying unconscious on the deck, Marla's face and throat were red and swollen, and she was barely breathing. They didn't know it yet, but Marla already had brain damage.

Paramedics rushed her to the ER and then to the ICU; she remained alive but in critical condition.

Sherilyn flew to Ohio, where a doctor told the family that Marla was in a coma after experiencing severe anaphylactic shock from the bee sting. He showed them her brain scans, which looked like the negatives of an icy moon, and pointed out the telltale signs of brain damage.

Marla was on life support for nine days. Sherilyn waited there for every minute, up to and including the moment a small committee of doctors told the family that they were sorry, but there was nothing more that could be done.

Sherilyn stayed by Marla's side as she was taken off life support and remained there as her sister continued to live for another eight or nine hours. Then, on September 25, 2007, she passed away.

Sherilyn spent the next few weeks helping to sort her sister's belongings and make funeral arrangements.

When she returned home to Eufaula, she was a broken soul.

AGENTS ASKED COLTON about his parents' plans to buy land, but he said he never heard them talking about it. "That must have been after I was gone."

"What about church? Did you guys go to church a lot?"

Colton found the question odd. "Not really."

They asked him more questions about his parents' sex lives, drug use, and marriage. He told them what he could.

Colton was silent for a few moments and then said, "Sir, may I ask you a question?"

Silence, then a slight nod.

"Have you talked to the man that was living with them after me? The lodger."

The agents looked at each other. They'd heard of this man from others.

CHAPTER 7

Persons of Interest

INVESTIGATORS BEGAN HEARING THE SAME story from several family members and friends, and it piqued their interest.

In late 2008 or early 2009, sometime after Colton moved out of their house, Bobby and Sherilyn took in a lodger who lived at the Eufaula house with them and worked part-time as their handyman.

One night while Bobby was away, Sherilyn began to feel uncomfortable with how the lodger was talking to her. A slow-burning hostility caught fire, and before long, the man was hurling racist epithets. When she called him out on it, he said that he was a white supremacist and that she and Madyson weren't "purebreds" because of their part Native American ancestry.

Apoplectic, Sherilyn pulled out her .22 and stuck the barrel against his ear, demanding that he leave the house immediately. She ended up chasing him out into the night and firing live rounds.

When police identified the lodger and looked into his past, they found a long arrest record. They also found the man's name— initials K.B.—on one of the prescription bottles in the Jamisons' truck. He immediately became a person of interest, and the FBI deployed US Marshals to track him down for an interview.

For the first time, Beauchamp felt they had someone with a potential motive for committing a crime against the Jamisons.

Last Encounters

During a newspaper interview, Sherilyn's mom Connie expressed concern over the ads that had lured her daughter and son-in-law to Panola Mountain: "We have since learned the land was not for sale because it was owned by an oil company. Were they for real?"

However, the Jamisons' broker, investigators learned, was a Panola landowner and year-round resident who claimed to have interacted with Bobby on the mountain the day before the disappearance. In an affidavit, she described the encounter to the Latimer County Sheriff's Office:

> He was upbeat and friendly. We talked a long time as I do with many folks. Most often I meet with people but he mainly wanted my GPS numbers so he could go to find the land. He said he had a Blackberry phone with GPS on and they were adventuresome and wanted to check it out themselves. Unusual as I generally meet the people first but it was a private person selling the property and he didn't want to trouble me.

Police interviewed another Panola Mountain resident who lived less than half a mile from where the Jamisons' truck was found and was believed to be the last person to speak with the family. This man told authorities that Bobby and his family stopped to chat. Bobby and Sherilyn allegedly asked questions about the area and the mountain, how to live on the land there, etc.

The man told investigators that he gave the family directions to their plot of acreage. Then, he said, they decided to return home to Eufaula before nightfall and drive back up the following morning.

He didn't see them again after that, he said. Nor did anyone, and a week later, the deer hunter reported their truck.

The Brothers Jamison

Of the disappearance of his nephew Bobby and kin, Jack Jamison told the local press: "It has me plumb puzzled. Nothing about it makes any sense."

After he learned of the disappearance, Jack knew it was imminent that investigators would pay a visit to his brother Bob Sr. He also knew Bob would start cursing if he had to find out his son was missing from either the cops or the TV.

Jack drove to the hospice care facility and requested that the nurses not let Bob watch the local news channels, all of which ran regular segments about the Jamison family disappearance and search effort.

This worked as a temporary delay, but there was still the matter of investigators coming to ask him questions.

News of this nature getting revealed to Bob in the form of a police question might be too much for his system. The toxin would have to be delivered in a friendly payload. Jack himself would have to tell him. And he did.

Bob Sr. was silent for a while. He looked angry.

Finally, he said, "Goddammit, they're gonna think I killed 'em."

"I'll help ya talk to 'em," Jack told his brother.

In addition to diabetes and kidney failure, Bob had early onset dementia. Even before entering palliative care, he'd needed Jack as his power of attorney for various court appearances and filings.

Jack was there with his brother when the investigators came. As expected, they asked about Bob Sr.'s escalating and increasingly vitriolic conflict with his son prior to the Jamisons' disappearance. There were rumors he'd threatened to kill Bobby and his family.

Jack later told the press: "He was either in a hospital or in a rest home. I just don't think he was involved. He was disturbed at the time, but I'm pretty sure he was not capable of being involved in that."

Investigators came to the same conclusion and cleared him of involvement.

Bobby Dean Jamison died three months later. His recently amended will, which excluded both his son Bobby and his ex-wife Starlet, named Madyson as the sole beneficiary of his estate.

Outlaw Country

Shortly after his brother's funeral in early 2010, Jack said to hell with it, jumped in his truck, and drove to Panola Mountain. He'd lived in Oklahoma his entire life—well over half a century—so he knew the reputation of the area.

Of the Sans Bois Mountains, some of the locals liked to say: "Don't go alone, don't go unarmed, and don't go."

When he reached the elevation of the clearing, Jack followed the access road to a handful of rustic cabin homes, each separated by miles of terrain. Jack slowed for an old horsehead petroleum pump demarcating a property line, and a rusted gate adorned with a political rally's worth of No Trespassing signs:

WE DON'T CALL 911, WE PROTECT THIS PROPERTY
WITH THE SECOND AMENDMENT

IF YOU CAN READ THIS YOU'RE WITHIN RANGE

TRESPASSERS WILL BE MISTAKEN FOR DEER

The signs were almost an art form in these parts.

He slowed again and peered sideways out his passenger-side window at a shack recessed into the woods. There was a woman sitting in front of the porch with a shotgun draped across her lap.

Jack lifted his hand off the steering wheel—an Oklahoma "hello"—but the woman just stared ahead.

He had similar encounters with the next few mountain dwellers. He didn't get the feeling they were bluffing when they said they'd open fire on a trespasser. Some of them might have long hoped for the chance.

He was alone. There weren't deputies or searchers out looking anymore, and the journalists and correspondents had moved on to new stories. The irony was rich: now that he no longer had to hide it from his dying brother, the case had virtually disappeared from the TV broadcasts.

But it made no difference. Petty concerns no longer mattered, if they ever had.

He approached another No Trespassing sign:

I CAN'T FORCE YOU TO ACCEPT JESUS BUT I CAN ARRANGE THE MEETING

The higher-elevation wilderness of southeast Oklahoma had always been known as "outlaw country"—a shadow biosphere of renegades and illicit commerce. When Jack was much younger, this phrase evoked nostalgic images of bank robbers and bandits, legendary fugitives like Belle Starr and Jesse James whose gangs were said to have evaded law enforcement by hiding in the network of caves in what is now Robbers Cave State Park, approximately ten miles from Panola.

Over a century later, a different kind of outlaw—meth manufacturers, mules, and cartel dealers—used this land, the frontal belt of the Ouachita Mountains, for their own subterfuge.

In the early 2000s, Oklahoma had one of the worst methamphetamine problems in the United States. As narcotics investigators cracked down, mobile meth labs migrated into the mountains. For a couple of years, it looked as if Mexico-affiliated traffickers monopolized the local source of supply. But despite competition with cartels, as well as bills passed by lawmakers restricting the sale of pseudoephedrine—a necessary ingredient for meth production—by 2009, labs were sprouting up again in the state.

The desolate mountain wilderness of southeastern Oklahoma was a known hotspot for this activity.

Dangerous People

Jack drove by another cabin, out of which a tall man wearing a dirty baseball cap, with mutton chops and yellow-tinted glasses, emerged with a pistol strapped to his side. The man stopped and stared him down as he passed. Hundreds of feet down the road, when Jack checked his rearview, he could see that the man was still standing there, staring after him.

He was able to speak to a few people eventually. One of them was a representative from the gas company who was there servicing the oil well. He told Jack that the man who had last talked to the family lived down the mountain, closer to the base.

Jack indicated he was going to go down and talk to him.

"Oh, I wouldn't do that," said the gas man.

"Why not?"

"Because there's dangerous people up here."

CHAPTER 8

The List

A FEW MONTHS INTO THE search, Niki woke up around
3:00 A.M. and listened to a heavy rainstorm squalling outside her bedroom. The pelting sheets sounded like waves of
creatures sprinting across the roof. The long, witchy appendages
of elm trees groaned in the wind, tapping and scraping at the
window.

She had dreamed of Sherilyn again, a recurring nightmare in
which her friend visited her from the mountain. Sometimes
Niki's dream self sensed her proximity, and when she looked out
her window, the outline of a figure would be visible on the dark
street below, silhouetted under a streetlight—just standing, staring up at her.

In other dreams, Sherilyn would come to her front door and
knock.

Careful not to wake her sleeping husband, Niki crawled out
of bed and looked out the window. It was hard to see the street
through the flapping branches and rain, but there didn't appear
to be anyone standing below.

She put on her robe and peeked in on her daughter, who was
sleeping peacefully. Of course she was. Niki still hadn't had the

talk with her . . . because how do you tell a six-year-old that her best friend has vanished?

She went downstairs and was about to make some Sleepytime tea when there was a knock at the door.

Niki froze.

Who could be here so late? She wondered, unable to read the time off the clock. It was just the trees, she told herself, puppeteered by the storm. An accident, it was just an accident.

She turned back to the stove, but a few moments later, the knock repeated—louder, slower, unmistakably intentional.

She walked over to the front door and looked out the eyehole. A dark, dripping figure stood there. A feeling of both terror and joy seized her, and she opened the door to find Sherilyn, soaked to the bone, trembling and sobbing uncontrollably.

Niki took her in, wrapped her in a thick quilt, and sat with her on the vintage couch they'd found together. Sherilyn curled up in her lap, and they cried together.

"How do you feel?" Niki asked.

Some of Sherilyn's hair, mixed with grime and debris, came loose in her hand. She was very ill. Niki realized she hadn't seen Sherilyn's face, those powerfully expressive, cosmic eyes, and as she tilted her friend's head and leaned down, a gasp escaped her lips. Sherilyn's eyes were sunk back into their sockets, clouded over with a bluish-gray film.

Niki woke up gasping to the sounds of the real storm. These meta dreams, dreams-within-dreams, were part of the recurrence. A psychologist might say they were constructs of her unconscious mind grasping for answers as she processed her grief.

But she couldn't shake the feeling that the dreams meant something more, that they were part of the puzzle somehow.

Another night, Niki dreamed she found Sherilyn, rooted into the forest bed, sobbing as she cradled and rocked Madyson's lifeless body.

Whatever the visions meant, she was always left gutted in the morning. Of the many dreams of suffering and death that she experienced during this time, these were the most painful—when she got to see her friend and hold her, only to wake up and have her ripped away all over again.

Find the Jamisons

After search efforts were called off, Niki was consumed with sadness. Her nightmares intensified. Almost out of necessity, she began organizing.

First, she collected all her correspondence with the family and any information, digital or paper, in her possession. She desperately wanted to look through Sherilyn's journal for clues, but she knew investigators had almost certainly already confiscated it. In fact, the journal may have been the impetus for the call from the FBI agent.

She created a Facebook page called "Find the Jamisons." Hundreds of users subscribed to follow the page, everyone from sympathetic observers and armchair detectives to trolls and provocateurs. In time, the page would become a community, a family Niki began to call her "Jamison warriors."

The goal, at this point, was simply to raise funds for continuing the search beyond the thirty-nine days that Beauchamp and Latimer County had put in. Whether through hiring private investigators or launching new search efforts, the private sector was the only hope now.

Shortly after law enforcement authorities designated the Jamison family investigation as a cold case, Niki and others sold T-shirts, posters, ribbons, and water during the Whole Hawg weekend, an annual Eufaula event. They raised 145 dollars.

Niki also organized a public vigil event at Posey Park in Eufaula, where a musician performed. With help from her husband and friends, as well as Connie and Starlet, with whom she had grown a bit closer by proxy of their shared grief, funds were raised by selling "Find the Jamisons" T-shirts.

Local news teams documented the affair, interviewing family members and friends, including Starlet.

"It's hard to face each day," Starlet said, holding the Jamisons' dog Maisy. "But Maize gives me hope, that and keeping the faith."

When interviewed by the local press, Niki called out those who stigmatized the Jamisons as reclusive and strange.

"Things are not always what they seem," she said, accompanied by her husband Wayne. "I don't want them to be judged."

She also called out law enforcement, saying not enough was done during the search.

"I'm not done looking. I'm not going to stop. They deserve that."

The Oklahoman reported that an unknown person, presumably a family member, said, "There is no greater agony than not knowing."

A few people gave speeches, including Pastor Geraldo Alonso from the Seventh-day Adventist Church of Muskogee, where the Jamisons had sought spiritual advice.

Alonso read from the Bible, Psalms 71:14: "But as for me, I will always have hope; I will praise you more and more."

At night, the group lit candles. As Niki looked out at the flames flickering in the shadows around the clasped hands and bowed heads, she recalled the trope about killers who attend their victims' memorials and funerals.

Could the person responsible be out there? she thought, studying the shadowed eyes of strangers.

The Intruder

Niki began developing a network of digital allies that included two of her personal friends from Arkansas, her cousins, volunteer researchers, web sleuths, and even psychics. As the case grew in popularity online, Niki received dozens of messages every day from all types of people: well-wishers telling her they prayed for the Jamisons' safe return; armchair detectives hawking geographic and topological maps of the search grid; mediums offering their remote viewing services; and total strangers talking up leads, suspects, and theories.

A friendly woman named Beverly, who was from southeast Oklahoma and knew the area well, reached out, wanting to get involved.

"This case is awful. I pray for Madyson every day. Please, how can I help?" she asked through Facebook Messenger.

"Thank you," Niki wrote back. "What kind of info do you have?"

"Well, my family has a cabin in the mountains there in Red Oak."

Niki thought about this and realized it could be useful in two different ways. One, it could act as a kind of command center or hub if she was able to organize a new search group. The area around Red Oak was vast and desolate, probably lacking reliable cell phone reception or anything even remotely close to nearby motel accommodations and amenities. Having a friendly home base would prevent them from having to drive back and forth from Wilburton or Kinta.

A friend with a local cabin could also be a source of information. From what she'd gathered, the few people who did live year-round in Panola and Red Oak were tight-knit, territorial, and fiercely private. But someone there knew something, Niki was certain of it. She needed to infiltrate the mountain community.

Niki hadn't even broached the idea of going to the mountain yet, as she knew her husband would object—and, from the sound of it, for good reason. Everyone she talked to about Panola said some version of the same thing: don't go.

She messaged more with Beverly and decided she was trustworthy.

Niki brought up her Google map, which had become the locus of her accumulated data. It was filled with notes and markings denoting the coordinates of where the Jamisons' truck was found, the perimeters of the grid searches conducted by Sheriff Beauchamp, and a variety of landmarks.

She wanted to mark the location of Beverly's cabin on the map, which was trickier than she thought. She decided to let Beverly do it herself and passed along her Google password. Beverly, excited to be helping, marked the coordinates.

The timeline of what happened next is hard to untangle. In real time, it shook out more as a blur of weirdness and panic than a series of discrete events.

Beverly suggested Niki and she meet up to plan a course of action, saying she could come to the cabin. Niki was open to this but didn't imagine it happening for weeks. She wanted to carefully organize her efforts.

She thanked Beverly for the offer and said she would get back in touch with her. They talked a bit more and then, before signing off, Beverly again mentioned that Niki should come to the cabin. This made her a little uncomfortable, but she chalked it up more to nerves and social awkwardness than anything bad.

The next day, Niki sat down at her computer wanting to reread an email she'd received about the Jamison case. But she couldn't find it. She searched her drafts, spam, and trash, but the email was gone.

It took Niki a bit to fully grasp what was happening. At first, she thought there was just a glitch or technical error in her email account. Gradually, it became clear that Beverly, who had originally contacted her with what seemed like a genuine desire to help with the Jamison case, had locked Niki out of her own Gmail account. The confusion turned into panic when Niki realized the woman— or whoever was behind the name Beverly—was deleting emails and files related to the Jamison case.

When Niki messaged her and asked what was going on, Beverly denied the activity. Niki did a quick online dive into her social media footprint and found that Beverly had a whole constellation of aliases and burner accounts. Initially, Niki figured she was the victim of a hacker, as the situation carried the classic signature of a phishing attack. But Beverly didn't seem to be harvesting any personal or financial information—she was only interested in the stuff that pertained to the Jamison case.

What in the hell is she doing? Niki thought.

As paranoia set in, she started to see the name of a man who was either Beverly's husband or friend popping up in random contexts. She wondered if Beverly was trying to protect someone involved in the Jamisons' disappearance.

Niki reached out to her Arkansas friends, Jan and her daughter Michelle, who had generously helped and supported her at the vigil in Eufaula. Jan and Michelle jumped on a three-way video call with her.

"She's inside right now," Niki pleaded, suddenly feeling like a character in a cyberpunk thriller. "Can we get in there and pull the files out?"

Eventually, Niki was able to regain control of her account and recover most of the deleted emails. But this was only the beginning, a broken signpost whirling alongside her as she descended into a vortex of chaos.

The Friend

Several months later, Niki still hadn't told her daughter Ronnie the truth. Because of the distance between their cities, it wasn't uncommon for months to pass in between visits, so she wasn't asking about her best friend...yet.

But Niki knew she couldn't push it off forever.

One day, Ronnie came home from school and asked, "Who was over here last night?"

Niki said that no one was.

"But I heard you guys talking."

Niki looked up at her and smiled. "That must have been Daddy and me."

"No, I saw her go in my bathroom," Ronnie pressed, insistent.

The second story of their house contained her daughter's bedroom, as well as a playroom and a half-bathroom.

"Who did you see in your bathroom?"

"Your friend."

"What friend, sweetie?" Niki asked, patiently. "What did she look like?"

"Skinny with brown hair, a pink shirt and jeans—old like you but no glasses."

Niki immediately thought of Sherilyn.

"I don't know who that could have been," she responded, casually. "I'll ask your dad if he had anyone over, okay?"

Her daughter nodded, and Niki watched her as she went off to play. For a time, the subject was dropped.

"Madyson Is Still Alive"

Another message popped up in Niki's "Find the Jamisons" admin console. This one came from a woman who said she had stumbled upon alarming information pertinent to the search for the Jamisons. It involved a white supremacist group called the United White Knights.

There was a book, the woman said, that contained the names of people who were to be killed. A hit list of defectors, snitches, enemies, etc.

"I saw the book, several pages," she messaged Niki. "I saw your friends on the list—their names, Bobby and Sherilyn Jamison."

Niki felt her face flush with anger, not about this supposed list but at the person messaging her. Because it had to be fake. She was about to respond with a short but strongly worded send-off when the woman sent another message.

"I know how they got on the list too," she wrote. "The lodger that lived with them. K.B."

This one paralyzed Niki in her seat.

At that point in the investigation, only the people closest to Sherilyn had known about the lodger story. Newspaper articles had referred merely to a family friend who temporarily lived with the Jamisons. There had been no published reports of his initials, much less what their conflict had been about. So if this person was just a troll, how did she know the initials, much less the significance of connecting the lodger—K.B.—to a white supremacist group?

"KB got their name on the list. He wanted revenge for the shooting incident with Sherilyn and WK [White Knights] was happy to oblige when they learned she had Cherokee blood."

The informant knew other personal details about the family, too. She knew that a peace symbol adorned Bobby's wedding ring. She knew things about Madyson, too. And it was the topic of Madyson that took the conversation into darker territory.

"Madyson," she wrote, "is still alive. There is a man in Laredo, Texas, his name is Charles Edwin Klein, a White Knights member. He is a pedophile ... and he has Madyson."

Niki's hands trembled as she typed: "How do you know this?"

"I spoke to him. He didn't know I knew. I tried to get him to say more, but ..."

She said the man had laughed as he described how Madyson liked to sit on his lap.

This new, hideous wrinkle renewed Niki's doubts about the story, and she stopped messaging the woman.

But the images were now imprinted into her synapses. That night, she dreamed about Madyson—the last phone picture of the girl alone in the woods come to life, but with no frame, only the ecology of the mountain in time-lapse as the seasons and geology changed. As Bobby and Sherilyn lay dying and rotting, slowly sinking into the understory, the photographer turned the camera onto his own pale, unaging face and smiled.

She awoke from the dream in the middle of the night and immediately threw on her robe, went downstairs, and got some water boiling for tea. As she waited for the steam, she Googled Charles Edwin Klein and found a press release from the Texas Department of Public Safety.

The top of the page said: "Texas Fugitive Still Wanted ... Charles Edwin Klein ... Up To $3,000 Reward."

Wanted for "Parole Violation and Failure to Register as a Sex Offender."

His computerized criminal history (CCH) included the following: "Sex Offense Against Child—Fondling, Aggravated Sexual Assault of a Child, Indecency with a Child, Indecent Exposure."

The man had a 1984 conviction for sexually assaulting an eleven-year-old girl and a 1991 conviction for indecency with a child. In 2004, he fled; three years later, the Dallas County Sheriff's Office issued a warrant for Klein's arrest for violating his parole. They called him "armed and dangerous."

The teapot started to sing just as nauseated panic shot through Niki's stomach.

But it was the mug shot that really broke her down. Klein's face was the same as the one in her dream.

Maybe she was dreaming *this*. She glanced at the front door, half expecting to hear a loud knock.

Upon further examination, Niki learned it would have been impossible for this man Klein to have been involved with the death of the Jamisons. He was incarcerated at the time.

And, like the email-hacking weirdo Beverly, who had essentially catfished her and then tried deleting her files, the bounty hunter's story and identity collapsed.

Who are these whackadoodles? Niki wondered. They seemed to be more than just trolls, hoaxers, or hackers. They were knowledgeable about intimate details of the Jamisons' personal lives and were using that familiarity to gain access to Niki.

The theories from these conspiracy yarns made their way into the family's thoughts. In the coming years, Connie would continually cite the possibility of a religious cult hit list.

In an interview with *The Oklahoman*, she said, "That part of Oklahoma is known for that ... cults and stuff like that ... from what I've been told and from what I've read. I was told (around the time of Sherilyn's disappearance) ... that she was on a cult's hit list."

What was the purpose of spreading these ideas? Niki wondered. It wasn't financial gain. So far, these games hadn't yielded any identity fraud or theft beyond deleted documents. It was almost like some kind of social engineering or LARPing mischief, but who gets their kicks harassing a missing family's loved ones? Who goes to this much trouble to trick a victim's friend and supply her with false hope?

Could it be the abductor/killer himself, getting sadistic enjoyment from playing mind games with his victims' friend?

Here she was reaching out for help, and it was as if she were being guided by vultures.

But she couldn't risk rejecting leads, no matter how improbable or insane they sounded. She couldn't afford to limit her search to conventional explanations and messengers, because this was not a conventional case. Something very strange happened on that mountain, something didn't make sense to anyone who looked at it.

A thought that kept Niki up at night was imagining that Sherilyn and/or Madyson were still alive and being held captive by their abductor. So the Klein story, however dubious, shook her to her core.

What if they had been taken by human traffickers?

It wasn't hard to imagine a scenario in which Bobby was killed and Sherilyn and Madyson were abducted. It happened all the time.

Everyone, starting with the police, had given up on finding them and were bullying the family into believing it was just an accident. But what if Sherilyn was in a room somewhere at that very moment—perhaps only miles away—praying to God that her friend doesn't give up?

CHAPTER 9

Small-Town Horror

Based out of Pennsylvania, Brett Faulds published a blog called *Keep the Search Alive,* on which he documented his freelance investigative journalism on missing-person cases. He wanted to help in whatever way he could.

His "expertise," he wrote, was in "being able to extract information from situations."

Brett launched a deep dive into the Jamison case at a time when the Google algorithm still equally favored small independent publications. As a result, his humble little WordPress blog was often the first search engine result that popped up when people looked for info on the case.

"Folks, dozens of people connected to this case and the Jamisons talked candidly about this situation to me," he wrote.

Initially, he believed the Jamisons were probably murdered. This view intensified when he learned of a mountain resident who claimed to have seen "fresh tire tracks" on the clearing that led away from the truck.

"This would now be the entire focus of my investigation," Brett wrote. "This to me is the only thing that made absolute perfect sense. They were there to look at land. Perhaps they met someone

69

that may have wanted to show them land somewhere else up there? Or maybe something sinister happened and they were forced into the other vehicle against their will?"

Brett wanted to speak with the Jamisons' real estate broker, Peggy Cooke, who was one of the last people to see and interact with Bobby on the mountain. Brett called her, pretending to be interested in mountain real estate, and then told her the truth, that he was investigating the Jamison family disappearance.

She kindly obliged him and repeated to Brett what she had told police, that Bobby declined her offer to show them the property—he just wanted the GPS coordinates, she said.

By early 2012, Brett no longer believed the Jamisons were murdered. In fact, his "birdies" had convinced him something entirely different took place.

"There is enough evidence to indicate that the Jamisons are not dead on Panola Mountain..." he wrote. "In fact, overwhelming evidence shows that the Jamisons staged their own disappearance and have 'walked away.'"

Brett cited an ambiguous statement made by Markus Ward, a deputy who worked on the Jamison investigation and was a candidate in the Latimer County Sheriff race: "I do not feel like they are in danger or left unwillingly," he wrote to Brett in an email.

Brett now believed the family left the mountain of their own free will and did not want to be found. But unlike Ward, Brett believed they were in danger.

"Morally," he wrote, "I have had to decide whether or not it is ethical to share all what I have uncovered in relation to this disappearance."

Anadarko

Elsewhere in Oklahoma, two particularly horrifying cases in similarly small towns rattled the public and sent authorities scrambling for answers.

A few months before the Jamisons' disappearance, residents of Anadarko experienced their own nightmare. Shortly after 11:30 A.M. on Sunday, August 23, 2009, retired Bishop Silkey Wilson Jr. and his wife arrived at the Worth Temple Christ Holy Sanctified Church.

On most Sundays, they were greeted at the door by Reverend Carol Daniels, who drove sixty miles from her home in Oklahoma City. Even though the church no longer had a formal congregation, the sixty-one-year-old woman still came every week without fail, hosting charitable events and making house visits to elderly parishioners who could no longer attend in person. She was a beloved member of the community.

On this Sunday, the pastor's car was there, but the pastor herself was nowhere to be seen, and the church appeared to be empty.

The Wilsons walked one block over to the Anadarko Police Department and asked for assistance.

Officer Ashley Burrus arrived at 12:02 P.M. and walked around to the side of the church, where he found that the south door was open.

A few minutes later, Officer Burrus emerged from the side door, looking pale and disoriented. He called for backup but struggled to speak coherently.

Detective James Howard, who took the call, knew by the inflection in the officer's voice that something was very wrong.

More officers arrived at the scene, as well as paramedics. One by one, they went inside.

Across the pews and behind the pulpit, Pastor Daniels lay naked and lifeless in a pool of blood. Her corpse was covered in gaping knife wounds—larynx and neck slashed nearly to the point of decapitation; hair singed off by fire, skin doused with cleaning chemicals.

An additional detail sent shock waves through the small religious community of Anadarko: the reverend's mutilated body had been staged with arms outstretched to make a ghoulishly bespoke human crucifix. After hearing this, many Anadarko residents believed the crime was committed as a satanic ritual.

Occult intent or not, the perpetrator did everything in broad daylight and got out only minutes before parishioners began arriving for the service. He left zero forensic evidence, and police never recovered the murder weapon nor the victim's clothing.

District Attorney Bret Burns called it the most horrific crime scene he'd encountered in seventeen years as a prosecutor.

Less than a year after the murder, the town demolished the church and built a memorial to Carol Daniels.

Three years after discovering the pastor's mutilated body, Officer Ashley Burrus drove by the memorial at 2:30 A.M. on his way to the Anadarko Police Department. The off-duty deputy entered the empty lobby, sat in a chair, drew his handgun, and shot himself in the chest. Paramedics arrived but couldn't save him.

Weleetka

Thirteen months earlier and two hours east, another brutal crime shocked an even smaller Oklahoma town.

On June 8, 2008, eleven-year-old Skyla Whitaker and thirteen-year-old Taylor Paschal-Placker woke up from a sleepover at Taylor's grandparents' home in Weleetka (population: 806). In the afternoon, the girls decided to walk the dirt road to the Bad Creek Bridge only a half-mile north. Thirty minutes later, Taylor's grandfather, Peter Placker, got worried and went looking for them. He found the girls laying in a ditch, their bodies riddled with bullet holes—eight in Skyla, five in Taylor.

Investigators believed the killer used two different firearms, but neither was located.

Two years later, Weleetka residents reeled again when another of its young citizens, Ashley Taylor, was murdered and cremated.

In a twist, the town's two major investigations eventually converged.

The McStay Family

One year after the Jamisons went missing, a California family, the McStays, disappeared in a case that shared a number of eerie similarities with that of the Jamisons.

On February 4, 2010, the McStay family seemingly vanished from their home in Fallbrook, California. Their sudden disappearance was particularly unusual, as the family left behind their beloved dogs, food in the refrigerator, and the children's toys. Additionally, their car was found abandoned near the Mexican border in San Ysidro, California, with no signs of foul play or forced entry.

Initially, authorities assumed the family had fled to Mexico and were involved in some sort of illegal activity. However, investigators quickly discovered that the McStay family had no criminal history, and there was no evidence to suggest that they had fled the country voluntarily. Instead, the investigation focused on the possibility that the McStays were victims of foul play.

When the family's home was searched, investigators found no signs of struggle or forced entry, but they did find clues that suggested the family had left in a hurry. There was still food on the table, and the family's computer had been left on. Additionally, investigators discovered they had stopped using their phones and credit cards.

Like the Jamisons, the McStay family case came to a grinding halt and turned cold.

CHAPTER 10

The Briefcase

SEVERAL MONTHS AFTER THE LAST major search, Sheriff
Beauchamp sat for an interview with *The Oklahoman*. Behind
him on his office wall was a giant topological map of the mountain. A constellation of color-coded pins and nodes represented
the locations of the various grid search and reconnaissance operations conducted during the previous six months; lines
crisscrossed the terrain between areas searched by humans, canines, drones, planes, and four-wheelers.

In terms of resources and search time, it had been one of the
most extensive manhunts in state history: over 400 experienced
searchers and volunteers; countless local, state, and federal
agencies; sixteen teams of K9 dogs; a dozen FBI agents, OSBI
agents, and private investigators. The state was nearing a one-mil-
lion-dollar price tag with nothing to show for it.

"I'm at my wits' end," Beauchamp said.

The sheriff looked as if thoughts were rapidly crisscrossing his
cognitive map, bouncing between different scenarios. He'd tried
everything. He interviewed everyone even remotely close to the
family; he allowed in FBI profilers and private investigators, always keeping his mind open to alternative narratives—still,

nothing seemed to make sense. He got so desperate at one point, he told the interviewer, that he even consulted with a psychic.

"A lot of investigators would love to have as many leads as we do. The problem is they point in so many different directions."

After the interview was over and the journalist left his office, Beauchamp stood before the wall, looking at the map for the millionth time. Bringing his face to within inches, he peered at the area around the clearing, noting the declinations.

Abruptly, he turned, walked back out of his office, and gathered the deputies.

"Y'all come on now," he said, grabbing his jacket and keys. "We're going back up there."

WHILE LOOKING AT the map, Beauchamp had suddenly remembered his hunting days, learning the secrets of whitetail bucks—practically a rite of passage for boys, and plenty of girls, growing up in southeast Oklahoma. They're taught that a big part of hunting is knowing how to track a wounded animal. After reading their reaction to the shot—*did they buckle?*—you go to the point of impact and look for bone fragments or hair or, if you think it was a paunch-shot, gut matter. They learned blood trailing, following the evidence of the animals' pain and desperation as they look for clusters of the tracks of their friends or something that reminds them of home.

Some of the earliest hunting truisms you learned were that wounded deer usually travel downhill and toward water. Incidentally, so do lost persons.

Beauchamp and the search teams had experienced colossally bad luck with water. It rained in perpetuity for the first few days on-site, then they had the false alarm with the water cistern, and then . . . there was the pond incident.

According to Brett's sources, during the investigation, a group of squatters got detained on the mountain. Squatters, who were usually either using or manufacturing drugs, were common on Panola, and they weren't the kind of people you wanted to stumble upon, even for law enforcement.

These detainees were in the process of being booted off the mountain when they played an unexpected card. One of them abruptly brought up the missing Jamison family and said they were killed on the mountain. The others added that white supremacists had done it, disposing of their remains in a pond.

They ultimately dredged one of the mountain's small ponds. Sure enough, they found animal remains, but not the Jamisons.

WITH HIS DEPUTIES in tow, Beauchamp wondered if, like the wounded whitetail deer, he could track the family's movements downhill and toward water. There wasn't much to be found, just a few small creeks that had already been checked off the grid by search and rescue teams.

But they could have missed something. *Somebody had to have missed something, because three humans can't vanish into nothingness.*

Lost persons sometimes seek higher ground to get a view of their surroundings or obtain cell phone service, but more often than not, they head downhill and toward water. Starting at the clearing where the Jamisons' truck was found, the sheriff and his deputies descended the mountain until they reached a creek bed, which they followed farther down the mountain. The going was tough, full of ridges, boulders, and shale deposits that broke apart under their feet.

After countless tours of duty, Beauchamp was in excellent shape. Military-training shape. His only injury—an ankle shattered into pieces when he accidentally shot himself as a young man—throbbed on occasion, but was no longer a significant burden. It still took him a good half-day to get anywhere out here. For the life of him, he couldn't understand how Bobby Jamison—with what was essentially a fractured spine and a six-year-old child in tow—could have covered so much ground as to completely disappear. It defied logic.

During one of the searches, they found a pocket knife. But it was clean—no blood, no DNA, no prints. That wasn't going to cut it. He needed forensics. Or ballistics. Or a sign of anything—literally, anything.

Sighing and stretching his neck, he looked up and saw a bulbous white shape perched beneath the branch of a pine tree.

"Welp, I'll be, would you look at that?" one of the deputies said, pointing.

Exasperated, Beauchamp walked off, heading back up the mountain.

Behind him, another deputy laughed. "How'd a dag nab balloon get out here?"

Revisiting the Footage

When he got back to his office, Beauchamp collapsed back into his chair between the map and his desk.

He brought up the security footage. He'd watched it at least a dozen times at least, but it's easy to miss obvious clues, even when you know what you're looking for. Cognitive psychologists say it's common, a natural byproduct of the way our mind categorizes the constant torrent of incoming data points. They even have a term for it—inattentional blindness, a kind of "misinformation by omission."

As he scrolled through the footage, Beauchamp focused on one of Sherilyn's trips from the house to the truck. There had always been something about this clip that bothered him. Due to the distance, angle, and low fidelity, not to mention the sheer number of trips they made, it had been challenging and tedious to identify every single object shown in the footage. But it made sense to scrupulously check for anything they packed that might later have gone missing.

He paused the footage, zoomed in on Sherilyn as she walked to the truck, and scrolled back and forth over a millisecond during which there was the slightest glimpse of something under her non-camera-facing arm. In another window, Beauchamp brought the same clip with the same matching timecode as seen from the second camera angle. As he zoomed in and toggled between the microseconds, the two parallel views didn't show much—a few pixels contorting and morphing like red-shifted galaxies.

He couldn't determine what it was at first. Between artifacting and pixelation, identifying the object was like a digital Rorschach test.

Eventually, he figured it out.

Beauchamp grabbed the inventory report of the items seized from the Jamisons' truck and began rifling through the entries. There was no line item for it.

There was no mention of the brown briefcase Sherilyn packed into the truck just before the family's departure.

CHAPTER II

The Plan

O N AUGUST 1, 2010, MADYSON turned seven years old in absentia. The police, who had returned many of the Jamisons' personal effects—including the 32,000 dollars, which was given to Starlet—had dramatically scaled back their search efforts. Heartbroken, Niki, Star, and Connie took to the "Find the Jamisons" Facebook group to raise funds for an independent search, partnering with community service projects and restaurants.

Niki felt like people had forgotten about the Jamisons. Even in their small hometown, news of the search and case updates had to compete with a range of other public concerns, from the aforementioned murder investigations to civic matters.

A month earlier, the Lake Eufaula Association organized an arguably tone-deaf murder mystery dinner fundraiser to benefit the road construction of a tourist and multicultural center.

The *Indian Journal* wrote a neo-noir preview for the event:

> The setting for "Murder on the Grill" will be the suburban home of Tom Dooley. While all the guests escape into the house to escape a thunderstorm, Tom stays behind to finish grilling. When the storm is over and the

guests return outdoors, they find their host's lifeless
body lying beside the grill which is smoking from
burned food. Several suspects are among the crowd.
Find out who they are next week.

A Ghost in the Bathroom

The Jamison family investigation was different from most cases.
For all the strange and suspicious details, there was no blood, no
bodies, no evidence confirming or disconfirming foul play. Police
didn't know if they were dealing with a crime or a tragic accident.
And despite the early media attention, without any new leads or
announcements from the police, the case faded from the papers.

But whatever luster the Jamison family's story lost locally, it
gained back nationally. About a year after the disappearance, a
producer for the Investigation Discovery show *Disappeared* contacted Niki and Starlet and asked to interview them for a full
episode on the case. They had participated in a number of brief
vignettes for the local news stations, but this would be the first
nationally broadcast show devoted exclusively to the disappearance of Bobby, Sherilyn, and Madyson.

Shortly before the day of her interview, Niki sat at her living
room table, looking nostalgically through her photos. The pro-
ducers had asked her to select a few of them for possible inclusion
in the show. She gazed at a picture of her and Sherilyn together
in the golden years and smiled—they were so young and vibrant,
they seemed to be glowing.

Suddenly, her daughter Ronnie came running over. Before
Niki could conceal what she was doing, Ronnie saw the photo.

"That's her," the child said, pointing at Sherilyn.

"Who?"

Niki was caught off guard, but she already knew the answer.
"That's your friend that was using my bathroom."

Niki could imagine Sherilyn visiting from the other side
and ending up in the bathroom, doing whatever it is that a

ghost might do there. For the first time, Niki felt that her
friend was dead.

She decided it was as good of a time as ever to tell her daughter the truth. She sat Ronnie in her lap and hugged her.

"Honey, there's something I want to tell you. Our friends—
Bobby, Sherilyn, and Mady—got lost. But lots of people are
looking and praying for them, okay?"

There was a momentary glimmer in Ronnie's eyes, but at six
years old, the meaning of her mother's words didn't fully process.

Off the Grid

The ID episode, entitled "Paradise Lost," opened with a reen-
actment of two adults and a child holding hands in a field as
they faded out of existence, over which a grim, laconic voice
narrated:

"A six-year-old girl and her free-spirited parents vanish in the
backcountry of Oklahoma..."

In retrospect, it was a pitch-perfect preamble for a broadcast
that would introduce the case to a much larger audience while introducing some of the more spooky and conspiratorial elements.

The show featured interviews with Beauchamp, Star, Niki,
and a variety of others, including private investigator Heather
Holland, who had traveled from Michigan to assist Beauchamp
in the investigation.

They talked about Bobby's back injury, Sherilyn's bipolar disorder and the death of her sister, and how all these events
converged to send the family into a tailspin. By 2009, Bobby and
Sherilyn were experiencing considerable strain—physically, psychologically, and financially. Unable to sustain certain kinds of
traditional employment, they supported themselves and Madyson and Colton with side work, disability insurance, and
settlement money from Bobby's car accident lawsuit.

The show claimed that because the Jamisons didn't trust
banks, they kept their money close to them in cash.

"When a person goes missing without a trace," the narrator crooned, "often the most critical information is hidden in their actions and words from the days before they vanished."

At some point early in the investigation, authorities became interested in the Seventh-day Adventist Church in Muskogee and what a pastor there remembered about the Jamisons' last week.

The Jamisons' haunted home, as well as Sherilyn's affinity with witchcraft, had already been out there in news stories about the case. In their ID interviews, both Bobby's and Sherilyn's mothers discussed the question of the family's spirituality.

"Sherilyn knew things about witchcraft," Starlet said. "Once she told me she had cast demons out of someone."

She added that Sherilyn believed she had a special ability to cast out demons because of a gold piece in her cheek.

Connie said: "They believed there were spirits in their house, and it frightened them."

The story took an even stranger turn when the show introduced a man by the name of Gary Brandon, who didn't appear on camera but was described as the Jamisons' pastor or spiritual advisor from the Muskogee SDA Church.

Pastor Brandon told FBI investigators that Sherilyn had written him a note saying her family was living under spiritual oppression and that three or four entities had materialized at their home in the form of children who communicated with Madyson.

In the weeks leading up to the trip to Panola Mountain, this spiritual oppression seemed to intensify. Pastor Brandon said that shortly after he received Sherilyn's note, Bobby also reached out, calling him over the phone to discuss a sensitive matter. Between the hours of two and four o'clock in the morning, Bobby told him, three or four demons would appear on the roof of their house. He'd seen them as recently as October 2nd or 3rd, only a few days before their disappearance.

Bobby and Sherilyn supposedly met with Brandon at a restaurant in Eufaula, where Bobby said he was reading *The Satanic Bible* for natural remedies and had looked online for "high-powered shells." He asked Brandon about obtaining "special bullets" that could kill demons.

The past couple of years had taken a toll on the Jamisons, their friends and family said.

"They didn't want to be around other people"; they "needed solitude," according to Connie.

They were fearful, and "it's hard living in fear," Star observed with tears in her eyes.

The show characterized the Jamisons as wanting a fresh start somewhere so they could escape their struggles and begin a new life. That somewhere was roughly an hour's drive away, at the end of an eight-mile climb into the rustic and secluded Panola Mountain.

"When it comes to off the grid," Beauchamp said, "this is about as far as you can get."

Heather the PI added that on a logistical level, the area makes septic systems difficult, and the only electricity comes from generators.

"Most of the people that come up and live in this area are people that are more or less interested in separating themselves from society," said Deputy Jeremy Anderson in a different video.

The Jamisons planned to buy forty acres of land and move there—that's why they went to the mountain. According to the authorities, Bobby and Sherilyn had taken Madyson out of Eufaula Elementary and planned to homeschool her on their new land, which they believed was "their ticket to freedom."

Their plan was to live in their moving container.

The Vigil

In October 2010, Niki and the family held a memorial/fundraising event for the one-year anniversary of the Jamisons' disappearance. This entailed another candlelight vigil at Posey Park followed by a private balloon launch on the Jamisons' lakeside property.

Niki watched the balloons sail into the sky, drifting like a susurration of white pigeons over the lake and then disappearing over the floodplains.

As night blanketed the land, Niki again found herself watching the candlelit faces in the crowd.

FBI profilers say killers sometimes attend their victims' memorials, join the search parties, help put up fliers, and get as close to the victims' families and case detectives as they can. Some killers will do this to keep tabs on the status of the investigation and make sure they're a step ahead of the police. More psychopathic minds try to extend and relive whatever sick thrill they got from the killing itself by observing the grief of their victims' loved ones.

With her daughter by her side, Niki scanned the faces, studying them for any suspicious behavior or glances. She didn't know what she was looking for—nervous eye contact maybe, an eerie grin, a fleeting over-the-shoulder glance from a departing lone wolf. Anything, even the most innocuous micro-expressions, that might suggest someone was reliving the final moments of Sherilyn's life.

She saw one man's face and imagined that he was the lodger. Another time, she thought she saw Klein facing away from her, but it was just an infant's bald head.

The sound of Ronnie sobbing interrupted her reverie. Niki looked down at her daughter's tear-covered face. It had been weeks since she told her the truth, but only now at the vigil did she finally break down.

At six, she had for the first time grasped the reality of death, the one force stronger than magic. Your friends could leave without saying goodbye; the people you love could disappear forever. The world doesn't keep us.

Niki took her daughter's hand and cried with her.

NEAR THE END of the ID episode, Beauchamp said the case was cold; law enforcement had no suspects, and "until evidence comes to light," it would probably remain that way.

He reiterated his belief that the family was "kidnapped or taken by force," but stressed that "you need to find bodies; whether alive or dead, to usually solve a case like this, you need bodies."

He concluded: "Every day I hear from somebody, 'Did you find that missing family yet...?' No. It messes with your confidence to not be able to solve such an important case."

The next year, Israel "Ish" Beauchamp retired as Latimer County Sheriff.

Niki wrote on her "Find the Jamisons" page that he'd told her he couldn't stand the guilt of not finding Madyson.

The Mexican Mafia Theory

The incoming sheriff, Robbie Brooks, generated a few headlines right out of the gate, arresting a Wilburton man who answered the door holding a lit marijuana joint.

Sheriff Brooks also appeared in a controversial local news segment that revisited the Jamison case.

Wearing an off-white cowboy hat, the boyish-faced sheriff said, "It doesn't make sense to anybody. None of their actions make any sense to anybody that's ever looked at the case."

Brooks stated the three most likely scenarios for what happened: "I believe she [Sherilyn] could have taken him [Bobby] out and committed murder-suicide on him and Madyson and then killed herself."

The second option, he said, was that they got lost: "I believe they were probably high on drugs, high on methamphetamine at the time they went to visit the property. They got out of their car and they wandered off into the mountains."

"From the information you've gathered, both were frequent meth users?" the interviewer asked, smartly following up on the sheriff's allegation.

"Yes."

"Every day?"

"Yes."

The interview concluded with one final inflammatory statement by Brooks, who said that if it wasn't murder-suicide or an accident, there was a third explanation.

"I may be wrong," he said with a slight smile. "The Mexican mafia could have done it."

"Why do you say 'Mexican mafia'?" the interviewer asked, surprised. "Where does that come from?"

"That's—that's the theory..." Leaning in, Brooks corrected his body language to a more serious tone. "Because Bobby's dad... it was alleged he was linked to the Mexican mafia, and they had burned one of his businesses down in Oklahoma City."

The broadcast, which won the Oklahoma Society of Professional Journalists third place General News award for 2012, also featured Niki.

Sitting on the Jamisons' dock on Eufaula Lake, she choked up when asked what she believed happened.

"Someone killed them... I think someone has Madyson, and I'm gonna find her... I'm gonna find her."

ALL THE TV airtime helped introduce the Jamisons' case to a national audience, something their loved ones desperately wanted. However, this attention was a double-edged sword, as it also popularized the story on a variety of Internet forums such as Reddit, Topix, and the recently launched Websleuths. The provocative stories of witchcraft, demons, murder-suicide, and shady backwood drug deals resonated in the online attention economy.

Before long, the burgeoning Internet ecosystem of true-crime coverage crowned the Jamison family case one of the most bizarre missing-person mysteries ever.

The Remains

As the case turned cold in 2011–2012, the Jamisons briefly disappeared from the headlines. Then, in January 2013, Pittsburg County Sheriff Joel Kerns announced that the skeletal remains of two people were found in Eufaula Lake. Receding water levels from years of drought left the bones partially exposed on a sandbar.

Sheriff Kerns said investigators also recovered a cinder block and a cable near the remains, which suggested the possibility of foul play.

However, testing soon revealed that the remains were not those of the Jamisons. In fact, the bones belonged to a single person who had died between 200 and 2,000 years earlier. Forensic scientist Angela Berg determined the potentially prehistoric age by studying the decedent's teeth.

"There's dental wear on these individuals, which is more consistent with the use of matates, which is what they use to grind corn. And it would have gravel and small bits of sand in their diet, and then it would wear the teeth down," she said.

It was another grueling false alarm.

Then, nine months later, in November 2013, Latimer County authorities announced the recovery of remains on Panola. Four years after a deer hunter had reported the Jamisons' abandoned truck, another deer hunter made an even eerier discovery in an area of the mountain known as Smokestack Hollow.

PART III

Consider Cult Deaths

activity along angle area around believe bobby buy case consider cult deaths degree disappearance drug eufaula evidence explanation fact family found home house jamison kill latitude line madyson meth miles missing mountains moving murder mystery oklahoma paranormal pastor people possession purchase read reported result satanic sherilyn spirits truck used witch

—KEYWORD CLOUD FROM *DAILY MAIL* ARTICLE

CHAPTER 12

A Perfect Triangle

ON NOVEMBER 6, 2013, SHERILYN and Tim Graham prepared for their thirteenth annual deer camp on Panola Mountain. Tim was particularly excited about this year's season. An avid hunter, he planned to introduce his daughter, Jessica, and his nephew, Lane, to the joys of predation.

That day they were headed to the camp to scout locations for a deer stand. Tim drove the family eight miles from their Quinton home to the mountain and another eight up into the high sticks, the higher-elevation hills that collectively form Panola. From the road, it was a short hike to their ceremonial hunting ground, a private tract of woodlands located in the Smokestack Hollow area.

They couldn't have picked a brighter, sunnier day. Even when the blue sky disappeared from view under the canopy, glints of sunlight studded the dead leaves and stones of the forest bed.

After only five minutes off the trail, Tim spotted a streak of white ahead in the tree line.

"Hey, you see that white thing on the tree over there?" he said to Lane and Jessica. "That's a rub right there."

"What's a rub?" they asked.

"Bucks grow a soft layer of velvet on their foreheads and antlers as they get big. Come this time a' year, they rub it off on tree trunks and use the scent to communicate to one another. Strips the bark off the tree and leaves a mark like that, which tells us stuff, too. How big the buck is, how old it is, even the paths it takes."

As they walked closer, Tim pointed at the ground, directing the kids' attention.

"Birds and other bucks eat the velvet, too."

"You can eat velvet?"

"If you're a bird or a buck you can—tastes like chicken."

The four of them laughed.

As they arrived at the spot, Tim took off his hat and scratched his head in confusion. There was no rub. In fact, there wasn't even a tree, only a small grove of dead brown vegetation, in the middle of which stood a single blade of grass perfectly angled to refract the light.

There's the rub—just a trick played by his own mind in cahoots with the sun.

As the kids looked up at him with blank expressions, Tim spotted something on the forest bed. It resembled a dead turtle, or the desiccated carapace of one—a dirty, bleached orb with green discoloration embedded slightly into the top layer of ground cover.

He picked the thing up. Its sun-baked surface had the hue of pearlescent necrosis.

"Hey," he yelled out to his wife, who was about twenty yards away. "I found a skull!"

"No, you did *not*," she responded in a sarcastic, matter-of-fact tone. When he didn't say anything, she walked over to him. "Is that human?"

They stood in silence for a few moments, and then he returned the skull back to the ground in the same position he found it.

Sherilyn turned to avert her eyes. But as she peered into the distance, her sights landed on another object about fifteen yards away.

As she walked over to it, goosebumps lined her arms.

"Here's another one," she said a few moments later.

Tim followed in his wife's footsteps and then traced the path down from her haunted gaze to the ground. There was another skull, lying face-up, nestled a few inches into the ground cover next to a log.

This one was smaller and missing its two front teeth.

"Let's get the hell out of here," Tim muttered. "Come on. We're gonna have to do this another day, guys."

Leading the way, Tim externalized his thoughts to break the nervous silence. "I swear that grass looked like a rub—"

He stopped in his tracks and, behind him, his family did, too, nervously bumping into each other from the abruptness.

"*What's goin' on, Tim?*" his wife asked with nervous agitation. He kneeled down. "My word . . . three of 'em?"

This third skull was the same size as the first, but as he narrowed his eyes, Tim noticed a distinctive feature.

"Alright, now let's get the hell out of here."

ON NOVEMBER 16, 2013, four years after the Jamison family disappeared on Panola Mountain, the Latimer County Sheriff's Department announced that the skeletal remains of three bodies had been discovered in the woods approximately 2.8 miles from the last-known location of the Jamisons.

Two days later, the *Daily Oklahoman* ran an article with the headline "Remains found could be missing Eufaula family." Gary Perkinson, the OSBI agent in charge of the Jamison investigation, stated: "There was nothing at the scene to indicate the identities of the deceased," nor was there anything that could "determine a cause or manner of death."

The *McIntosh County Democrat* ran a story a few days later with the headline, "Skeletal remains possibly those of missing area family." In the article, Sheriff Jesse James, Latimer County's third sheriff in as many years, said the proximity of the remains to the location of the Jamisons' truck made authorities feel it was "possible" they had found the missing family. James also remarked that the case file on the Jamisons "is very, very thick" and included numerous interviews by multiple law enforcements.

On November 27, the LCSO released an incident report stating that the remains consisted of three skulls, bones, bone fragments, and bits of clothing. The report also revealed the GPS coordinates of the discovery, which was described as "an extremely remote area about nine miles south of Kinta."

When the family implored the authorities for more info, Connie Kokotan was told by an OSBI agent that a child's shoe was found with the remains.

"I asked them what it looked like, what color it was," she told *The Oklahoman*. "Madyson's favorite color was pink. She always wore pink."

She added: "I think [law enforcement] knows more than they're saying; they've implied that over the years."

A newspaper article that appeared shortly thereafter contained a brief interview with the hunter who made the discovery, a local man named Tim Graham.

Mr. Graham told reporters that he saw a hole in one of the skulls.

An OSBI agent was quick to state that any damage to the skeletons could have been caused by scavenging animals like coyotes.

When the interviewer mentioned this to Mr. Graham, he responded, "Ain't no coyote did that."

The Office of the Chief Medical Examiner sent the remains to a university in Texas for specialized DNA analysis.

Almost immediately after the discovery, Niki had a strong feeling about it.

On the 17th, she wrote to the Jamison warriors: "It's with a broken heart that I report... today. Not really sure what I'm feeling. One minute, I'm sobbing, the next I'm in a fog. I was sure Madyson was alive out there somewhere... I was wrong. Expect more from me on this later, just can't really handle it right now."

"In my heart of hearts," she added, "I don't feel they have been there the whole time. I think they were dumped after the searches stopped."

Niki called the medical examiner's office several times and eventually spoke with one of the pathologists there, but all she was told was that the remains were in Texas and the autopsies probably wouldn't be completed for nine months.

Sure enough, the Office of the Chief Medical Examiner completed the autopsies of the Jamison family on June 6, approximately nine months later. But after consulting extensively with forensic anthropologists, the medical examiner, Joshua Lanter, M.D., couldn't establish a cause or manner of death.

For four years, it seemed like Bobby, Sherilyn, and Madyson had vanished into thin air. One by one, each investigator had said some version of "I don't know." Then they reemerged as nothing more than a few bones, and the only explanation that could be offered was "Undetermined"—yet another "I don't know."

No Coyote

I learned about the results of the autopsies in the news in 2014, back when I wasn't yet writing true crime, just obsessively researching it. Five years later, I woke up in the middle of the night with a phrase stuck in my head. It was disjointed and unordered, the words wriggling through my sleepy mind.

It had something to do with a coyote, or the absence of a coyote.

I imagined it like a neon marquee in the blackness: "That ain't no coyote?" I muttered. The marquee flickered and went black.

As you can probably tell, I was burnt-out and living with my parents at this time. We were out in the East Mountains of Albuquerque, New Mexico, a community in which coyotes had been known to snatch small pets out of yards. My mom told me about an elderly woman who was walking her dog when a coyote snatched him away and carried him off shrieking into the woods.

I was peering out my window at the dark, snow-covered trees, hoping not to see bioluminescent eyes, when it hit me.

Neon letters lit up high desert: "Ain't no coyote did that."

I remembered the article I had read with the line by Tim Graham. There aren't many times in life that you're going to wake out

of a dead sleep doing word jumbles about scavengers and disartic-
ulated skeletal remains.

The next day, I found the article in a November 2014 edition
of *The Oklahoman*. Rereading it, I was a little surprised at the lack
of detail with regard to the Graham story. Most of the article re-
hashed other elements of the case. There were only a few short
quotes from Mr. Graham followed by the unqualified, unnecessary, and premature rebuttal offered by one of the OSBI "lawmen."

I looked through newspaper archives for any other interviews
with Tim Graham and was surprised to find that there were none.
There were dozens of articles referencing the information from
the discovery, but no additional info or details.

I sent a couple of messages to email and social media accounts
associated with Mr. Graham.

Bupkis, for weeks.

Then I tried some public databases and phone numbers. I
reached someone through text that may have been Tim's son or
nephew. Maybe it freaked him out to get a random message asking about the bones he once found; I saw the bouncing dots of a
reply bounce for a moment and then stop.

The next day, I received a voicemail message from Tim Graham.
The man who found the Jamison family's remains was down to talk.

MR. GRAHAM WASN'T alone that day back in 2013, I learned. He
and his family discovered the remains together. His wife Sherilyn
joined us on the call and helped Tim recall the experience.

Tim told me the story that opened this chapter, in which he
confused a sunlit blade of grass for a buck rub before encountering the skulls in close proximity.

As I listened to the second half of the story, I thought about
how unnerving it would be to go out into a familiar tract of the
wilderness with your family and find three human skulls. I imagined the profound dread and claustrophobia as the church of the
wild becomes a padlocked ossuary.

"I turn back towards the trail down the road," Tim said, "which
wasn't far—we're talking maybe a hundred and fifty yards off the

road—and when I turned and walked down, I said, 'God dang, there's another one.' And I picked it up, and it had a hole in it."

I was intrigued by the hole, of course, but another detail, the proximity of the remains to the road, stood out to me, as well. This was something that he would stress a number of times. The overall area was secluded, but this particular spot wasn't prohibitively remote. They were approximately 150 yards from the road, which is the same road—the only road—that connects to the well pad and all the other mountain properties.

In other words, it was hard for him to imagine how three people didn't manage to follow that road until they found a property.

As for the hole, I asked, "Could this have been made by an animal—say, a coyote—as the OSBI suggested?"

"Look, I know what a bullet hole is," Mr. Graham said, with an edge that suggested this question was the bane of his existence. "This was a bullet hole—it was frayed and had jagged edges. The bullet had come from the inside out of the top of the head. It wasn't an entrance, it was an exit hole. If it had been an entrance, it would have been perfectly rounded. I'm not a doctor or nothing, but I been around animals my whole life and I shot many a-critters. We're talking about a damn specialist conducting an autopsy—if he didn't know that was a hole, he shouldn't be an examiner."

Tim's words were full of fiery implications, but before I could ask my follow-up question, he moved on.

"Didn't we also see a femur bone?" he asked his wife.

"Yeah, we did. There was a large femur bone right by where we saw the big skull. We were just trying to leave."

"Yeah, we were trying to get the hell out of there."

After the Grahams returned to the road where their truck was parked, Tim called their friend, who was also named Tim—Tim Turner, who worked narcotics cases for the Stigler Police Department and had gone to the same Quinton church as the Grahams for many years. Turner would go on to be the Haskell County Sheriff.

Sherilyn got inside the truck with Jessica. As Tim placed his call, his jittery nephew jumped up onto him in a piggyback position and remained there as long as he could.

"Three *what?*" Turner asked.

"Skulls. Three human skulls."

"How do ya know they're human?"

"Oh hell, they could be gorilla skulls then," he grumbled. "Whaddya want me to do? I'm here with Sherilyn and the kids. You want I should collect 'em in a bag and bring 'em to the station?"

"No, don't touch a thing. Just hang tight until I can get the right people up there. Where are you?"

"The deer camp; ya know where that is?"

"Yeah. But not sure about the county lines there. Is that Pittsburg County or Haskell?"

"It's technically in Kinta, so that's Latimer County..."

Sherilyn held Jessica in her arms in the back seat. She wasn't sure if Jessica had been close enough to the skulls to know what they were, or if her silence was more reaction to their nervous body language and impending nightfall.

The family had been coming to this spot for over a decade. And just like that—three sets of human remains appear maybe twenty yards from one of their deer stands. How had they not seen them?

Sherilyn remembered the photocopied pictures of the Jamison family on the walls at her work four years earlier. When she saw that the wife's name was the same as hers, she felt a little like Sarah Connor in *The Terminator*.

In the four years since the case was in the news, she and Tim had never discussed it. She was pretty sure her husband didn't know anything about the Jamisons.

Outside the truck, his frustrated voice carried. "...Kinta's not in Haskell County, bud...no it ain't..."

After the Tims finally got off the phone, the Grahams waited in their utility vehicle with the doors locked as the blood-red tree line succumbed to the brood of civil and then nautical twilight.

The kids were on edge, and so were the adults, further unsettling the kids. Tim had hoped some light tunes on the radio might throw off the macabre yoke of their discovery, but it only made the situation eerier. As it turns out, country love songs don't pair well with human skeletal remains.

Mrs. Graham closed her eyes again and visualized the missing poster she saw on the wall at work from what seemed like ages ago. The last-known image of Madyson was taken somewhere near their current location (a sobering thought in and of itself). In it, she made a strange face, an open-mouthed expression that exposed her recently lost two front baby teeth. The first thought that had come into Sherilyn's head when she found the smaller skull facing up to the sunny sky with its missing front teeth was *Please don't let this be that little girl.*

She hugged Jessica, tightly.

THE NEXT HOUR felt like an eternity, during which the Graham party sustained several jump-scares as creatures of the night trundled from their bedrooms to their kitchens. Though Tim threatened several times to just drive home—"Oh, to hell with this," he blurted every ten minutes or so—they waited, because both he and his wife knew it would look bad if they left.

Finally, Tim Turner arrived with the cavalry, an "army" of cruisers and county service vehicles. The Grahams let out a collective sigh of relief. Each of them had shuddered at the idea of waiting around for several more nighttime hours in the woods.

Tim led a procession of deputies to the remains. This time, without his family, the wilderness felt alive, like trees were scarecrow-like figures that moved when he wasn't looking. For years, he had expressly avoided two things—cops and these here woods at night—and now here he was, marooned in the latter at the command of the former.

Tim pointed out all three skulls, and then-Deputy Turner spun around and faced him: "And y'all was huntin', you said?"

"Scoutin' locations for to, yeah... *we been coming here since 2000, Tim.*"

The deputies hung long strips of yellow tape blocking off the trail and began processing the scene. Turner accompanied Tim back to the truck and listened to his full account of the discovery. He quarantined the family to keep them from corroborating details with each other, and deputies took statements from Sherilyn, Lane, and Jessica individually, one at a time. He gave them a pencil and paper to transcribe their verbal stories.

For the first hour or two, there was no doubt that deputies were suspicious of the Graham family.

"How did you come across all three skulls?" Turner asked Mrs. Graham.

This pissed Tim right off, and he threatened to leave again. By one in the morning, they had gone through the story a half dozen more times, and Turner wanted them to stay longer.

"No, we're done. This is bullshit," Tim finally said. "I got a child who needs meds. You know where I live."

The Grahams drove off Panola Mountain, never to camp there as a family again.

THEIR NEXT POINT reminded me of a comment made by Connie in a newspaper interview. She'd claimed the family learned the area in which the Jamisons were looking was owned by an oil company and wasn't for sale.

"If you research this enough," Tim Graham told me over the phone, "you'll find there wasn't a damn piece of property up there to sell."

"No," his wife echoed. "At that time, there was no property up there to buy."

"I know Kinta Mountain because I been on it for ten years."

"You mean Panola Mountain?" I asked, confused and for good reason.

"No. Panola's on the other side . . . you see, Kinta is the point where four counties meet on this mountain. It's not a mountain, really; it's a hill."

Tim said they were told that troopers would search the area where the remains were found "like a fine-toothed comb." But he, his wife, and one of their neighbors went back to the spot the very next day.

"And I'll be damned if we didn't find a kid's tennis shoe and the femur bone . . . in about twenty minutes."

Again, he'd called Turner: "'We found more bones, bud!' But they didn't search that damn ground," Tim scoffed. "Gimme a break."

They were also told there was a thousand-dollar reward for their discovery.

"There wasn't no damn thousand bucks, neither."

"Sure wasn't."

"I mean, it's not like we was looking for money, but they said what they said."

Perhaps the most surprising thing Tim told me came when I finally asked my follow-up question concerning the location of the hole in the skull.

"If you take your finger right now, put it on your nose, and take it to the top of your head and go to the right maybe two inches, that's where it was. I remember like it was yesterday."

"And you said you thought it was an exit hole on the top?" I asked.

"Yeah. The one skull had a perfect hole on the top of the head like he put a gun under his chin and shot himself. I'll tell you my theory—because the other two skulls didn't have no holes—"

"That we could see."

"—that we could see. I think he killed his wife, the kid started running, and he shot her . . ."

"Murder-suicide."

". . . and then he couldn't take it and killed himself." Tim paused for a moment. "That's what I think, but it could have happened a million other ways. Yeah, some people thought wild animals could have dragged them down, but you know what, bullshit, because there was no chew marks. And animals might have dragged something, but there's no way in hell animals would have dragged them so close together, fifteen yards apart, in a triangle pattern. The skulls made a perfect triangle."

"Hm-hmm. A perfect triangle."

THERE WERE MANY intriguing aspects of the Grahams' story, but the most immediate question I had was the same one Mrs. Graham asked herself: how did they not discover the remains earlier?

Their family had been going to that spot for over a decade. They knew Smokestack Hollow inside and out and had thoroughly explored it in the course of scouting the best spots for camping and deer stands. Inasmuch as they were able to quickly and easily spot all three partially submerged skulls in 2013, it's odd that they missed what would have presumably been three fully intact bodies on the surface of the ground cover in 2009, when the Jamisons had only been missing for a month, and then continued to miss them for the next three years.

The multiple search operations on Panola, which purportedly covered an area of ten miles, also missed them. While tasked with a much larger search vector proportionally, they also had several thousand times more people and equipment at their disposal.

Did all these people really miss seeing three family members lying dead in a forty-five-yard triangle formation? Or is it possible that no one saw the remains there because they hadn't yet been deposited?

CHAPTER 13

Butterfly Kisses

DOWNTOWN EUFAULA HAS ONE THOROUGHFARE of small municipal buildings and businesses and, fittingly, that's Main Street, which extends for just a few blocks.

One of the buildings, the Kelley Memorial Chapel of Hunn, Black & Merritt Funeral Home, was built in 1937, when Eufaula, or "Eufoley," as locals often called it, was a much different place. The town folk still used potbellied stoves and got bed sick with scarlet fever. It was the dawn of the land acquisition rush when most of McIntosh County's acres were gobbled up by speculators hungry for mineral rights.

A few years later, Eufaula got war bond fever. Children walked up and down Main Street selling red poppy cards and collecting scrap metal to support the war effort. Military convoys from Muskogee County's Camp Gruber trundled by the new funeral house, and the kids in uniform waved at their younger selves.

Inside the storied chapel, a small funeral service was held in July 2014. Members of the Jamisons' immediate and extended family, including Star, Colton, Connie, Dana, Jack, and Jack's brothers and sisters, occupied the first two rows.

Niki Shenold sat in the back row with her husband and Melanie, a mutual friend of the Jamisons. In the last year or two, a rift had formed between Niki and Star. There was no clear account of how it happened, but Star had made it clear prior to the funeral that she didn't want her in attendance. Niki came anyway, but did not speak a word to anyone. The mourners faced forward, looking to the front of the chapel, where flower bouquets surrounded three ornately designed urns at rest on a table. Behind this display stood three white columns, each crowned with a framed photo of the family arranged to form a triangle.

At the beginning of the service, music was played briefly, the country song "Butterfly Kisses," whose lyrics include:

> *I must have done something right*
> *To deserve a hug every morning*
> *And butterfly kisses at night*

Bobby's cousin Dana Jamison, who had traveled in from out of state, found herself sitting next to Starlet. Dana had always had a cordial enough relationship with her, but they'd never been particularly close. She was a little surprised when Star held onto her arm and broke down, sobbing uncontrollably. Caught up in the moment, Dana extended to her all the grace she had, for the woman had lost her only child and her only grandchild.

They say that there is relief in knowing that for the families of missing persons, it's better to learn their fate—even if the news is horrific—and get some kind of closure.

After the remains were found, Sherilyn's mom Connie said: "...I hope those remains are [the Jamisons]. I know that sounds strange, but I need closure. All the people who've been affected by this need closure."

But Dana remembered Starlet talking with confidence about how Bobby, Sherilyn, and Madyson would pop up someday, perhaps returning from Mexico—the whole nightmare would turn out to be a huge misunderstanding.

Maybe Starlet needed that hope. Maybe she needed it to be unresolved because the truth was just too horrifying. Dana turned her head to look down at her moaning and holding desperately to her arm and wondered if maybe it would have been better for her not to know.

Starlet later told one journalist that close to the time the remains were found, she had prayed for a miracle.

"I think that God knew that I needed something," she said. "It's just given me a little bit of peace just knowing that they have been found. I know that they are with God and they are in a better place."

Shortly after the OCME released the Jamison family's autopsies, former Sheriff Beauchamp went to the office of one of the OSBI investigators assigned to the case and talked to her about it face-to-face.

"I just kinda wanted to check in, now that the bodies have been recovered, ya know, what the status of the case is at this point?"

The agent looked confused at first, then said, matter-of-factly, "Well, the case is closed, Israel."

"Oh, okay. So, how did they die?"

"All the evidence suggests it was natural causes, an accident—they got lost out there and probably died of exposure. Hypothermia, most likely."

"What about the bullet hole?"

"The pathologist didn't see anything more than damage caused by animal scavengers after the fact." She saw the doubt in his eyes. "But, talk to me, what do you think it was, a murder-suicide?"

"No, if it was murder-suicide, they woulda found her gun—the twenty-two pistol. Did y'all take metal detectors up there?"

Beauchamp was frustrated. When he retired as sheriff, he assumed the investigation would remain ongoing until more evidence could be developed. He didn't think the case would simply be shut down.

"We took everything. There was no gun."

"Then that's a murder," he said with a grin.

CHAPTER 14

Under Suspicious Circumstances

T HE FIRST RECORDED AUTOPSY WAS conducted on Julius Caesar after his assassination by Roman Senators on the Ides of March of 44 b.c. The doctor, Antistius, inspected each of the dead dictator's twenty-three stab wounds to determine which one had killed him. When he was finished, Antistius reported his findings to the citizenry from the Forum, which is how the Latin words "from the forum" gave us our modern-day term "forensic."

For the bulk of the first two millennia a.d., medical science and pathological discourse were dominated by the four humors, Hippocrates' theory that the health of the human body depended on the proper equilibrium of four fundamental substances: black bile, yellow bile, blood, and phlegm. Physicians were still invoking the debunked humoral theory as late as the mid-1900s.

The first known autopsy completed to determine whether or not a crime was committed—what became known as a "medico-legal" autopsy—was in 1302, when the Italian physician-philosopher Bartolomeo da Varignana presided over the anatomical post-mortem examination of the "black Azzolino," whose presumably poisoned body turned olive- then black-hued within hours of death.

The first autopsy conducted in the New World was ordered by the Catholic Church to determine if the conjoined twins Joana and Melchiora shared a soul. The priest baptized them both just to be on the safe side.

It's easy to take something like an autopsy for granted, but for much of human history, causes of death weren't understood. One can't help but wonder how many people got away with murder. Even when the medical establishment did regularly conduct medico-legal investigations and autopsies, their diagnoses were as likely to be wrong as right. In 1912, American physician Richard Cabot audited 3,000 autopsies and found that over half of them were incorrect.

The field of physical anthropology was in its early development at this time, and though it had to weather the pseudoscientific scourges of criminal anthropology, phrenology, and eugenics, the widespread study of skeletons led to anthropometry and the ghoulish but necessary body farms where scientists studied human decomposition. Eventually, in the 1950s and 1960s, forensic anthropology emerged, buoyed by the high-profile case of the paraphiliac cannibal and serial killer Ed Gein.

In the decades that followed, forensic anthropologists assisted law enforcement and medical examiners in identifying and unearthing the mass graves of genocidal war crimes and the burial sites of sadistic murderers. One such case was that of the West Mesa "Bone Collector," Albuquerque's very own serial killer.

The Bone Collector

The high desert plateau of the Rio Grande Valley, once the sacred home of countless Native Americans and diverse wildlife, became the "War Zone," a high-crime neighborhood known for murder, homelessness, drug use, and sex workers.

On February 2, 2009—incidentally, the same year the Jamisons went missing—Christine Ross was walking her dog Rucca through the morning shadows of the West Mesa subdivision community named Paradise. Rucca dug up a large bone and presented it to her. Disturbed, Christine texted a picture of it to her sister, who was a nurse. Her sister said it looked like a human femur bone.

Police investigators arrived on the scene and discovered the remains of multiple human bodies buried across 100 acres of barren land. The Albuquerque Police Department (APD) launched a massive effort, methodically excavating the entire site using heavy equipment, hand sifting, and satellite pictures to study ground disturbance and determine possible grave locations.

It turned into the largest crime scene in American history, requiring around-the-clock work for nearly three months. Ultimately, the APD recovered the skeletal remains of eleven bodies and one fetus. Detectives suspected the work of a serial killer (Albuquerque's first), who was dubbed the "Bone Collector."

Dirk Gibson, an expert on serial killers, called the unsolved West Mesa murders Albuquerque's "crime of the century." West Mesa, however, was not the crime scene, Gibson asserted, only a "dumping ground." Additional "ongoing" murders could involve different grave sites and possibly even additional killers.

Because only bones were recovered, Albuquerque investigators had limited evidence to examine. It took forensic anthropologists nearly a year to identify all the victims, who were likely killed between 2004–2005.

The medical examiner designated the manner of death as "undetermined," but the cause of death was "homicidal violence," likely strangulation or suffocation.

What I would learn was that the medico-legal investigation mirrored the Jamison case. Though the two cases were significantly different in many regards, both had four-year gaps between the victims' deaths and the discovery of their remains, and both required the work of forensic anthropologists.

Forensic Clues

The field of forensic anthropology is based on the idea that the skeleton is a kind of time capsule. Like the growth rings in a tree trunk or the geologic layers of sediment underneath the Earth's surface, the bones of the dead provide a window into the past.

Forensic anthropologists are called upon to assist in medical examinations when decedents are considered missing persons or the victims of crime and the only biological remains are skeletons or partial skeletons. Their methods help to estimate primary indicators—namely, the age, race, gender, and height of the deceased. This doesn't 100 percent identify the person, but it narrows the possibilities down. Combined with other methods and identifiers—DNA analysis, fingerprints, comparing ante-mortem and post-mortem dental and medical records, anthropometry, and pathologies (deformities)—examiners can get pretty close.

Pathologists study anatomical features to estimate characteristics like age. For example, it is easier to determine a more exact age of death in children because of their predictable growth rates. With adults, examiners must make broad guesses based on the degeneration of the skeleton. This is why in some autopsies, one might see "all cranial sutures are open, including the spheno-occipital synchondrosis," because an unfused bone can indicate a subadult or child.

Determining the cause of death based only on skeletal remains is a different story altogether and requires evidence of injury: a knife wound that penetrates bone and leaves a signature striation pattern; strangulation that fractures a particular bone in the neck; blunt force trauma that leaves telltale fracture patterns; a gunshot wound that leaves behind ballistics. But in each of these examples, the bones alone may not contain conclusive enough evidence on which to make a determination.

These examples are skeletal remains that contain clear injuries. But even in cases of brutal murder, bones aren't necessarily affected. And when bones do contain fractures or damage, it can be difficult for pathologists to determine whether they occurred before or after death.

The autopsies of the eleven women and one fetus recovered in West Mesa concluded that the manner of death was homicidal violence. But based on what has been publicly released, there were no specific injuries that enabled them to determine the cause of death.

"Unless a number of women independently decided to walk there to die, there is no other explanation besides serial murder," Gibson said in an interview with the *El Paso Times*.

The Jamison case was starkly different in its context clues. Smokestack Hollow was almost certainly not a serial killer's burial ground; it wasn't the repository for a sequence of targeted killings committed by one or more psychotic predators over several years.

A different kind of nightmare played out on Panola Mountain—a mysterious confluence of events that looked more like a hallucinatory logic puzzle than a criminal investigation.

I wondered if the autopsies contained any clues, anything that could shed some light. There had to be something in the raw material facts that could bring us closer to the truth.

The laws around releasing autopsies vary by state, and I assumed—wrongly, it turned out—that because I was not a Jamison family member, I would have to file either FOIA or the Oklahoma State equivalent. So I did that—I looked online, filed, emailed, etc. At one point, I found abstracted versions of the autopsies by looking through probate court records. But I wanted the full documents.

Then I went to the Oklahoma State Medical Examiner's website and learned that all I had to do was email them requesting the documents. I did that and received the full autopsies a few days later.

It was the journalistic equivalent of struggling for hours to pick a lock, only to find out the door was ajar.

But I had my reading material for the evening—three autopsies, replete with the forensic anthropologist's consultation reports.

The Jamison Autopsies

Sherilyn's report stated the decedent's name as Sherilyn Leighann Jamison, age forty-five (the forensic pathologist, for some reason, included the years they were missing into their age), who was "injured or became ill," and listed the location of discovery as "heavily wooded" premises "south of Kinta." Under "Manner of Death," he checked: Unknown.

Type of Death: Under Suspicious Circumstances

CAUSE OF DEATH: CAUSE OF DEATH UNKNOWN (INCOMPLETE SKELETAL REMAINS)

MANNER OF DEATH: COULD NOT BE DETER-MINED

CIRCUMSTANCES OF DEATH: These human re-mains were recovered on the northern side of San Bois Mountains south of Kinta (Latimer County) on November 16, 2013.

I. CIRCUMSTANCES OF THE EXAMINATION: The postmortem examination of Sherrilynn Leighann Jamison is performed at the Office of the Chief Medical Examiner, Eastern Division, Tulsa, Oklahoma, on 6/12/2014 commencing at 1300 hours. Assisting in the examination is Angela Berg.

II. CLOTHING AND PERSONAL EFFECTS: Re-covered with the remains includes a bra cup and a green/brown colored leather-like boot. These clothing effects are further delineated in the forensic anthropol-ogist's consultation report.

External Examination: These skeletal remains consist of a cranium with 10 maxillary teeth and fragments of the left humerus, left ilium and left femur. These remains represent 1.8% by number and 27.18% by weight of a total human skeleton. The skeletal remains are bleached and weathered and no residual tissue or odor is identified.

> Injuries: No perimortem trauma is noted to the remains. Due to the absence of the skin, soft tissue, internal organs and the remaining skeleton perimortem trauma cannot be excluded. Carnivore damage is noted to the cranium and proximal and distal ends of three long bones. Rodent damage is noted to all the skeletal elements.

The "Anthropology Consultation" report restated much of the same with some additional information:

> Postmortem Interval: 18 months to 5 years
>
> The skeletal materials are bleached and weathered, with no tissues or odor, and green discoloration. There is carnivore and rodent activity on all bones. The shoe is discolored, has tearing from animals and the glue has detached. The bra cup was under a leaf litter layer. This suggests these items have been in place prior to the previous fall season.
>
> Positioning: The staining of the cranium and the limited damage to the nasal bones and nasal conchae suggested that the cranium had limited movement. A map based on the GPS coordinates shows the locations of all the recovered items, suggesting that these individuals decomposed in a nearby location. (See attached GPS coordinates and mapping.)

By number, less than two percent of Sherilyn's bones were recovered; by weight, under thirty percent. Of these, the medical examination found no evidence of "perimortem trauma," meaning injury prior to death, but noted that because of the limited remains, it cannot be ruled out.

Bobby's autopsy listed the decedent as Bobby Dale Jamison, age 48 (again, lost years were counted in the age).

CAUSE OF DEATH: CAUSE OF DEATH UNKNOWN (INCOMPLETE SKELETAL REMAINS)

MANNER OF DEATH: COULD NOT BE DETERMINED

CLOTHING AND PERSONAL EFFECTS: Recovered from the scene include a left boot, right insole of a boot, tongue of a boot, a clothing label and a fragment of a flexible material with a cloth material on one side.

External Examination: These remains consist of a cranium with one maxillary molar, bilateral femora and a right humerus. These remains represent 2.2% by number and 35.09% by weight of a total human skeleton. These remains are completely skeletonized, bleached and weathered and there is no residual soft tissue or order.

INJURIES: No perimortem trauma is identified to the remains. Carnivore damage is noted on the cranium and proximal and distal ends of the bilateral femora and right humerus. Due to the absence of skin, soft tissue, internal organs and most of the remaining skeleton, perimortem trauma cannot be ruled out.

Madyson's autopsy listed the decedent's name as "Madyson Stormy Star Jamison" with the age noted as 10 (perhaps because they were unable to determine an approximate time/date of death).
The conclusions reached were the same as for Bobby and Sherilyn:

Due to the incomplete skeletal remains, the cause and manner of death were "undetermined." Due to the lack of skin, viscera, and the remaining skeleton, perimortem trauma [or foul play] could not be ruled out.

The anthropologist report added that only the calvarium of her cranium was recovered, but the open sutures helped determine her young age.

The short list of Madyson's personal effects found at the scene included "a white shoe with rhinestone embellishments and a dried flower (undetermined if natural or man-made)."

ONCE AGAIN, A major discovery—arguably the most important, the recovery of their family's remains—had concluded with a now-familiar refrain: undetermined—we don't know.

Two major time-based hurdles had hindered investigators, including the coroner's office, every step of the way. One was the duration of time—approximately nine days—between the Jamisons' last-known sighting and law enforcement arriving at the scene and declaring them missing. The other was the four years between when the Jamisons went missing and the discovery of their partial remains.

IN MY LIMITED capacity to understand an autopsy report, a few thoughts occurred to me after reading and rereading the documents. One, of course, was that there was no specific mention of any hole in a skull. Pathologist Joshua Lanter wrote that "postmortem carnivore damage and rodent damage is noted to the cranium," and this was the same for all three reports. There was nothing marked for one skull in particular suggesting even the potential for anomalous damage.

But the reports also stated that "perimortem trauma cannot be excluded," which brings me to my next point.

Very few of their bones were recovered. The way various publications described the discovery over the years, one might have thought authorities recovered near-full or partial skeletons, but there wasn't anything close to that. They really just found a few bones and personal effects.

The remains represented only 2.2% of Bobby's skeleton, less than 2% of Sherilyn, and 0.6% of Madyson's (for whom only one bone, the calvarium of her skull, was recovered). The logistics of this—particularly the fact that all three of their skulls were found but little else—struck me as strange. More tangibly, it underscored the relative meaninglessness of not finding evidence of injuries consistent with homicide. Consider all the ways there are for a person to be killed, and then imagine how many of them could be conclusively determined from looking at just one or two of the victim's bones four years later.

Was it possible that because of the totality of damage, Dr. Lanter simply couldn't issue a conclusive determination as to the nature of the hole? Could prudence and due diligence have dictated that he ascribe the damage to postmortem scavenging rather than bolster a narrative of foul play that couldn't be substantiated?

I tried several times contacting both Dr. Joshua Lanter and Angela Berg through the Oklahoma State Medical Examination Department, but never received a reply. I even left a message with the department's press secretary, asking simply for a statement regarding the claims of a gunshot wound. No response. Without hearing from them or seeing a photo of the skull, there was little more I could do but set the question aside until I could at least speak with someone knowledgeable in wound ballistics.

Another passage that stood out to me regarded the time and positioning of decomposition. The pathologist wrote: "The bra cup was under a leaf litter layer. This suggests these items have been in place prior to the previous fall season." According to Dr. Lanter's analysis, how long the items were in that specific location couldn't be narrowed down any more than to at least since sometime before the previous year. He noted the postmortem interval in a different section as anywhere from "18 months to 5 years." He also wrote that characteristics of the cranium suggested it had "limited movement" and likely "decomposed in a nearby location."

These details are important in considering whether this was the location where the Jamisons died or whether their remains might have decomposed in another "nearby" location in Smokestack Hollow, or somewhere elsewhere entirely.

There was also something about the position and ratio of the bones that seemed strange. If the location in Smokestack Hollow was the site where they died, and the accident narrative is true, the way the Grahams claimed the remains were found, in a triangle, is obviously strange, but more specifically, if they died together, wouldn't you expect to see Madyson's remains mixed with or close to the parents' bones?

The expected rejoinder to this would be that after the Jamisons' accidental death due to exposure, the remains were pilfered and scattered by scavengers. So then which spot are we looking at in Smokestack Hollow: was this the spot where they originally died, with the remains recovered representing what was left over after scavengers did their thing, or was this simply a spot to which those few remains were dragged?

If this was the location where their full bodies had once laid intact, why weren't more of their clothes and effects found there? If this was simply a location to which animals dragged a few of their remains, it strikes me as weirdly coincidental that all three of them were represented, including all three of their skulls.

One of the most haunting statements in the autopsies came in the forensic anthropologist's notes and pertained to Madyson's personal effects—her "white shoe with rhinestone embellishments and a dried flower." The image of this little girl, the Jamisons' miracle child, reduced to a small, bedazzled shoe, was a gut punch.

Then there was the dried flower, which, in a series of reports largely devoid of surprises or curveballs, was unexpectedly chilling. The notes stated it was unclear whether the flower was "natural or man-made."

I couldn't help but wonder about the context in which investigators recovered this little artifact. Did they collect other vegetation or leaves from the area, or just this one dried flower? Did they at one point consider it to have evidentiary value? Where was it found, inside the footwear or lying on top? Was it Madyson's prior to her death, perhaps affixed cosmetically to her shoe like the rhinestone embellishments?

Was it possible someone left it for her after she died?

Body Dump

According to trained investigators and search and rescue experts, there are two main circumstances in which a body or skeletal remains will turn up in a previously searched area. The most frequently seen one is that the search teams simply missed it.

After reading Robert Koester's *Lost Person Behavior* and speaking with him, it became clear to me that it is not uncommon for search and rescue operations to narrowly miss finding bodies, even when that area has received multiple inspections, especially when they are tasked with covering expansive, mountainous terrain. Offhand, 2.7 miles may not sound like much, but as the crow flies (a phrase I would start hearing a lot), it's a pretty significant chunk of land.

The second reason why searchers and K9 teams could have missed the remains is that they weren't there at the time of the search. This falls into the "body dump" theory. In his book *Geographic Profiling*, veteran detective D. Kim Rossmo wrote that "the forensic-conscious murderer" may dispose of his victim's body in a remote location that is different from the actual murder site in an attempt to confuse investigators. Over time, exposure to the elements and scavenging animals disarticulates the skeleton, erodes trace evidence, and complicates the recovery process.

"Homicide detectives consider such a case the hardest type of murder to solve, stripped as it is of chronology and physical evidence."

With respect to the Jamison case, I couldn't help but think that if a perpetrator wanted to slow-play the depositing of the bones so that the remains would eventually be found, but not in a way that could be incriminating or make the authorities more suspicious, this is the way he would do it: wait a few years until the investigation has died down, take the skulls and a few bones and personal effects, and toss them in a popular but remote hunting ground, where it is inevitable that someone will stumble upon them.

———

AT SOME POINT, I realized that my interest in the case was venting from greater depths than just a criminal inquiry. I wanted to know what happened to the Jamisons that day in the woods, but I also wanted to know the truth about their lives. It's easy for a person's visceral day-to-day reality to be distorted when retroactively translated for outside analysis.

If, in the blink of an eye, you suddenly disappeared, and someone were to come along and try to explain your life and the circumstances of your disappearance based on your movements, diaries, purchases, conversations, texts, web searches, etc.—what would they conclude? If police investigators, journalists, and mobs of online sleuths began looking back through all the loose ends and rough edges of your life, would they find anything provocative or anomalous?

I began reaching out to Bobby and Sherilyn's friends and family members to try and learn the unvarnished truth of this story.

CHAPTER 15

Scorpio Rising

N IKI REMEMBERED A DAY BEFORE Sherilyn had even met Bobby when the two of them walked the quaint backroads in Oklahoma City to a tarot and crystal shop. They browsed the calcified stones and tarot decks, giddily pointing out overpriced occultnik and bargain esoterica. There was a clearance sale on intuition stones—two for the price of one.

Sherilyn inspected an amethyst with the intensity and scholarship of a professional appraiser, lacking only the loupe or magnifying monocle by which she might assess the crystal lattice for iron impurities, transition metals, and trace elements.

The semi-precious violet quartz, named after the Greek word for "intoxicate," was a healing stone preferred by those with spiritual abilities.

"My daughter will be an indigo ..." Sherilyn breathed, her eyes glowing with intensity.

Niki looked at her thoughtfully. She didn't know Sherilyn wanted another child.

Though they had both generally eschewed traditional religion, they shared a faith that some benevolent cosmic force lay in and behind the scenes of the clown's autopsy that was modern life.

This extended to an interest in more neo-pagan themes and the belief that certain people had powers, affinities—*abilities*—linking them with that source energy.

Before leaving, Niki and Sherilyn swooped up some witchcraft books to put on their respective coffee tables, largely as a joke to see peoples' reactions when they came over.

THE YEAR 2004 was a titanic one for the Jamisons: Sherilyn and Bobby married, gave birth to Madyson (against the odds), and moved to a new home in a new town about two hours away from OKC.

Eufaula was a small lakeside hamlet that had everything the young family of four needed: privacy, a respite from city life, and more natural wilderness than they could ever explore. Their house overlooked Eufaula Lake; their backyard was literally a private beach of white sand leading down to a small dock and pier. Mortgage payments would be tight—renovating the gutted infrastructure would take some serious elbow grease—but it was, in many ways, their dream home.

Around the same time, Niki, who had also remarried, gave birth to her daughter. Though Sherilyn's new home was a four-hour round-trip drive, Niki made the trip often, and, like Chrissie before her, took the journey of motherhood with Sherilyn.

Over time, their daughters became best friends, while Niki grew to think of Sherilyn as her sister.

SHORTLY AFTER THE Jamisons had settled in at their new lakeside house, Niki visited and from the moment she arrived, Sherilyn was in constant motion, flitting around the house with the kinetic energy of a caffeinated waiter. She was practically glowing with joy, her face flushed with inspiration.

Niki recognized this state.

A few months earlier, she watched an impassioned Sherilyn attempt to start a garden after abruptly deciding that she wanted to grow corn and possibly other vegetables. Donning dusty overalls, her auburn hair concealed under a faded blue bandana,

Sherilyn turned into the living embodiment of *The Old Farmer's Almanac*, extolling the virtues of living self-sufficiently off the land and, someday, off the grid.

When Sherilyn was genuinely excited about something, she had the magnetism of a leader. The next month when Niki returned, however, Sherilyn had cooled on the garden idea and was on to something new.

From the excited utterances echoing through the hallways and rooms, she gathered that Sherilyn had come up with a business idea. Niki sat on the couch in the center of her friend's wild migratory orbits around the living room. She glanced at the coffee table, which was plumaged end-to-end in loose-leaf pages of notes and financial estimates.

A fragment of the front cover of the witchcraft book she bought from the crystal shop protruded from underneath. Niki had gotten rid of her copy years earlier—Sherilyn must have held onto hers.

Leaning over to look at some of the notes, Niki struggled to decipher her friend's distinctive handwriting, but she made out enough to know it was research on business licensing and commercial real estate properties available in Eufaula.

Sherilyn plopped down beside her on the couch, grinning as she buoyantly configured her legs into the yogic easy pose. Then she took a deep breath and closed her eyes, as though passing into the eye of the hurricane.

"Did you win the lottery or something?" Niki asked, with a confused smile.

"We all did." Sherilyn bounced on the sofa cushion, arms and face genuflecting to the heavens, as though she were receiving fresh manna. "There's like a one in a trillion chance that any of us would even be here—and yet, here we are!"

"Okay, lady, how many cups of coffee have you had?"

Sherilyn then explained, in a non-linear and tangent-filled soliloquy, her decision to rent a storefront in Eufaula's business district and convert it into a hair salon. By the time she concluded, her excitement and energy had hardened into sober self-possession. "I'm gonna start my own salon. I know everything I need; why work for someone else when I can do it better and make more money?"

For as long as Niki had known her, Sherilyn had always been a diligent researcher. They sometimes half-ironically attributed this to her zodiac sign, as Scorpios are known for being intensely observant and studious. A meme that periodically circulated online joked, "How a Scorpio's brain works," with an image of a light switch and its two settings: *utterly obsessed* and *uninterested.*

She had seen this capricious nature in her friend before, but only in short bursts—flights of fancy and spontaneous ideas infused with euphoria. It's one of the things she loved about Sherilyn: her love and embrace of the moment, the trust she placed in her own intuition and instincts.

She was most certainly a Scorpio, a "creature with the burning sting." Her endless curiosity and attention to detail felt like a force of nature at times.

Sherilyn was fiercely, unstoppably spiritual. She often said, "Synchronicity is the universe telling you you're on the right track."

She believed God was all around us, infused into all particles of matter. Everything was a sign. There was no such thing as a coincidence or accident.

Once, when she and Bobby were having relationship trouble and arguing more than usual, Sherilyn looked down and saw a rubber band in the shape of a heart by her foot. This was all she needed—a single portent reminding her that love would guide the way.

Sherilyn's favorite books were *The Secret* and *The Seven Spiritual Laws of Success*, works which reinforced her belief in the power of intention and the law of attraction. Positive thoughts attract positive outcomes; dark thoughts attract negative outcomes.

Almost every time Niki visited Sherilyn, she was working on some big new idea or project. She did her homework, too; she conferred obsessively with sources, crunched numbers, and planned meticulously. If she didn't have an answer for something, she hunted it down. But usually, by the next time they talked, Sherilyn was on to something new, equally convinced it was the next big thing.

Chrissie had seen and felt these qualities back at the salon in OKC. Though she was amazed at Sherilyn's energy, it often felt unstructured and "manic." She'd wondered more than once if her friend had adult ADHD.

Niki now wondered the same.

Normally, Sherilyn's feverish plans and ideas didn't require squandering money or resources. Normally, there weren't palpable negative consequences. This time, however, she had pushed the envelope. After convincing Bobby that the hair salon would be a hit, they paid six months of rent in advance for the storefront space. Bobby spent even more time, effort, and money on costly renovations, installing a wash bowl and salon chair, painting the walls, and cobbling together a marquee that they hoisted above the entrance.

Then, almost overnight, she lost interest in the whole endeavor. Niki asked her about it over the phone a few weeks later, and she barely even remembered. She murmured, "Oh yeah" with a disinterested "meh" and said she had scrapped the idea, before quickly changing the subject.

This pattern repeated over and over again, and Niki started to wonder if it was symptomatic of a deeper issue.

The next time she visited, Sherilyn was a different person. As soon as the door opened, Niki could see that the fire in her eyes was gone, replaced by a cold, distant glaze.

Their time together was usually vibrant and celebratory, full of hugs, spontaneous dances, and uninhibited soul-spilling. But during this visit, Sherilyn didn't hug or greet her, didn't smile or make eye contact, and when Niki tried to ask her questions, she whispered one-word replies. Eventually, she disappeared into her room and didn't return until the next day.

The behavior was a saddening but predictable part of the pattern, and Niki didn't take it personally. She had long suffered depression herself. Briefly, she considered whether it could be the culprit in Sherilyn's case. But as she read anecdotes about the stormy vicissitudes of what at that time was still referred to as manic depression, she realized her friend was struggling with something other than just generalized depression or ADD.

Sherilyn's episodes would come on like an epic spring-cleaning frenzy applied to anything and everything, a ceaseless succession of explosive ideas, convictions, and grandiose plans that would keep her up for days at a time. This inspirational cleanse was followed by an intense crash, a period of darkness in which Sherilyn had no energy or motivation and could barely bring herself to leave her bed, much less engage with the world.

For most of her life, Sherilyn hadn't been aware of her condition in a concrete way. When she met Niki, she was still in the dark, and, in the 1980s and 1990s, the medical community was, too. Doctors considered drastically fluctuating moods to be a medical pathology, but their clinical diagnoses were limited, and it was routinely confused for schizophrenia or psychosis.

Although Niki and Sherilyn rarely spoke about her condition specifically, the two did address its reality, utilizing the gentle, sometimes unspoken channels of information transfer that close friends develop after years of mind-melding.

Sherilyn found that on both ends of the spectrum—the hypomania and the depression—the illness impaired her relationships, particularly with Bobby, with whom she argued intensely and often. Something as simple as how the toilet paper roll was affixed to the holder could provoke a yelling match that persisted deep into the night.

After years of struggling, Sherilyn eventually went to a doctor, who diagnosed her with bipolar disorder and prescribed her mood stabilizers and psychiatric medications to help manage the rapid cycling. Sherilyn took these meds, and for a time, her condition improved: her highs weren't so high; her lows weren't so low.

"[Sherilyn] was like two different people," Starlet said of her daughter-in-law. "When she was taking her meds, she was like the happiest person on Earth."

But Star, Niki, Colton, and others could only watch as another familiar pattern emerged: Sherilyn would take her meds, start to feel better, and then think, *I feel good and things are under control—I don't need these pills anymore.*

Once she was back on track and feeling better, she would stop taking them, and the cycle soon returned, sending her right back to square one. She sometimes experienced "mixed episodes" in which she descended into aggressive, dark states and poured her thoughts onto paper. Family members believed such an episode likely precipitated her "hate letter" to Bobby.

THE NIGHT THAT Sherilyn absconded to her bedroom, Niki waited patiently on the living room couch. She was alright with the alone time, because she had a stomachache . . . again. Over the years, Niki had gotten these periodically, but that night, she realized something—the stomachaches only happened when she was at the Jamisons' house.

I'll Never Be Normal

I first started communicating with Niki over Facebook, and this turned into a series of phone conversations over several years. She had taken a vow to herself and her family that she was done trying to solve the case. Her involvement a decade earlier had become so all-consuming and destabilizing that she swore to her husband she was done with it for good.

"There were stretches of three to four days in a row where I wouldn't sleep. Psychics, names of property owners, Facebook pages. I was neglecting everything else—family, friends, etc. because this was my life twenty-four-seven. My health was so bad, but I couldn't see it while I was in it. Bless my husband's heart, he was so patient with me," Niki said, noting that the issue was still a sensitive subject. "He thinks if I pick the case up again, I will go back down that rabbit hole. And I've had to fight it. As we move, I come across notes and get back into it—*why did I write this name down? What does that word mean?* But I've had to fight it. I pray about it a lot. If I'm meant to know, then God will let it happen. I've been feeling like he's nudging me."

"I'm interested in what happened on that mountain, of course," I said to her, "but I'm more intrigued with the real story behind this family—who they were and your experience with them. We don't have to go down any rabbit holes of what happened on the mountain."

I asked her about Sherilyn's experience with bipolar disorder. Niki recalled a time after she had discontinued her meds and experienced a particularly brutal cycle. Sherilyn finally broke down in front of her.

"I'm never going to be normal," she cried. "I'm going to have to take pills the rest of my life."

Niki, who had struggled with depression in her own life, understood the stigma placed on mental illness, the sense of shame in having to adhere to a daily pharmaceutical ritual just to feel "normal."

As did I.

From the time I turned eighteen, I knew I had some type of psychiatric imbalance. Throughout my twenties and much of my thirties, it was treated as generalized depression and anxiety, for which I tried just about every SSRI, SNRI, atypical antidepressant and benzo known to Western civilization, including Prozac, Lexapro, Zoloft, Wellbutrin, Venlafaxine, Xanax, Klonopin, and many more. I also tried amphetamines and the non-stimulant drug Strattera for my ADD.

While some of these meds helped allay my depressive symptoms, I long suspected there was something else going on. Because my aunt Jill had had bipolar disorder, I began to look more closely at its symptoms.

By the time I began researching the Jamison case, I was only about a year removed from my own diagnosis of "probably bipolar II," which I had at first heard as "in addition to generalized depression and anxiety, you probably have bipolar, too." But my doctor actually meant bipolar type II, the newly minted DSLM designation that grouped less severe cases of bipolar disorder into a constellation of hybridized affective disorders, including anxiety, substance abuse disorder, attention-deficit disorder, and various configurations of dual diagnosis. Currently, there are up to five different versions of bipolar disorder.

Unlike the majority of illnesses, injuries, and conditions that can be physiologically diagnosed and treated, mental illness doesn't show up in x-rays or brain scans. It can't be objectively quantified. Scientists can point to phantom traces of how mental illness demotivates synapses—for example, a depressed person's brain scan shows fewer nerve fiber connections—but there isn't currently a way to diagnose mental illness just from looking at the brain. It's like a black hole of the mind—you can't see it, but you can intuit its presence from the destabilizing effects it has on surrounding systems.

Further complicating the discourse is the fact that scientists still don't know what causes mental illness. For many decades, it was a decided medical fact that depression was a neurochemical problem involving depleted serotonin levels. In recent years, however, this idea has been strongly challenged by studies showing there is little to no connection between depression and serotonin levels. While the regulation of this and other neurotransmitters through psychiatric medications, usually SSRIs, has been shown to help diminish the severity of symptoms, many scientists no longer view the cause of depression or other psychiatric conditions as primarily neurochemical. Instead, they believe it is an amalgam of biological or genetic predisposition, psychosocial contagion, personal trauma, and possibly even epigenetic memory.

Bipolar disorder has long been a problematic psychiatric condition to diagnose and treat. The condition involves two polar opposite settings, one of which, hypomania, often feels enjoyable. Bipolar is particularly tricky in this way because feeling good— sometimes really good—is part of the illness. The hypomania of the up cycles can generate prolonged periods of epiphanic clarity and feverish energy, which, from the outside, can resemble drug intoxication. Internally, for the affected, the experience feels lucid—organic.

It's hard to convince yourself you're sick and need medication when you're riding a wave of euphoria, a seemingly inexhaustible natural "high."

The problem, though, is it's not natural, and ultimately, it often causes people to do unnatural things, including spending sprees, drastic reactions, and risky sexual behavior. Like a superpower that can't be controlled, the up cycle warps reality. People with severe untreated bipolar may only realize the true nature of their illness when it lands them in a hospital or prison, and they realize that the invincibility of their mania is just as destabilizing and dangerous as the hopelessness of their depression.

One of the most difficult aspects of bipolar disorder is exemplified by Sherilyn's pattern of going on and off her meds. Sherilyn, it seems, wanted to believe that her internal strength of spirit and faith—her soul—was enough to overcome an illness of the mind. Despite knowing the pills stabilized her in some way, she was troubled by the idea of developing a lifelong dependence on psychiatric meds.

She based so much of her thinking on the law of attraction and the power of intention and positivity. But for Sherilyn, whose moods were unpredictable, it was not always possible to be positive.

THE MURDER-SUICIDE narrative of the Jamisons' disappearance seemed unfair to me initially. I couldn't help but get defensive when someone with bipolar was suspected of perpetrating something as heinous as murder-suicide. Mental illness can be an indicator of violence, but it's myopic to suggest a direct correlation. The reality is, statistics show people with bipolar disorder are more likely to be the victims of a crime than the perpetrators.

But severe cases can cause violent impulses and behavior, especially when untreated and/or compounded by other factors.

"Bipolar patients are prone to agitation that can result in impulsive aggression during manic and mixed episodes," an article in the *Psychiatric Times* stated. "However, depressed states can involve intense dysphoria with agitation and irritability, which can also increase the risk of violent behavior."

More indicative symptoms, the article continued, involve "paranoid delusions or command auditory hallucinations," as psychotic episodes, which can stem from bipolar disorder, are "associated with a higher risk of violence."

This made me think of the statements Bobby and Sherilyn supposedly made to Gary Brandon about their "spiritual oppression." This storyline remained one of the strangest unanswered questions for me, because it ostensibly involved two adults hallucinating similar things independently from each other on multiple occasions during the final weeks and days before they went missing.

One question that had gnawed at the back of my mind ever since I first read about this story involved this notion of Bobby seeing demons.

In its most severe iterations, bipolar disorder can produce delusions and hallucinations. So it's not improbable that Sherilyn, who was on and off her meds and naturally inclined to dwell on the spiritual realm, would have described vivid experiences with demons and spirits.

But what explained Bobby's claims? Where did his demons come from?

CHAPTER 16

A Dangerous Man

Dana Jamison couldn't remember a time when she didn't know her cousin Bobby. They saw each other often as kids, at the near-monthly Jamison family reunions. Bobby's father, Bob, and her father, Jack, were two of twelve siblings who grew up poor in rural Sallisaw, Oklahoma, picking cotton to survive.

As a kid, Dana wasn't allowed to stay the night, because Granddad was mean—scary mean. Bob and her other uncles relayed childhood stories: if they weren't doing the right thing—forget spankings, Granddad would chuck a hammer or pick up a board and hit them with it.

Dana still loved going to her grandparents' house, though. They lived on a big farm, and she and Bobby would go on adventures down the railroad tracks and get in trouble for swimming in the creek.

Bobby and Dana were each only children and accustomed to a certain standard of solitude. The other cousins were either older or younger, so Bobby and Dana gravitated to each other and quickly became inseparable. When I talked to Jack, he called them "thick as thieves."

Dana's parents divorced when she was around ten, after which she spent summers with her dad. This meant frequent visits to see Bobby, who spent the hot off-school months working at his dad's gas station. Dana would come to stay for a week and work at the gas station, too. It was exciting to handle cash transactions and pump gas for customers. They were a part of the real system of the world, fueling America's motorists. And they had fun together, working hard and fast with grins on their faces and springs in their steps. They even had fun closing down and cleaning up, gamifying menial tasks as only kids can.

Dana remembered Uncle Bob drove a hard bargain and liked to pontificate on the values of hard work and self-reliance, the virtue of not expecting handouts in life. When she showed up for her week of summer employment at the gas station, he would tell her, "You're gonna work for no pay because I'm providing you food and shelter." But at the end of the week, he'd always give her the money. He had a tough exterior and occasionally teased her to tears, but underneath, Bob was a softie when it came to his little niece.

With his son, however, it was different. Bob was harder on Bobby because he wanted his boy to be tough.

But Bobby was painfully shy and sensitive, the sweetest kid Dana ever knew in her whole life. He never once hurt her feelings. Bobby had a protective instinct but struggled to be assertive and communicate. He was tender at heart and when he got in trouble, he cried. Bob really didn't like this.

One day, Bob showed Dana and Bobby how to ride a horse. Dana, who was athletic and fearless, jumped right on and took a decent trip around the pen. When it was Bobby's turn, he struggled to bring his leg around the saddle and was visibly trembling.

"What is wrong with you? Get on the horse." Bob said with a look of disgust.

Feeling the weight of his father's gaze, Bobby slipped right off, got his foot stuck in the stirrup, and fell on his bottom. He started tearing up.

His dad laughed. "The girl's tougher than you are."

As they got older, Dana and Bobby remained close, and she saw that the tension between Bobby and his father didn't diminish. Bobby was still kind and soft-spoken and, in his teenage form, introverted; once he knew someone and trusted them, he would open up and share his thoughts, but he wasn't one to chat with strangers.

Dana remembered that Bobby was also a bit effeminate at this age. His father wanted him to play football, but that wasn't going to happen. Even were it not for the athletic requirements, Bobby was far too shy and reclusive to play a team sport.

Uncle Bob had a preternatural ability to repair just about anything, and he taught Bobby how to fix things, how to be scrappy with his hands and troubleshoot. From a very young age, Bobby helped his dad out on jobs, big and small. By sixteen, Bobby worked for his dad full-time at the gas station as well as varying jobs with Bob's many business ventures, which included a Christmas tree farm and a tow truck company.

Bob was always enterprising and seemed to have a golden touch. He brought Bobby with him to town auctions on the courthouse steps and bought up undervalued properties—always with cash—that he would fix up and resell for four to five times what he paid.

He also took Bobby along for searchlight jobs and taught him how to operate the old World War II-era apparatus, which was originally designed for use in bombing raids. The retro sci-fi-looking contraptions found a niche in local marketing and publicity events.

"This is a sixty-inch 'carbon arc,'" Bob said, proudly swiveling the mirrored parabolic reflector toward his son. "Only ten thousand of these were made, and most ended up in Europe after the war. These rods suck a hundred and fifty amps at seventy-eight volts, and burn at three thousand degrees."

Bobby liked knowing the secrets behind the magic. When it was activated, he marveled as a one-inch arch of magnified electricity somehow transformed into twin stalks of white light blasting into the night sky. The so-called "artificial moonlight" sliced past the corn fields, instantaneously outrunning the backcountry highways to tell every wayward motorist within thirty-five miles, "Here we are—something big is happening!"

Of the twelve Jamison siblings, none had more than one child, and most, including the Sallisaw brothers, worked hard to earn fortunes they could have never imagined growing up.

Like his brother, whose scrimping and industriousness netted a sizable savings, Bob Sr. had a good head when it came to financial matters. But whereas Jack was a lifer who worked for an electric company for many years, Bob was a freelance entrepreneur who liked to flip properties and businesses and earn a quick buck.

Bob aimed to retire in his fifties, and as that mark approached, he started liquidating his assets, selling off his companies one by one. But he always retained a business for Bobby: when he sold the gas station, he kept the tree farm, and Bobby worked there; then when he sold the tree farm, he kept the searchlights, and Bobby lugged the things around in his truck and did jobs.

He continued doing them even through two bouts of cancer, when he was so emaciated and sick no one was sure he would make it. Even after his car accident, when his back was, for all intents and purposes, broken, he kept working for as long as he could.

As adults, Dana didn't see that much of Bobby anymore. Distance and parenthood reduced their relationship to brief conversations at bi-annual family gatherings, at which they immediately sought each other out. She still loved Bobby; she just didn't see him very often and had her mind focused on the visceral and immediate necessities of life. They were at that age when the old worlds fell and, if you cling too tightly, you go down with them.

In 2009, Dana experienced a major health scare that required five surgeries. The experience took her out of commission in terms of keeping up with news of the family. But while Dana lost the thread of what was going on between Bobby and Bob, she was aware that in recent years, a major rift had taken place. When she heard the shocking news of the family's disappearance, she conferred over the phone with her father and other family members and gradually learned more about the nature of the Jamison conflict.

It was much worse than she had imagined.

The Rift

As with so many family conflicts, the central tension seemed to be over money. For many years, Bobby worked at and helped manage the gas station his father owned. He claimed he had worked for low or no pay under a verbal agreement with Bob that he would be compensated in future ownership shares when the company was eventually sold. But Bobby claimed this didn't happen, and when he found out that the sale had gone down, he filed paperwork to sue his sixty-seven-year-old father.

The situation devolved further when Bob Sr. amended his will to exclude Bobby, as well as his then-ex-wife Starlet, from receiving any of his estate or inheritance.

In May 2009, six months before the Jamison family vanished, Bobby filed a protective order against his father in the District Court of McIntosh County. His petition claimed that on November 1, 2008, shortly after he amended his will, his father came over to the Jamisons' home, where another vicious argument ensued, during which he threatened to kill Bobby and his family. Afterward, as Bob Sr. tried to drive off, Bobby had stood in front of his vehicle, blocking him. His father surged ahead anyway, barely missing contact. In his petition, Bobby wrote that Bob had tried to kill him right then and there.

Early in the next year, Bob Sr. allegedly repeated the death threat during a bathroom break while they were both at the courthouse for a hearing on the petition. Bobby wrote to the judge that he and his family feared for their lives at all times, describing his father, Bobby Dean Jamison, as a "very dangerous man who thinks he is above the law" and has been involved or associated with "prostitutes, gangs, and meth."

Dana couldn't square these claims with the father-son duo she had known her whole life. They might not have shared the closest or most loving relationship, and Bob could certainly be an insensitive hard-ass, but he had always taken care of Bobby financially and given him jobs. She just couldn't imagine what falling out they'd had that would have precipitated Bob making death threats and writing his already financially strapped son out of his will.

Over the course of several conversations with Dana, it became clear to me that she was baffled by this question. She spent a considerable amount of time thinking out loud, and at one point, she proffered that perhaps Bobby had unwittingly become a pawn in the protracted divorce battle between Bob Sr. and Starlet.

"[Starlet] kind of shielded Bobby from consequences. She came from a well-to-do family and from what I understand, they weren't thrilled with her marrying a local guy [Bob Sr.]. I've heard she wanted the money and fought my dad, so maybe she was trying to protect the money for Madyson. But for the Jamisons, if you were middle class you came from money."

This was a roundabout way of speculating that Bobby's legal moves against his father could have been influenced by Starlet. But the truth was, she didn't know and couldn't understand it.

As far as the bigger question of what happened to the Jamisons on the mountain, Dana was at a loss.

"Nothing makes sense," she said, echoing with authentic bewilderment a sentiment I'd heard from so many others. "The last we heard from the FBI, they were saying it was an accident."

"Do you believe that?"

She sighed. "Not really."

"What do you think happened?

"Somebody did something to them . . . but I don't know who, and I don't know why. I don't think Bobby had the fortitude to be a drug dealer. He would help someone in distress, so I can't see him selling. I don't know if they came upon something. He was always kind of gullible, so maybe somebody lured him there."

Uncle Jack

I also spoke with Dana's father, Jack Jamison, about the case. His daughter had described him as a soft-spoken, understated man (more akin to Bobby than Bob himself), and this tracked with how

he answered questions—with the bare minimum of words necessary to convey a point. In a way, he reminded me of my Grandpa
Harry and many of my relatives from Arkansas and Missouri.

Jack said that shortly after the remains were recovered, authorities requested a DNA sample from him as the closest male
relative. While he was there, the FBI told him Bobby, Sherilyn,
and Madyson had most likely gotten lost and died from exposure.

He said he believed them, which tied into the subject for
which Jack had the most to say: Bobby. And he had a different
take on things.

I asked him about Bobby's claims that he and Sherilyn were
scared of Bob Sr. and felt threatened by him.

"I think that's a bunch of bull," Jack said, "because she's the one
that carried a gun. And she lived in a house with him once, so I
wouldn't share a house with someone I was scared of, would you?"

"So you don't think your brother was capable of something
like that?"

"Absolutely not. When I was in his house with him and his son
would come cursing and a-ravin' at him and I was surprised he
even took it, but he did ... I don't think he would hurt them at all
unless he had to do it to defend himself."

I asked him about the business fallout regarding the gas station: "From your perspective, do you think they were in the right
to be upset about this?"

"No. They mooched off him all the time, that boy did. Now I
don't know a lot about what she got off him. He'd give that boy
stuff, and they prolly didn't even mention the searchlights. He
gave them searchlights to advertise with, and he had a tree farm
and'd get him to plant the trees an' sell 'em. But no, he'd give and
give and give to that family ... [Bobby] was spoiled."

Jack recalled the court hearing for Bobby's petition for a protective order against his father. While sitting in the court gallery,
he met a woman who worked for the Department of Human Services (DHS).

When Bobby entered the courtroom, Jack leaned over and
said, "You reckon that boy's on something?"

She responded: "You let me talk to him, and I can tell you what he's on."

The court ultimately rejected Bobby's protective order request. A few months later, the Jamisons went missing.

Jack said that in the hysteria of what followed, not only was his brother accused of being involved, but he himself faced suspicion.

"They were accusing me because I was his power of attorney. They said 'follow the money,' you know what I'm saying.... If you read all them conspiracy theories, they was saying I hid them in coal pits."

Jack claimed that the accusations didn't bother him, but when I asked Dana about it, she recalled finding her father weeping as he read the rumors.

"My dad is the most honest person I've known in my life and is very tender-hearted. He's kind of like Bobby in that way," she said. "My dad would read things on the Internet and it would make him sick. I told him, 'You can't read that stuff anymore.' He probably aged ten years in those few years..."

CHAPTER 17

Colton

TOWARD THE END OF HIS FBI interview, Colton faced harder, tougher questions. The agents remained polite but seemed to have some needling suspicions about his parents.

They asked him about their plans to buy land and move to the mountains. They asked about their drug use. They even asked about their sex life, or lack thereof.

Finally, they asked why he moved out.

Colton fidgeted and leaned back in his seat.

BY THE TIME I reached out to Colton, over fifteen years had passed since his family went missing. Early articles about the case had attributed to him a few select statements, but he was only thirteen at the time, still very much a child. There weren't any long-form interviews with him, and he hadn't spoken publicly about his family or the investigation since the funeral in 2014.

I had just about given up on reaching him when someone finally answered one of his listed numbers.

A gruff voice distractedly mumbled the name of a car dealership.

In a moment of panic, I realized I had called Colton's workplace. I asked if he was available and while waiting, I debated whether I should hang up. It was unutterably rude to bother him at work, but the reality was, I might not get another chance to talk to him. Also, calling someone to the phone while they're at work and then hanging up is rude, too.

When Colton answered, I apologized for interrupting him at work and said I was calling him to ask questions about something that he probably would rather not think about—his experience growing up amid the turmoil of his family's disappearance.

I had been expecting a hostile or at least unenthused reaction, which, frankly, would have been justified. But after I speed-explained to him my interest in the case and my own experience with how mental illness can fracture families, he was receptive. To my surprise, he agreed to speak to me, but later, after his shift.

Only a few minutes into the call, he said, "It's time for closure, time to heal. I've never talked to anyone about it—people have reached out to me over the years, but I didn't give them the time of day."

I decided to start by getting Colton's thoughts on the accident narrative: with Bobby's mobility issues from his back injury, could he have walked through miles of this terrain?

"Yes—I mean, it wouldn't be comfortable for him. But there was one time, he and my mom got into a big fight while in town and—she would do stuff like this—she just left him there. He had to walk home. And you can look it up, downtown Eufaula to Sandy Bass Bay, you're talking fifteen or twenty miles on foot. He left during the day and didn't make it back until eleven that night."

"Had your parents ever gotten lost hiking or in remote spots before?"

"No, and to be honest, that just doesn't sound like them," Colton said. "Especially my stepdad—Bobby was an experienced outdoorsman, with tactical and wilderness training and whatnot. Him getting lost out here is just shocking to me, there's no way he would let that happen. Even on the lake, he could have driven you all around without lights or navigation. I don't see him getting confused as to north, south, east, and west."

Colton said that Bobby's comfort and familiarity with the outdoors verged into nerd territory. His stepfather could instantly identify different species of trees and plants (knowledge he'd used to help run Bob Sr.'s tree farm for years), as well as different rocks and land formations. He truly loved being out in nature. That was the whole point of moving to the lake house, Colton said, to be immersed in nature.

"I don't believe he could get lost," Colton added. "He always knew the backroads, the quickest way to get somewhere."

Bobby was also always prepared and did his due diligence on a place before showing up, Colton said. He always mapped out his endeavors, which is why investigators had found detailed documents and maps about the Panola land on his computer.

Sherilyn was shrewd and scrappy, too. Maybe not a bona fide lumberjack like Bobby, but she was even more zealous when it came to research. For Colton, there's simply no way they went up to that mountain after weeks of planning and then suddenly left their truck, cash, and dog behind to get hopelessly, inescapably lost with their six-year-old daughter's life on the line.

Bobby must have been comfortable enough with the area and his ability to find the acreage that he left the GPS and navigation devices behind.

Colton also had problems with the way his parents had supposedly left the interior of the truck, of which he had been shown photos.

"They wouldn't have left things like that," he said, referencing the way their belongings were supposedly left in a pile. "Bobby's wallet would have either been in his hand or in the center console. His phone probably would have been in the door of the truck or on him; the keys would have been in the ignition or on him."

The dog, Colton said, would not have been locked up in the truck. She was always with the family, as she and Madyson were inseparable.

Colton said the location of the truck itself—parked on a cramped incline with three-foot drop-offs on either side—indicated unusual circumstances.

"I know damn well my mom wouldn't have let him park somewhere that was inconvenient for her to get out."

Nothing about it sounded natural to Colton. Even the way the house was left, unlocked with all the lights on, struck him as strange.

"It's like they were rushed out of the house," he said. "Also, supposedly the area [where their remains were found] was thermally searched, then they are found within the radius that was searched, so that's interesting. Were the bodies dumped after . . . ? The way they were laid seems weird. If they were dying of hypothermia, you might see Bobby on top of Madyson to keep her warm and dry, but I guess there was time to scatter the remains and animals pick them up."

His last point was one I hadn't heard before, but it carried a certain logic.

The first thing Colton said that surprised me was in response to a question about the plan to move to Panola. He said he never heard his parents mention anything about moving or buying land or living in a moving container. All of these ideas occurred after he moved out, which was about six to nine months before their disappearance.

Colton described the last few years that he lived with his family as a downward spiral.

"My mom always blamed herself for not patching things up with Marla before she died," Colton said. "And it ate her up inside. That's when things started really going downhill."

Sherilyn, who had been diagnosed with bipolar disorder a couple of years earlier, was known to go a bit off the rails sometimes when she was off her meds. But the trauma of her sister's death triggered a new, more serious stage of her mental illness.

The first six weeks after Marla's death was a time of unmitigated darkness. Sherilyn cocooned herself away from the world and slept around the clock in a bedroom devoid of light. She didn't speak to anyone and didn't eat. Had it not been for Bobby limping up the stairs and feeding her sandwiches, she might not have eaten at all.

Months later, when Sherilyn finally began to reconstruct some semblance of a life outside her bedroom, Niki visited and spoke with her about grief, and how she had struggled with the death of her father in 2002. Sherilyn asked her if it was possible to move on after someone she loved so deeply disappeared so suddenly. Niki tried to be as encouraging as possible, but there were no magic words or special cures for this kind of grief, especially at such an early stage. For Sherilyn, the acute pain never really went away; the damage never healed. Researchers now believe that psychiatric pain functions very similarly to physical pain and that trauma is often a major factor in the onset of severe mental illness. The trauma trigger in bipolar disorder, for example, has been noted by clinical psychiatrists for years.

Sherilyn, who had always believed so fervently in the power of intention and positive attraction, was lost in grief, inalterably consumed by the finality of her sister's absence.

It affected each member of the household uniquely. With Madyson, who Sherilyn believed had special gifts and abilities, she channeled some remnant of control through what remained of her unshakeable faith. Madyson, she believed, could communicate with spirits, just like her mom. She had passed on the gift, the torch, as she knew she would.

While Sherilyn spoke to the spirit of her sister Marla, who visited their lakeside home from beyond the grave, Madyson spoke to two new friends, Michael and Emily. Only she could see them, but that didn't make them any less real, her mom said.

For Colton and Bobby, Sherilyn's grief converted into increased arguments, fighting, and hostility. Colton began having intense disagreements and verbal altercations with his mom during the day only to listen to her and Bobby yelling at each other at night.

The tension grew worse when Bobby, who was already dealing with chronic pain and depression from his back injury, began receiving death threats from his father.

It reached the point where Colton overheard them yelling about divorce on a daily basis. They had separated their money, which, as a thirteen-year-old, he remembered hearing as around sixty grand each. Bobby hid his share in his truck, accounting for the likelihood that Sherilyn would kick him out.

One night, Sherilyn came into Colton's room and had him stow her money under his mattress. It stayed there for about a week until she took it back while he was at school.

He never learned what this had been about, but it was part of the escalating cycle of paranoia, fear, and anger that reached a fever pitch in 2009.

COLTON BELIEVED HIS family was most likely killed, and his best guess as to the perpetrator was the lodger in a hybridized version of the white supremacist hit list theory.

He recalled a moment of lucidity when his mother regretfully explained to him what happened with K.B., how she'd just flipped and chased him with her pistol, firing live rounds.

"She was ashamed, but really she was scared. And she admitted that she said and did things she shouldn't have."

Colton never developed a cohesive theory, but he thought: If this guy is an ex-convict, he might come back. And if he's an ex-convict who's part of a white supremacist group, he might come back with some friends.

"If he was in the White Knights—you do stuff for rankings, to prove yourself. You're not in the gang unless you do something to get your laces," he said.

It was quite possible his mom had made a fool of a man whose comeuppance was based on revenge killing.

Colton never met the lodger and admits he doesn't know what happened to his family. But he doesn't believe the story about them driving up the day before and then returning. And in his gut, he's always felt they were rushed out of the house and probably followed to the mountain.

"The people up there know what's up. But you keep your mouth shut, or they'll come after you."

CHAPTER 18

The Lodger

WHEN I WAS RESEARCHING THE West Mesa case, I interviewed a man named Ron Erwin, who Albuquerque police investigators briefly considered a person of interest in the search for a serial killer known as the "Bone Collector."

At 8:30 A.M. on a Tuesday morning in 2010, Ron went to work at his business like he had every weekday for the last sixteen years. He was working on a supply order for a client in Tulsa, OK, when one of his employees said there were some customers waiting for him upfront.

He walked out expecting salespeople, but the "customers" turned out to be two police detectives, a man and a woman. The nervous male detective (who acted "as though he were talking to Ted Bundy," Ron quipped) informed him they had a warrant to search his office, adding that Ron had no recourse—they could legally kick down the doors if they so desired.

"You don't need to do that; here are the keys," Ron said as calmly as he could, even though he was numb from shock.

Because the investigation crossed state lines, the FBI ultimately came to Ron's home to confiscate his personal belongings. They shut his business down and prohibited him from

going to his home until the search was done. They also confiscated both his work and personal vehicles, and forensic
specialists audited his company's computers.

At 10:30 A.M., Ron's mom called and said the Associated Press
had contacted her. Ron instantly knew what that meant: there
were already headlines in the papers naming him as a suspect in
the West Mesa serial murders.

Why were the police suddenly investigating him for the murder of eleven women?

In his earliest days as a photographer, Ron had toured Albuquerque and snapped some pictures of the "street life." Within a
few months, he realized they were bad photographs, but he always
kept his work—three copies of each—so they were still around in
2010 when somehow the police heard about them. Ron believes
they were tipped off by someone with a grudge against him.

He'd allegedly snapped seven specific images of Albuquerque
women that concerned investigators. They were able to identify
and account for five of the women, but two were unknowns, and
this prolonged suspicions.

Of course, the pictures were taken years before the West Mesa
killings. But neither Ron nor the investigators knew this until
later. On the day FBI agents executed a search warrant on his
home and business, they didn't give him any information about
why he was under suspicion, or even the nature of the charges for
which he was being investigated.

Ron compared it to a *Twilight Zone* episode. Though he knew
he was innocent, he watched the true-crime shows. He knew
people with solid alibis still get indicted all the time by overzeal-
ous prosecutors who are under pressure to solve big cases.

And his lawyers told him the situation was "dead serious,"
that he should prepare himself for the possibility of being tried
for murder.

Fortunately, though the police confiscated all his files, Ron had
retained a spare thumb drive with backups, including the meticu-
lous diary he'd kept for the past twenty-two years. Behind the scenes,
he was able to prep his defense by using his contemporaneously

written entries to reconstruct where he was on any particular date in 2004, which was a critical year in the investigation.

Swept up in the Kafkaesque nightmare was the most important relationship in Ron's life. He had only recently met the woman who would one day be his wife.

"How do you explain something like that?" he said with a slightly weaker tone.

Beyond the awkwardness of introducing the words *serial killer suspect* into a one-year romantic relationship, Ron's wife lived in Vietnam at the time, and because his passports had been confiscated, he wasn't able to go see her for nearly the entire second year of their courtship.

Their marriage flourished anyway, and after nine months, authorities finally returned all of his belongings and released a statement saying that he was no longer being investigated. Ron conducted his own reputation management efforts online, but even today, you can find articles and videos portraying him as a suspect in the West Mesa case.

It's a cautionary tale about the speed at which misinformation travels and the irreversible nature of Internet speculation.

In the course of researching the Jamison family case, I heard so much about the lodger that he, like so many other characters in the story, began to take on an almost mythical status. Even after all the intervening years, the lodger, whose name was Kenneth Bellows, still frequently surfaced online as a potential suspect. And as I learned firsthand, Colton saw him as the best guess for who murdered his family.

But was there any evidence at all to base this suspicion on? In the early weeks of the investigation, both local and federal investigators considered K.B. a person of interest. But then they cleared him.

I was hoping to speak to Kenneth himself, but I soon learned that was not possible. He was essentially on his deathbed, his sister Kellie Hurst told me—in hospice care and unresponsive.

"We're just kind of waiting for him to pass," she said, matter-of-factly.

I offered my condolences, thinking that would be the end of the conversation. But Mrs. Hurst was both personable and talkative, and when she inquired about my reason for calling, it turned out her brother and her had spoken extensively about his experiences at the Jamison house. In fact, at the time the police were looking to question K.B. about his connection to the family back in 2009, he was living with Kellie and her husband.

The story she told me aligned in some ways with what others have said about the Jamisons. In other ways, the portrayal diverged. And with regard to the night of the pistol-wielding incident between Sherilyn and Kenneth, I heard a markedly different version of events.

She vividly remembered the night investigators came to her house and interviewed her brother. They had seen it coming.

The night the US Marshals and investigators came looking for him, Kellie said that they'd gone out to hear some live country music, which they did every weekend. While there, she received a call from agents in Wilburton who said they needed to speak with Kenneth. Kellie told them it would be late by the time they got home; that's all right, the agents said, reiterating that they really need to speak with him.

So it went that at close to 11:00 P.M., Kellie found herself opening her home for and hosting a small get-together of law enforcement agents and deputies who questioned her brother until two or three in the morning.

Kellie wasn't particularly worried, because she knew her brother couldn't have had anything to do with the Jamisons' disappearance. She also knew the agents had already done a thorough background check, because they had a huge file on him; they would know that her brother had a drug rap but nothing violent, and soon they would know he had a rock-solid alibi.

"It was quite a deal, but they did determine he had nothing to do with it. Because he had been here with us," Kellie told me. "I mean, he didn't drive, didn't really go anywhere. If we went any-where, he went with us."

On the day the Jamisons disappeared, Kenneth was with his sister all day and night.

"We were working at the Bible school," she said.

I wanted to know how Kenneth had met the Jamisons and moved in with them, which had always struck me as strange. Ev-idently, Kellie had found it strange, too.

"I still can't believe they hired my brother to take care of that little girl," she told me. "That's what they wanted him for."

"They hired him to take care of Madyson?"

"Yes! He helped around the house, too, but mainly they needed somebody to get her up, get her ready for school. And I was think-ing, 'You don't even know this man.' Now my brother would never hurt a child—but with his history? He'd been in prison for drug-related charges . . ."

Kenneth's arrangement was for room and board and a weekly stipend that may have been a few hundred dollars, though Mrs. Hurst isn't sure if he was consistently paid.

He took over the upstairs room that Colton had grown up in before he moved out.

"[The Jamisons] had property in Cancun and would go and stay in Mexico for days or weeks at a time. . . . We thought they was pretty nice people at first. Then, geez, they turned strange."

I asked what she meant by that.

"They were . . . strange. People don't act like that." She was really trying to find the words, but they eluded her. "They were cut from a different cloth."

"Is there an example that comes to mind when you think about what made them so different?"

Mrs. Hurst sighed and said, "She was just saying the strangest things, spiritual things. They didn't believe in God, but I don't know what you call it . . . it was something else . . ."

"Satanism?"

"No."

"Paganism?"

"Maybe. But they were all about this spiritual world. That's what was going to save them. [Sherilyn] would leave for a few days because of the spirits. And she had this sister that died … she was gonna go there and save her spirit and bring her back to Oklahoma. That's what she talked about doing, she was gonna go bring her sister's spirit back and protect her. Kenny would tell me this stuff, and I just said, 'You need to get out of there.'"

She recalled hearing that Sherilyn had an explosive temper and had to be in control. Kenny once saw her jump on Bobby's back in anger.

"[Kenneth] found a dead cat in the chair. And she, Sherilyn, put oregano all over the house to keep the spirits out …"

"Wait, I'm sorry, can we back up a second—what did you, uh, say about a dead cat?"

"Ken kept smelling something horrible in the house. And he looked and looked and looked, and finally, he pulled the chair over and found a dead cat under the chair."

After hearing about the Jamisons' suspicions that neighbors poisoned their cats, this little detail gave me pause.

"I said to him, 'You need to get away from there.' I feared for my brother … and the little girl, Madyson. They had a name for her, some kind of child …"

"Indigo?"

"Indigo! That's it."

I asked Kellie about the infamous altercation between Kenneth and Sherilyn and whether her brother had ever expressed any racist sentiments.

Absolutely not, she said, adding that her brother had married a woman with Native American ancestry.

"He probably said something about [Sherilyn] being crazy … or that she was the Antichrist. What she started to do that night"—Kellie sounded irritated—"was tell Bobby that Kenny had hurt that little girl—Kenny did not hurt that little girl, he never did. She was doing that to get Bobby to come back to do something to Kenny."

After the shots were fired, Kenneth called his sister, terrified.

"They had been fighting, and I think at this point [Bobby] wanted out, a divorce, and was running away from her ... it had been a bad relationship for a long time."

When they saw on the news that the family was missing, Kellie and her brother talked about what might have happened. They both had a sinking feeling that it was murder-suicide.

A FEW WEEKS later, I learned from Kellie that Kenneth Bellows had died at the age of sixty-six.

The lodger was moving on.

Kellie seemed credible to me in terms of her memory and honesty. She had no idea I was going to call her and ask her about this stuff, so it's not like she had time to prepare her answers.

I wasn't sure what to think of Sherilyn's supposed accusation of Kenneth hurting Madyson, but it's a detail that was notably missing from her own version of the story.

As a base-level takeaway, it occurred to me that the most disturbing details of the lodger story no longer had anything to do with the lodger. The most galling part may be that Bobby and Sherilyn hired a man they barely knew to take care of their six-year-old daughter. For a period of many months, they gave a veritable stranger, an ex-convict to boot, daily unsupervised access to their daughter.

CHAPTER 19

A Digital Prayer

THANKS TO THE UNLIKELY TAG team of a wonderfully named SSRI medication, Viibryd, and Clomipramine (my first tricyclic antidepressant!), by October 2019 I was stabilizing psychologically for the first time since the late Obama years. It was only after taking Clomipramine that I realized for most of my adult life, I'd experienced severe anxiety in near perpetuity. The tricyclic balanced something in my brain and gave me a new baseline, allowing me to neutralize compulsive thought patterns.

I was finally ready to get back to the Pacific Northwest, the land of rainy trees, ex-Californians, and lonely unsolved mysteries, when on the day before Halloween, I fell and broke my hip.

I wish I could say the injury was the result of me doing something heroic or epic, like running into a burning building to save an elderly lady's dog or surviving an avalanche or something. Unfortunately, the truth is just about the opposite of epic. I was standing at the counter of a gas station when, unbeknownst to me, the looped shoelace from one of my hiking boots latched around the metal hook of the opposing shoe. When I finished the transaction, I turned, hands and arms full of sundries and provisions, and tripped, stumbled, and lurched for what felt like ten feet before crashing Elvis-the-pelvis first onto the hard linoleum floor.

I'll spare you too many details of what came next—such as not one person stopping to help me except for a store employee who irritably dragged a chair out and set it beside me as I lay writhing in pain. My dad took me to the hospital, where I learned I had a fracture on the femoral neck of my hip. I would have to get pins put in, which resulted in me sweating deliriously for four hours with no water as I awaited surgery.

On the plus side, I got my first morphine shot.

When I first woke up from surgery, I distinctly remember thinking my leg had been cut off—amputated. I could see and feel that I had both legs, but I couldn't believe how much pain I was in.

The next day, I spent Halloween in a hospital for the first time. Late at night, I thought I saw a blood-drenched nurse walk by my room, but I'd been smacking the Dilaudid button like a *Jeopardy!* contestant, so it might have just been delirium and not a wildly inappropriate workplace costume.

I had some recovery ahead of me, a nurse practitioner told me a few days later while showing me how to ambulate with a walker.

Before the hospital staff discharged me, the surgeon looked over my x-ray and told me everything looked perfect (later, I posted the image to social media, unaware that the faint outline of my testicles was visible).

"You'll be on crutches for about six weeks, but then it should heal up nicely without any problems."

AFTER TRIUMPHANTLY FINISHING my book and trying to leave the mountain, I was instead hobbled and bedridden in a secluded house on a snowy mountain with an intensely devoted nurse watching my every move. It was almost the exact plot of *Misery*, except that the nurse was my mom.

Granted, she took amazing care of me, as did my pops, but immobility and pain had not been on my bingo card for the year.

The silver lining was that I had plenty of time to read the online forums on the Jamison case. There were plenty to choose from, but I focused on Reddit and Websleuths. I tried in vain to find archived copies of threads from Topix, a viper's den of a forum that had been popular for talk on the Jamisons in 2009 and 2010 but was now defunct.

You may wonder why a journalist or writer wanting the truth of a story would want to plumb the depths of the Internet's most conspiracy-laden correspondences for information. It's the same reason that seasoned police investigators do it: the Internet hive mind is a great place to find clues and leads.

Murder Theories

There were two periods of time during which speculation over the Jamison family reached a fever pitch: after the disappearance in 2009, and after the recovery of the remains in 2013. Throughout this period, the two major camps were those who believed the Jamisons got lost and died of exposure and those who believed they were killed.

The accident camp rightly pointed out that the temperatures on Panola Mountain were low enough to cause hypothermia, especially given that the Jamisons were believed to not have any jackets or supplies with them. Many commenters pointed out the statistics on lost persons and how frequently even trained experts and veteran hikers get lost and die.

In defense of searchers not finding the bodies, one commenter directly invoked Koester's seminal book, *Lost Person Behavior*, which states that most unsuccessful searches don't include inspection beyond the median statistical distance, which guarantees a fifty-percent chance of failure.

Another sleuth added the "formula" to the Jamison search, whereby searching a three-mile radius from the truck would equate to over twenty-eight square miles. Combined with Oklahoma's never-ending wind, which threw off the dogs' scent, the search was doomed from the start.

The most popular murder theory was that the Jamisons either witnessed something they shouldn't have seen (most likely drug-related) or were in a drug deal gone wrong. But there were several sub-camps of the foul play theory. A fair number of sleuths believed the Jamisons were killed by one or more Panola residents who lived on the mountain and knew their way around.

The most familiar characters were Peggy the Realtor, who had earned the moniker the "Lady on the Mountain," and D.C., the man alleged by police to be the last person to speak with the Jamisons. These neighbors had the GPS coordinates where the family planned to be the following morning. Sleuths, including the prolific and level-headed OkieGranny, wondered who the neighbors talked to overnight.

After posting topography maps of the Smokestack Hollow area, OkieGranny concluded that the lost narrative didn't make sense. The area was flat and close to roads, she said, easily accessible to a local perpetrator.

OkieGranny also criticized the way the family, particularly Sherilyn, had been stigmatized as "crazy." She rejected the murder-suicide theory in which Sherilyn killed Bobby and Madyson.

"It's all BS to me," she concluded. "I still believe they were in the wrong place at the wrong time that day, and someone is getting away with murder."

The blog *Prairie Chicken* wrote: "It looks to me like they could have been taken to that part of the mountain on that dirt road by the creeks, robbed . . . and someone or ones told them to start climbing and probably shot them."

A Mr. Noatak described what he believed to be a "sensible method" of silencing three people: carbon monoxide poisoning, which would leave no traces or discernible cause of death.

"This was a crime committed by a non-member of the family. A crime of passion, after the fact," he wrote.

The biggest differentiator in the murder theories was motive. While most believed it was money, others wondered if there was some kind of territorial beef among residents of the mountain who felt threatened or exposed by the Jamisons.

One sleuth, SolitaryOne, described a kind of distorted self-preservation instinct that exists in some of the more rural and remote Southern communities, where "outsiders" are seen as a threat to their way of life. In this scenario, described as "the *Deliverance* factor," locals view the elimination of such threats as a God-given, constitutional right.

One poster, who believed the Jamisons were ambushed while leaving, shared an alarmingly similar experience that he had in the southern part of the county during the second weekend of February 2013 (which was, incidentally, only a month after the discovery of the Jamisons' remains). While he was looking at forty acres of land, he said, locals pulled up in a truck, blocked his exit, and accused him of trespassing. He had to drive around them to exit, and the ambusher still tried to "ram" him by accelerating in reverse.

This person claimed to have relayed his story to both the Realtor and then-Sheriff Jesse James. There were a number of posts alleging malicious Oklahoma mountain cliques.

Mtrooper

One sleuth, Mtrooper, claimed to be a private investigator who was working on the case. In a series of posts starting in early February 2010, she speculated about the role Bobby's dad played in the Jamisons' deaths. After claiming to have confirmed his links to the Mexican mafia, she wondered if the family was abducted out of revenge.

Mtrooper made a list of the most likely scenarios, which included: a family murder plot fueled by money; a random murder fueled by money (she cited Bobby flashing his money around); a Mafia abduction; getting lost and dying of exposure, which she found unlikely; the family still being alive and hiding out in a timeshare; and finally, murder-suicide.

Not only did Mtrooper defend the mountain residents, but she also began questioning the motives of some of the Jamison family members. She described an experience on the mountain in which she was impressed by the local Panola neighbors; conversely, she described the family's effort as suspiciously lacking

except in probate court. She cited a specific conversation in which
Peggy said that Jack, Starlet, and their significant others defended
themselves by claiming they didn't want to leave fingerprints behind and increase their criminal exposure.

After looking into the family's financial issues, she wondered
about the amendment of Bob Sr.'s will, which excluded Starlet as
a beneficiary, and asked a loaded rhetorical question: "Why would
you put a reward out for your missing loved one if you knew what
happened to them, or worse yet if someone else found out about
it and was actually able to produce a body?"

Some sleuths believed the perpetrator was not a local at all,
but someone who either followed them from Eufaula or otherwise knew their destination.

SolitaryOne conflated the local and non-local theories to suppose that someone like K.B. could have had links to the
Panola/Red Oak community.

Questioning the location of the remains, others pushed the
body dump theory. On the absence of teeth at the recovery site,
one poster questioned how they could have sifted the ground and
not found anything, suggesting it was a secondary burial location.

Like other sleuths, including myself, OkieGranny viewed the
location of the remains as a dump spot where the perpetrator
could have surreptitiously deposited a few bones in a safe place
that someone would have naturally stumbled upon—and it
would look like they'd been there all along. Only a local suspect,
who knew the terrain well, could pull this off.

Throughout the forums, there was the pervasive sense that
something wasn't right with this case. More specifically, there was
frustration at what was perceived to be a vagueness in the autopsy.
One wondered why more wasn't said about the damage to the
skulls and the distribution pattern, or "spread," of the remains.
After speaking with the Grahams, I definitely craved confirmation of the so-called "perfect triangle," which, if true, seems like a
detail worthy of inclusion in the autopsy results.

In other troubling aspects of the case, more than a few web
sleuths, as well as family friends, questioned Madyson's bleached

hair. For some, it indicated that the Jamisons were on the run from something and trying to conceal the child's identity.

NIKI CROSSED OVER and began posting and interacting on Websleuths, where she said she felt connected to Sherilyn somehow. Supporters posted candlelight tributes and prayers for the Jamisons, including a Prayer of Roses to the Virgin Mary of Guadalupe. In 2012, one of the Jamison warriors lit three candles in a digital prayer that caught on and was replicated and shared by other members.

Niki had learned from tough-won experience to be more judicious in her choice of rabbit holes. At this point, it was a matter of preserving her own mental health, which at times teetered on the brink of collapse from chronic sleep deprivation and anxiety.

When a poster in a Topix forum claimed that the Jamisons were buried under a bridge in Marble City, Oklahoma, Niki didn't take the bait. Instead, she rewatched the clip of the surveillance footage—and noticed something that surprised her.

On July 28, 2012, she posted a screed to her Jamison warriors in which she asserted her belief that the video shows two different men: Bobby and someone else wearing a brown shirt. Initially, she'd thought he changed shirts. But the footage had always bothered her, and after "freezing each frame" and studying the pixels, she was "99 percent positive" it showed a second man who wasn't Bobby.

What was this mystery man doing there? Was he holding the Jamisons hostage, as Colton suggested?

Private Investigators

During this time, then-Sheriff Beauchamp brought in at least two private investigators to help him.

One of them, Tim Miller, had been requested by the OSBI. He was one of the searchers who had scoured Panola Mountain on horseback. Miller ran a nonprofit search and rescue organization called Texas EquuSearch Mounted Search and Recovery, which focuses on missing-person cases, including high-profile abduction victims such as Natalee Holloway.

Miller founded Texas EquuSearch because of his own devastating personal experience with a loved one disappearing. In September 1984, his sixteen-year-old daughter Laura went missing; two years later, boys riding dirt bikes discovered her body propped under a tree in a swampy oil field in north Galveston County, Texas. This roughly twenty-five-acre swath of land along Interstate 45 between Houston and Galveston is now known as the Texas Killing Fields. Between the 1970s and 2000s, multiple killers used the remote bayous and retention ponds here to conceal the bodies of at least thirty-three women and girls who were abducted, raped, and murdered.

Miller has spent the last four decades of his life hunting his daughter's killer.

In 2015, he told the Houston Press: "There is one thing worse than having a murdered child. And that is probably knowing that your child is out there dead somewhere and never being able to say good-bye."

He set out to develop an independent investigative unit that would cater to families experiencing what Miller himself went through—and continues to go through every day of his life.

The other private investigator tapped by Beauchamp was Heather, a Michigan-based social worker who headed a volunteer search and rescue group. By night, she was an amateur sleuth, who used the Internet to conduct deep dives into cold cases.

Her career as a missing-person investigator started as a passion project and then metastasized into a natural side job. For many years, she was more of a hobbyist, working cases pro bono outside her full-time work hours. But over the next decade, Heather put together an impressive track record with a list of accolades and commendations from both victims' families and seasoned detectives.

Heather's focus was on helping families who were out of resources. She was a missing-person investigator but, more importantly, she was an outsider, not professionally affiliated with any law enforcement body or firm. She counts this as one of her assets.

"Sometimes people are more willing to talk to an investigator who's not a police officer," Heather said.

She brought a few more assets to the table. One was her experience taking on special projects: cold cases that law enforcement agencies have abandoned; missing-person cases whose agency of jurisdiction have, for whatever reason, suspended or terminated their investigative efforts. Though this wasn't entirely the situation with the Jamisons, by late 2009, the larger search efforts had dwindled considerably.

Another advantage was Heather's tactic of closely following paper trails and digital records, which resulted from her early career effort to master the use of the National Missing and Unidentified Persons System (NamUs) database. In previous decades, investigators had to conduct laborious, time-consuming, and sometimes travel-heavy physical audits to track down files and correspondences; a digital doyenne, on the other hand, lets search algorithms do the courier work.

In addition to NamUs, Heather utilized Freedom of Information Act requests, court files, ancestry records, and police and autopsy reports. She also has access to her own team of cadaver dogs, one of whom doubles as her pet.

I REFINED MY focus further and looked at Websleuths threads from early 2010, when the search for the Jamisons was largely suspended but the investigation was ongoing.

Starting January 8, 2010, Mtrooper posted a series of messages over several weeks. At first, she half-jokingly reminded law enforcement that its job was to investigate. Then she angrily chided police for the lack of updates.

The second post voiced a pretty popular theory at the time, championed most fervently by Brett Faulds on his blog *Keep the Search Alive*, which had posited that the Jamisons weren't dead and that they had either faked their deaths or were in some kind of witness protection program.

In forum posts, he characterized the Jamison "mystery" as "just a program in reruns [that] will continue to cast a dark shadow on innocent people…" and ridiculed "idiots [who] will always think someone got away with a crime."

Niki clapped back, characterizing Brett as a grifter who had misled his readers about his sources and abilities and made it harder for people like her to get taken seriously by law enforcement.

Mtrooper's next post was about Bob Sr.'s will, and "the plot thick[ened]." The probate documents he left behind "could be a motive," she wrote. "Wife (Starlet Jamison) of Bobby's father has Bobby and his family killed knowing that her soon-to-be divorced husband is about to die and she would get nothing. She has filled probate to be the executor of his will. How convenient."

It took me a bit to figure out what Mtrooper was talking about in her third post, but eventually, I realized it was referring to Bob Sr.'s will and the execution of his estate after his death in 2009, shortly after the Jamisons' disappearance. This was only the very beginning of a long-running collectivized probe into the entire Jamison family's financial and legal matters.

Shortly after Mtrooper's posts and dozens of others, an account named Jamisonssister97, which purported to be a member of the Jamisons' extended family—Sherilyn's ex-sister-in-law, specifically—began posting. In her first message, she confirmed that Bobby Sr. died of a heart attack while in a nursing home. She also confirmed that Maisy the dog was alive but had barely made it after suffering severe dehydration. The dog wouldn't have survived another day.

"Sherilyn would never leave her dog," she wrote.

This note of tenderness didn't hold long before she confirmed Sherilyn's mental illness in crass terms, describing her as "severely bipolar" and "medically crazy." Jamisonssister97 said Sherilyn had visited her only a month and a half before she went missing and was fighting with Bobby and on the verge of divorce; they openly discussed how they would split their money.

Sherilyn's ex-sister-in-law summarized what she and Starlet believed—that the clearing where the truck was found was not

A DIGITAL PRAYER   161

the crime scene. Whatever happened, she said, happened else-where, and the truck was put there as a decoy.

A couple of days later, Jamisonssister97 wrote that Sherilyn carried her purse everywhere and would have never left it behind in the truck. Then she made two interesting statements:

1. If they were murdered, we all think they knew the
   person.
2. We need to know more about Bobby.

A few days later, Jamisonssister97 stopped posting entirely, which caused Mtrooper to spend weeks openly worrying that something had happened to her. She wrote:

It's easy to forget that there is a GOOD chance that SOMEONE out there made the Jamisons disappear and they probably don't want anyone helping us figure out exactly who that might have been.

The Cell Phone Log

Mtrooper, who for weeks had claimed she was working directly with law enforcement on the case, appeared to prove her inside role when she released the Jamisons' phone call log, which pur-portedly showed the final incoming and outgoing calls on Bobby's cell phone. Okiegranny collected info from Mtrooper and, over the years, added to it to produce an almost Steinbeckian timeline of the Jamison family's life.

I wasn't able to fact-check every statement. For example, in Oc-tober 2009, Okiegranny wrote that "Bobby made phone inquiries about buying homeschool materials for Madyson and also called Sylvan Learning Center"; she wrote that on October 5, only days before their disappearance, "the Jamisons had planned a trip to Panola Mountain with church friends to look at land, but the trip was postponed due to bad weather."

However, I corroborated enough of them that I believed she was posting the info in good faith.

The cell log began on October 7, after the family bought gas in Porum, OK, and made their first trip to the mountain.

Oct 7, 2009—Jamisons took first trip to the mountain, stopping for gas in Porum, OK

8:55 A.M.— Call to out-of-state landowner

9:18 A.M.— Bobby checked his voicemail

9:19 A.M.— Bobby called an unidentified Eufaula number (thirty-seven minutes)

9:26 A.M.— Received a call-waiting call from a different unidentified Eufaula number

9:57 A.M.— Two consecutive calls to a Muskogee cell phone number

12:41 P.M.— Bobby checked his voicemail

12:42 P.M.—Bobby called the church family (eleven minutes)

1:38 P.M.— Bobby called the out-of-state landowners (two minutes)

1:40 P.M.— Bobby called the out-of-state landowners again (two minutes)

1:55 P.M.— Bobby checked his voicemail

1:56 P.M.— Bobby checked his voicemail

1:58 P.M.— Bobby called the previous unidentified Eufaula number again (one minute)

1:59 P.M.— Bobby checked his voicemail

2:02 P.M.— Bobby called the previous unidentified Eufaula number again (one minute)

2:06 P.M.— Bobby called the out-of-state landowners again (one minute)

2:07 P.M.— The out-of-state landowners called Bobby (three minutes)

2:15 P.M.— The out-of-state landowners called Bobby (two minutes)

2:16 P.M.— Bobby may have called the Lady on the Mountain (PC) but misdialed (one minute)

2:18 P.M.— Bobby called the out-of-state property
                 owners (one minute)

Okiegranny wrote that the Jamisons reached a stopping point
on the mountain at about 6:00 P.M., at which point they spoke
with "the neighbor (DC)" for about an hour. According to the
neighbor, after this conversation, the Jamisons decided to drive
home and return in the morning.

The next day—the day they disappeared—the Jamisons woke
up early, hit the gas station in Porum again, and made their second trip to the mountain. The call log continued:

8:09 A.M.— Bobby called the Lady on the Moun-
                 tain (101 minutes)
12:53 P.M.—Photos of two well site signs taken
                 on the Blackberry. The Jamisons
                 stopped and spoke with neighbor
                 DC again
1:50 P.M.— Bobby dialed voicemail, but his
                 number was listed as BRISTO OK in-
                 stead of VMAIL
2:47 P.M.— Final photo of Madyson taken on the
                 Blackberry

This is when we fall past the event horizon, into an intractable
blackness that conceals the final glimpses of the family's fate. At
some point after 2:47 P.M., October 8, whatever happened to the
Jamisons happened.

Then, four days later on October 12, the cell log reportedly
showed Blackberry activity and odd voicemail calls.

6:00 P.M.— BRISTO OK
8:00 P.M.— Incoming call
8:50 P.M.— Incoming call
8:51 P.M.— BRISTO OK

The next day, on October 13, there was a final incoming call on the Blackberry at 5:27 P.M.

The phone records were a hot subject in the threads for a while, as they appeared to show that Bobby's mobile phone made an outgoing call to voicemail on October 12, even though it was ostensibly locked inside the abandoned truck at the time. The two-part anomaly further vexed web sleuths, because instead of showing up as "VMAIL" like his earlier calls to voicemail, this outgoing call appeared in the records as "BRISTO OK."

New threads of commenters attempted to parse the meaning with several arguing the possibility of "dog dialing." One commenter was adamant that after the Jamisons left the truck and got lost, Maisy could have easily pawed the Blackberry's main power button and then stepped on the track wheel that scrolls to the voicemail pop-up.

Other commenters said that their phones showed the city instead of VMAIL when the phone was roaming—i.e., taken out of service range, presumably in a different area. Did this suggest that someone had taken the Jamisons' Blackberry phone during this time and then returned it before police found the truck? They certainly had plenty of time to make the trips.

More granular threads ranged from the nuances of precipitation levels/temperature and soil density and sink rate analysis to moonshot speculation about whether the Jamisons had their teeth pulled prior to death.

Some sleuths had, like me, found it odd that the dried flower noted in the autopsy supposedly stayed on Madyson's shoe for four years, despite the chaos of scavenger activity and disarticulation.

The Line of Tragedy

In my painkiller-fueled haze of late-night research, I also went down some of the more extreme rabbit holes. One of the more bizarre elements of the Jamison case was how it attracted fringe conspiracists and tapped into a longstanding undercurrent of satanic panic, both locally and online.

Years after the case had gone cold, websites like Strange Outdoors, Mysterious Universe, and Anomalien published new articles repopularizing the Jamison family disappearance and expanding on the mythology. Somehow demons, cult hit lists, meth cartels, and white supremacists weren't provocative enough, and hungry content publishers began referring to some "occult psychic/Cabalist" named Sollog and a "pattern" of tragedies, murders, and mass death events occurring along the 35th-degree latitude. Sollog called it the "Line of Tragedy."

On a lark, I messaged Sollog on Facebook, where his description reads "Greatest Mystic in History." Listed in his web of cursed coordinates were a smattering of mass killings, terrorist bombings, natural disasters, and homicides, including the local cases of Pastor Carol Daniels, the disappearance of Tommy Eastep, and the Jamison family.

According to Sollog, the 35th degree is Eufaula's spirit lay line, which runs through the Avenue of the Dead and comprises just one vector of the Pentagram of Blood that encompasses North America.

When I was writing my first book, a kind and earnest man named Mark painstakingly tried to explain to me what happened to Elisa Lam, a young woman recorded in the elevator at the infamous Cecil Hotel before police discovered her body in the rooftop water cistern. He believed, honestly and literally, that a group of largely invisible puppet masters had staged a ritualistic murder.

He was one of the few investigators who could see this covert reality, and he used a special web tool to zoom in on the pixels of the security footage and find the patterns.

Mark continued messaging me long after I was done with the book. When I told him I was working on a new story, the Jamison case, a couple of days passed, and then he came back with some marked-up pics of the Jamison security footage zoomed in to show blurry pixels. He wrote that based on Sherilyn's involvement with a seance, the only logical conclusion was that a cult of killers—"specifically a satanic cult, the most dangerous and frightening of all killers," had pulled the Jamisons into a ritualistic human sacrifice.

The demons that Bobby saw on his rooftop were just the cult visiting in the night.

Mark said he'd seen such figures pull up in a van once with all four doors open and abduct someone in only ten seconds.

They're "organized and experienced," and "they take great pleasure in torture."

The Jamisons' killers thought they got away with it, Mark said. "They didn't count on an old retired guy examining the video so closely..."

Satanic Panic

Mark's conspiratorial fever dream is, strangely enough, well-grounded in recent American religiosity. So too are the overtures of satanism and witchcraft in the Jamison case, which were taken seriously in Oklahoma, where a predominately Christian population has a long history of fearing and rejecting the occult. But the movement to instantiate Satan into the fabric of reality was not local to Oklahoma or even the South. In the 1980s, a wave of moral hysteria started in America and spread across the world, convincing millions of people that Satanic cults masquerading as middle-class suburban daycare centers were systematically kidnapping children for the purpose of sadistic ritual abuse.

This "satanic panic" was triggered by conspiracy theories, misinformation, and false accusations stemming largely from the discredited psychotherapeutic practice of recovered-memory therapy (RMT). Researchers have said that based on reports from lawyers, social workers, and therapists, there were around 12,000 unsubstantiated claims, many of which were the direct result of false memories created during hypnotic regression.

A new wave of satanic panic, buoyed by the currency of conspiracy theories laundered through the Internet, can be seen in a wide variety of true-crime cases.

But the spookiness of the Jamison case wasn't only the result of satanic panic. There was an undeniable high strangeness that threaded through the story that I could no longer in good faith avoid.

It was time to reckon with the so-called paranormal activity in the Jamisons' lakeside home.

CHAPTER 20

A Demon Familiar

"What haunts are not the dead, but the gaps left within us by the secrets of others."
—"NOTES ON THE PHANTOM,"
NICOLAS ABRAHAM (1987)

WHILE MANY OF THE PEOPLE I interviewed about this case had divergent opinions about the Jamisons' cause of death and a host of other data points, one of the few consistent refrains was the haunted nature of the Jamison home and the ghosts and demons who lived there rent-free inside the family's consciousness.

In a 2014 interview with the *Daily Mail*, Connie Kokotan was asked about the Jamison family's house and the allegations of witchcraft.

She said, "[Sherilyn] definitely started trying to find out whether it was built on an Indian burial ground. I do not know what she discovered."

From the very beginning of the Jamisons' time in Eufaula, it seemed Sherilyn was at odds with the house, like an unstoppable force meeting an immovable object. She believed their Eufaula

The clearing on Panola Mountain where the Jamisons' truck was found on October 17, 2009. Inside were the family's cell phones, wallets, and dog—malnourished, but alive—and $32,000 in cash. *Photo by Niki Shenold.*

The desolate landscape offered few clues as to the family's fate. *Photo by Niki Shenold.*

The bluff against which the Jamisons' truck was found. Investigators said the driver had probably been compelled to stop or pull over by an oncoming vehicle. *Photo by Niki Shenold.*

An old horsehead petroleum pump, which demarcated property lines during Oklahoma's oil boom. *Photo by Niki Shenold.*

An abandoned vehicle punctured with bullet holes and covered with graffiti sat in the clearing near the Jamisons' last-known point. Family friend Niki Shenold recognized Sherilyn Jamison's message of "God Rules" and other of her messages spray-painted over the occult symbols. *Photo by Niki Shenold.*

Niki came to believe a convicted murderer had become angered by Sherilyn's use of his "target practice" and may have been involved in the family's disappearance. *Photos by Niki Shenold.*

The last image of Madyson. Friends and loved ones believe the child looked frightened and that someone other than her parents took the photo.

Niki Shenold found this spot, near the top of the bluff, where she believes Madyson's last photo was tal
Near this location authorities found a child's footprints when they first searched the area.
Photo by Niki Shenold.

The view of beautiful Eufaula Lake from the Jamisons' backyard. Slightly east of its southernmost arm, 100 feet below the water, lie the relics of a ghost town—the original Eufaula settlement, which was called North Fork Town. *Photo by Laura Dormanen.*

Sherilyn Jamison called Madyson an "indigo child" and believed she had special spiritual abilities, such as communicating with the dead. *Photo by Niki Shenold.*

Niki Shenold said Sherilyn Jamison was like a sister to her. After Sherilyn's disappearance, Niki devoted years to searching for the truth of what happened to the Jamison family.

After viewing the security camera footage from the Jamisons' property, Sheriff Israel Beauchamp described Bobby and Sherilyn's behavior as "trancelike." Friends and family believe the Jamisons may have been forced or coerced out of their house.

Latimer County Sheriff's
ce is located in the remote
ntain town of Wilburton, OK.
county, like the rest of
ahoma, operates under the
riff system," an antiquated
el of law enforcement still
wed in some Southern states.
o by Laura Dormanen.

The Eufaula graveyard, where the Jamisons are buried.
Photo by Laura Dormanen.

MISSING PERSON

Peggy McGuire
White Female

Peggy McGuire was last seen on November 16, 2015, dropping her son off at school, outside Eufaula, OK. She had spoken to her step-father while on her way to the home she shared with her son and his father. Peggy has not been seen or heard from since. Her Toyota truck was recovered on November 18, 2015, from the parking lot of TJ's Ice House Bar in rural McIntosh County.

If You Have ANY Info About This Case Call
INMATE ACCESS #20
800-522-8017
Submit online at tips@osbi.ok.gov

Subsequent to the Jamison family's disappearance, two more people went missing in Eufaula in separate incidents: Peggy McGuire in 2015, Tommy Eastep in 2013.

2 UNSOLVED HOMICIDE

Tommy Raymond Eastep
Native American Male

Tommy Eastep was last seen on July 7, 2013 in Eufaula, McIntosh County. On September 27, 2013, his abandoned and locked 2003 Silver Chevy Silverado pickup was found in the woods near Holdenville, Hughes County, south of county roads 120 and 374. On April 8, 2017, the remains of Tommy were found near the recovery site of the truck. Any information about the events leading up to his death are needed.

If You Have ANY Info About This Case Call
INMATE ACCESS #20
800-522-8017
Submit online at tips@osbi.ok.gov

"dream home" possessed a dark energy—and everyone who came over and stayed for any length of time felt it. For Niki, it manifested as nausea and stomach pain, which became so common that Sherilyn had peppermint tea ready for her whenever she came to visit.

Colton, too, noticed it from the beginning—a heavy dread, a negative, repellent force. It was an old house, so at first, he attributed the feeling to the residual creepiness left over from the home's previous inhabitants, the most recent of which, he heard, was a family of ten strung-out squatters who smoked crack on the roof every night and left the house in such a state of disrepair that the city condemned the property (which had a collateral benefit of significantly lowering the price).

When they began remodeling, the Jamisons knew they had their work cut out for them because of the previous tenants' years of neglect. But Bobby had the knowledge, skill, and temperament to get it done. He told Colton that his own dad, Bob Sr., was an "alcoholic asshole" of a father but did at least one thing right: he taught Bobby how to work with his hands and fix things.

Bobby and Sherilyn wanted to add Formica granite countertops, which required a special glue to make the laminate sheets adhere properly to the underlayment. But when they applied the adhesive and laid the Formica down, a foamy goo bubbled up to the surface between the fissures. It was like a sea of foam had suddenly materialized below their feet. In all his years of home repair, Bobby had never seen anything like it before, and it frustrated the hell out of him. No brands of glue would work—each time, the anomalous substance came bubbling up like angry magma from the depths.

Other unsettling occurrences transpired during remodeling. Random tools and appliances abruptly stopped working or made strange noises.

This *Home Improvement: Paranormal Activity* episode escalated to the point where Sherilyn began writing on pieces of paper, "Satan, get out, you're not welcome here" and "This house serves Jesus," and taping them around the house.

She also began intensely praying and only then, she believed, were they able to get things to work. Everything fell into place, and eventually, they prevailed in revamping their home.

However, two years later, in 2006, a fire burned down a sizable portion of their house. No one was injured, but it destroyed much of their renovation work. The fire department blamed the conflagration on squirrels in the attic above Bobby and Sherilyn's master bedroom.

Sherilyn didn't buy that; she blamed evil forces.

When I spoke with Colton, he recalled a memory of his mom shortly after their fire. Determined to get answers about what was going on in their home, Sherilyn went to a "palm reader."

Not yet a teenager, Colton didn't have all the words for it yet, but he knew his mom was into paranormal stuff, haunted things—the "other side."

The psychic told her that the cause of the fire that burned down their house was a demon from one of her past lives.

When she got home later that evening, she told Colton and Bobby of her psychic medium's conclusion: it wasn't a squirrel, it's a demon from my past.

It probably wasn't going to pass as an insurance claim, but Sherilyn was deadly serious. She invoked a spell: "I rebuke this evil in our home in God's name."

As he came of age, Colton's burgeoning curiosity tapped into conversations between Sherilyn and Niki. He sometimes flipped through the pages of the witchcraft books they brought home. Some of their conversations stuck with him enough to commit them to memory, and as he grew older and more committed to his Christian faith, he came to suspect that his mother had been playing around with forces that are better left alone.

Out-of-Body Experience

In an interview with the *Daily Mail*, Niki said, "In all seriousness, that house was haunted. I don't want to sound crazy, but when-

ever I went there, I felt a horrible presence; I would leave feeling
so down and depressed, it's hard to describe."

Niki told me several paranormal stories, including her daughter seeing Sherilyn in the bathroom. In article interviews, she also
described seeing a gray mist coming down the stairs at the Jamison house. There was a bit more to the mist story, though.

Her husband Wayne was there, she told me over the phone
while on a twenty-minute work break.

She explained that Wayne was a very logical type, a twenty-
two-year military veteran who was not into ghost stories or urban
legends at all. When Niki saw the gray mist, however, Wayne suddenly froze. He abruptly stopped talking and stared ahead as
though paralyzed.

Niki was so surprised by his expression and demeanor that
she laughed and said, "What is going on? Wayne, talk to me!"

Later that night, she asked him about what had happened. He
said he didn't know—what he remembered from the momentary
state was being outside his body, floating up and looking down
at them from above. He remembered Niki saying, "Talk to me,"
but from the vantage point of the ceiling.

The experience terrified him, Niki said. She believed it was
the house. It does strange things to your mind.

Ghost Town

I would be curious to know what Sherilyn found out in her research on the history of her property. As I began to delve more
into the history of southeast Oklahoma, and Eufaula more specifically, I was impressed by the very literal sense in which their
home was built on a kind of burial ground.

While the visitors enjoy the scenery and water activities, many
are unaware that just east of the lake's southernmost arm, nearly
a hundred feet down, at the bottom of the lake, lie the submerged
relics of the original Eufaula: North Fork Town (aka, Old Town,
or Micco).

Founded by Creek Indians centuries prior to Oklahoma's statehood, the territory of North Fork Town played an important strategic role in the region during the early to mid 1800s. The Five Civilized Tribes chose North Fork Town as the site for their intertribal council meetings, which drew representatives of both Upper and Lower Creeks, Choctaws, Chickasaws, Caddoes, Seminoles, Delawares, Shawnees, Quapaws, Seneca, Osages, Pawnees, Kickapoos, Wichitas, Kichahi, Piankashaws, Tawakonis, and "Isterhutkeys" (white men).

The prairies and woodlands on which they met held a fortuitous geographic location as the fork between two major rivers, the Canadian and North Canadian, and the nexus of two historic routes, the Texas Road, which was used heavily by the Cherokee, Creek, and Choctaw Nations, and the California Road, a federally protected passageway that ushered tens of thousands of prospectors through Oklahoma toward the West Coast during the California Gold Rush.

By the mid-1800s, North Fork Town had grown into a bustling trading center with all the trappings of a typical frontier town: a general store, a post office (the Micco Post Office was built, named after the Cherokee word for the town), a saloon, and a few scattered homesteads and blacksmith shops. It was a small but thriving community, with a population of several hundred people. The Methodist Church even scooped up an eighty-acre chunk of farmland and constructed the Asbury Manual Labor School, a three-story stone-and-brick dwelling built to accommodate 100 students, twenty-four teachers, and one preacher.

Then the Civil War arrived. Caught in the middle of a "fratricidal bloodbath" fought on their own land, the Five Civilized Tribes and the communities of Indian Territory were decimated. North Fork Town served as a little more than a Confederate supply base.

After the war, during the Reconstruction, the Asbury Manual Labor School, as well as much of the town, was destroyed by a fire in 1869. Creek Chief, Samuel Checote, petitioned for federal money, and the town set to work rebuilding their school. They rebuilt it three times, in fact—in 1868, 1881, and 1887—and all three times, it burned down.

As the winds of industry shifted and the "Ironhead" took over, the new Kansas and Texas Railroad (MK&T, often called Katy) supply depot became a major commercial draw, around which a "tent city" soon popped up. Urged even by its most influential local newspaper, the *Indian Journal*, to follow the path toward growth, it wasn't long before North Fork Town experienced a substantial exodus as its businesses and families migrated to and joined the "tent city," which was soon renamed Eufaula. Appropriately enough, "Eufaula" originated from a Creek phrase meaning "here they split up and went many places."

After the widespread displacement of the Civil War, the original North Fork Town still had a few residents, but it was now largely a ghost town of overgrown prairie grass, bridge culverts, and abandoned outhouses. Nowadays, ghost towns make for modest tourist draws, which may have been the case for North Fork Town had it not been for a final death knell.

In the early 1950s, the US Army Corps of Engineers began work on the Eufaula Dam, which was a controversial and hotly debated issue at the time. The dam was built to help control flooding in the area and to generate hydroelectric power, and it required the flooding of several thousand acres of land, including North Fork Town.

Residents were given notice that they would need to evacuate, and many of them did so, but some were reluctant to leave their homes and their community. In the end, the town was flooded, and North Fork Town disappeared beneath the waters of the newly formed Lake Eufaula.

For many years, the town lay hidden and forgotten beneath the surface of the lake. However, in recent years, interest in local history has been rekindled, and efforts have been made to document and preserve what remains. One of the most intriguing aspects of North Fork Town is the fact that, in spite of being submerged for over half a century, many of its structures and artifacts have been remarkably well-preserved due to the lake's relatively cold and oxygen-poor water, which has helped to slow the process of decay.

One of the most prominent structures still visible at the bottom of the lake is the old Asbury schoolhouse. Although it has been severely damaged by the flooding and the passage of time, the building still stands. The roof has collapsed, and the walls are heavily encrusted with underwater growths. At depths of up to 100 feet, where visibility is reduced by all the suspended silt and algae, the site is difficult to access. But scuba divers reported that the desks and chairs are still visible inside, as are a few tattered textbooks and other school supplies.

Other structures that can be seen at the bottom of the lake include the remains of a general store and the Micco post office. Both buildings are largely collapsed and covered in silt and debris, but the outlines of their foundations can still be seen, as can a few scattered items of merchandise and mail.

Did Sherilyn learn about the submerged ghost town that her home overlooked? Had she looked into other dark legends of Oklahoman history?

The Indigo Child

One of the more unsettling paranormal stories concerns Madyson, who was said to have at least two imaginary friends that she believed were spirits. In one interview, Starlet said her daughter-in-law believed "the spirits of a long-dead family lived with them" and that Madyson "spoke with the youngest spirit."

When I asked Niki about the reports of Madyson's spirit friends, she said she wondered about the extent to which Sherilyn had put those ideas into her head.

"I loved Sherilyn deeply, but there were times I wondered—hmm...how to even put it into words," she said, pausing. "Madyson may have had a friend, but I do know that kids are very perceptive, and she may have heard her mom talking about her having imaginary friends and then perpetuated it. When Ma-

dyson was born, Sherilyn wanted her to be gifted in that way so badly, and she thought that she was a ... oh, I can't remember—"
"Indigo?"
"Yes! She thought Madyson was an indigo child from the time she was very young. We were so into crystals and the metaphysical/paranormal, and I think she was projecting. Or maybe she did have a friend or special powers."

The "indigo child" is a vestige of 1960s New Age philosophy and before that, the Spiritualism of the nineteenth century, which popularized the idea that certain chosen souls are born with special extrasensory abilities—healing, clairvoyance, telepathy, and communicating with spirits of the dead. These early psychics, who were predominantly women, used spirits as a kind of Trojan horse for their social-religious movement, which advocated for causes like the abolition of slavery and women's suffrage. They believed the spirit world was constantly growing and evolving, and "spirit guides" represented an intelligence more advanced than humans that could lead us toward an enlightened state.

The 1960s appropriated these ideas of transcending the corrupt human establishment. Indigo children were seen as the vanguard of that new world—healers, guides, old souls, system-busters, etc.

The canon expanded over the decades, differentiating between the successive generations of indigos, the crystal and rainbow children, who are the kids and grandkids of indigos, respectively. But the unifying descriptive traits among this clade of mystics remain similar: they are highly empathetic and possess an extra-sensitive emotional intelligence. From an early age, indigos demonstrate an innate, almost subconscious, spiritual affinity and are usually resistant to traditional systems of social control or authority.

In recent years, psychiatrists and pediatricians have argued that many of the so-called indigo children are kids with potential learning disabilities or mood/personality disorders, conditions that can be worsened by their parents' resistance to medical diagnosis and treatment.

Like most children, Madyson had imaginary friends. She held tea parties with them on the family's front lawn. But unlike the vast majority of kids, Madyson was told her imaginary friends were something different, something more important. She came to believe her friends, Michael and Emily, were not only real but guides from the spirit realm, the souls of dead children.

On other days, Sherilyn said her "friends" weren't what they appeared to be—they were the form taken by the demons who visited their home.

Hauntology

I began to consider the psycho-emotional components of these stories, as well as the role trauma played in the Jamisons' spiritual visions.

Some studies have shown a significant correlation between trauma and the development of paranormal beliefs, but what is more illuminating is the way in which the traumatized mind is biochemically wired to be more conducive to paranormal interpretations. In her thesis entitled "Haunted by History: Interpreting Traumatic Memory Through Ghosts in Film and Literature," Gina Nordini described how a "traumatic memory is remembered differently" and has a different effect on the brain than a "non-traumatic memory."

She cited psychotherapist and trauma specialist Babette Rothschild, who said that the two parts of the brain that deal with memory are the amygdala, which controls the emotional effect, and the hippocampus, which organizes our memories into a proper linear timeline and narrative. When a person has a traumatic memory, a powerful "unconditioned stimulus" generates synaptic sensory messages that circumvent the cortex and bombard the amygdala and hippocampus. They break down, no longer able to process new sensations or information. This allows the foxes to rule the hen house, so to speak; as trauma powerfully dominates the present, memory itself becomes scrambled and meaningless.

In her article, "Narratives of Disembodiment: How Ghost Stories Teach Us About Trauma," Mary McCampbell wrote about author Bessel van der Kolk's concept of "the essence of trauma" being in dissociation. The "overwhelming experience" of one who has undergone trauma is "split off and fragmented, so that emotions, sounds, images, thoughts, and physical sensations related to the trauma take on a life of their own."

In his essay "Ghosts, Trauma and Travel Fever in Psychoanalysis," Michael J. Feldman writes about the broad historical trauma passed down through generations and the gaps in the narratives we use to describe our personal and collective narratives. He argues that ghosts are ruptures in memory caused by traumatic disassociation. They "represent unspeakable unknown secrets buried in the unconscious."

I BELIEVED THERE was more going on here than just spirits or demons. This isn't to say they can't be real, of course—they might be surrounding me at this very moment. But human suffering represents a more visceral fright. Murmurs of a demon familiar were a part of the tapestry of the Jamison household, like height lines or family pizza night, but this doesn't fully explain the dynamic that was going on.

Kellie Hurst, K.B.'s sister, who had been so pained to describe the family's unusual spiritual beliefs, told me Sherilyn planned to travel to Ohio and bring back the soul of her sister. This was a recurring theme in her talk of the spirit world—reuniting with Marla through various supernatural means.

Somewhere in the haze of these conflicts, some kind of osmosis or memetic transfer took place. It was no longer just Sherilyn and Madyson discussing spirits and demons. Now Bobby spoke of them, too. He saw them on the roof; he felt their presence enough to feel threatened and ask for outside help.

When I spoke to Bobby's cousin Dana, she said she had no idea what to think of the reports of his demon talk.

"Bobby's family was not religious," she told me over the phone. "He wasn't really into that, so it was probably brought by [Sherilyn]."

Considering all the ghost stories, satanic panic, and supernatural visions in the case led me back to a basic question I'd had for a while: Why was Bobby seeing demons on the roof? Why was he contacting a spiritual advisor about protecting his family from spiritual warfare with special bullets to kill demons?

Why was the entire family sharing the same hallucinatory and delusional material? Was it just some sort of tulpamancy or a collective externalization of the family's trauma (Madyson was naming characters, like her imaginary spirit friends Emily and Michael)?

Or did the situation escalate into *folie à famille*, or shared psychosis?

There was an ongoing trauma alive in the Jamisons' lives, warping their experience of pain into a story they could explain to themselves and perhaps others.

At some point, the story began to evolve—out of desperation—into a plan.

What Was Wearing Bobby?

The thread took a darker turn during one of Niki's last ghost stories, which marked the point at which I could no longer meaningfully differentiate between the family's supernatural beliefs and their ongoing mental health crisis.

Sherilyn told Niki about an experience one night in the house when she tried speaking to Bobby, who was standing at the top of the stairs like a statue. After spinning her wheels a little longer, Sherilyn realized Bobby wasn't moving or reacting at all.

Annoyed, she climbed the steps and got up in his face.

"Hey, I'm talking to you," she said, inches from her husband's eyes.

Bobby had a frozen look on his face, as though he were daydreaming about eternal nothingness. Suddenly, when he turned his head to look at her, his eyes were different. They'd lost their normal sweet brown hue and were now big and black.

Sherilyn had never seen Bobby like this before, and it scared her. He wasn't looking at her—he was looking *through* her.

Then, in a sudden burst of agitation, he pushed her. Only Sherilyn's quick reflexive grasp of the railing prevented her from falling down the stairs.

She was more shocked than angry. She yelled in Bobby's face and locked herself in the bathroom. When she emerged a bit later, he was back to his "usual self" and didn't remember the incident.

"It wasn't him," Sherilyn told Niki. "I know it wasn't. That was a demon wearing him."

Sherilyn and Niki both claimed that this was extraordinarily uncharacteristic of Bobby.

But it was supposedly not the only incident like this during their last months at the Eufaula home. And it should go without saying that many seemingly even-tempered men resort to abusive behavior behind closed doors. Some domestic assault survivors have said that during their abusers' rages, their eyes look black and "predatory."

Additionally, opioids, which Bobby was known to be taking, stimulate the parasympathetic components of the autonomic nervous system, which dilates the pupils and makes them look especially large and black. Opioids can also cause erratic, aggressive behavior, especially if someone is withdrawing or coming off the medication.

There are other explanations for the Jamisons' spiritual visions and strange behavior. In due time, I would be presented with a particularly compelling one.

But before that, I learned more from Colton about why he moved out from the Jamisons' house after fifteen years of living with Bobby and Sherilyn.

CHAPTER 21

The Downward Spiral

AFTER RECOVERING FROM HIP SURGERY, I moved back to Portland in 2020 right as the pandemic hit its stride. The city was clogged with noxious toxins from Washington wildfires. On my second day back, the Air Quality Index tallied a 477 (the previous high being 157), meaning that if you stood outside, you'd become seriously ill within minutes. Between covid and the fires, it felt like I wasn't supposed to be indoors or outdoors.

Additionally, in the wake of George Floyd's murder, the city was exploding with protests and civil chaos in response to police brutality and systemic racism. While an insurgent group of anarchists tried to occupy the federal courthouse, provocateurs from right-wing militia groups like the Proud Boys and the Oath Keepers roamed the streets. Mysterious paramilitary squads rode around downtown Portland, detaining random protestors.

Somewhere in this miasma, I began to experience intense chronic pain in my right leg, which I presumed was related to my hip injury. It started at the femoral neck, which tenuously balances the upper and lower half of the body, and radiated throughout my leg, affecting every muscle group from buttock to ankle. The pain was a throbbing, bone-deep sensation that jumped around my limb

like a whack-a-mole rodent. I developed a limp, and as the pain worsened, there were times I could barely put weight on my leg.

I began wondering if the surgery on my hip had inflamed the
major nerve that runs through that area of the leg. I went to doctors, physical therapists, and chiropractors, trying to figure out
what was going on. Eventually, I learned it had something to do
the T-band muscle being inflamed.

Chronic pain is exhausting and demoralizing. No matter how
much you meditate, no matter what mantras of positivity you repeat to yourself, the pain slowly but inexorably eats away at your
will, focus, and patience.

Like mental illness, pain is subjective. It can't be seen or meas-
ured by scans, but we know it's real. Acute pain is an evolutionary
defense mechanism by which the brain informs the body it's
doing something detrimental. It's a "multi-dimensional" sensation
run by a network of nerve fibers with special receptors called no-
ciceptors, which are responsible for creating the perception of
pain. These receptors, along with A-delta fibers, C fibers, peripheral A-beta nerves, and brain-based networks activated in the
brainstem, the thalamus, and part of the cortex, comprise a system known as the descending pain modulatory system, which
works to communicate and then suppress pain signals.

When this system gets hijacked and rewired, chronic pain results. Scientists believe this happens when a person's A-delta and
C fibers become damaged and permanently activated, causing the
brain to receive constant pain signals. The signals are "amplified"
as the nociceptor routes get "sensitized."

Recent studies have suggested that cognitive and emotional
factors—part of a biopsychosocial model that includes exposure
to trauma—can play a role.

To quell the pain, I began using enormous quantities of kratom, a powder made from the plants in the coffee family, which
has a powerful narcotic effect. It's not an opioid, but it stimulates
the same receptors in the brain and essentially acts as substitute
for strong painkillers. Kratom also helps greatly with anxiety and
depression.

I sang its praises and even advocated for its use to help with the over-prescribing and overdosing of pain meds.

The only downside was choking down the green powder, which is so fine that the slightest inhalation could line my throat and sinuses with chunky wet green guck and leave me coughing my lungs out and throwing up. I got very efficient at consuming enormous heaping spoonfuls of the stuff and washing it down with water in timed stages.

I was the guy at restaurants asking for spoons and then disappearing into the bathroom, the guy with a backpack full of utensils covered in a skein of dried-over powder slobber.

A Violent Cycle

The experience gave me some newfound insight into the psychology of Bobby Jamison, who, between two bouts of testicular cancer and his back injury, had lived with chronic pain for the bulk of his adult life and was prescribed strong painkillers.

In the final years, as his back pain persisted and Sherilyn's mental instability and grief worsened, pain relief became a fundamental directive. It was no longer just Bobby using his prescribed opioid painkillers. Colton told me that Sherilyn regularly, even chronically, consumed the meds. It got to the point where Bobby had to hide them—both the pills and the patches—because she was stealing them, overdosing, and having seizures. She was also taking prescribed Xanax at the time.

Colton described it as a "violent cycle [of] being pilled out and depressed and ... secluded. It got really bad."

The erratic, paranoid behavior and fighting intensified, as well. Colton told me that although he was very young at the time, he remembered a period in which Bobby and Sherilyn were talking seriously about divorce.

"They would fight and not talk for two days. Bobby would go work; they would storm by each other and not talk, then fight at night; Bobby would sleep on the couch, angry, or sleep in the spare bedroom."

For teenaged Colton, the writing had been on the wall for some time. After the death of her sister, Sherilyn spiraled into substance abuse and a darkness that unilaterally changed her.

The second time we spoke on the phone, Colton described childhood memories I was initially hesitant to include. Ultimately, I concluded that what Colton told me was probative and relevant, and that if he had the courage to be transparent about the truth, then I had a duty to reflect that truth in my reporting.

"[Sherilyn] was starting to get abusive and starting to actually lay hands on me and hit me, throw things at me." Colton feared he might be provoked into saying or doing something that he couldn't take back.

He knew this wasn't her; he knew his mom didn't truly want to hurt him. This was about *her pain*, which flowed through her as a conduit. But intent hardly mattered anymore. His mom was sick, untethered from reality. The situation was beyond dysfunctional; it had become toxic. Dangerous. The ship was unmoored and irretrievably off-course.

"I always told her that if things didn't change that I was going to go move in with my dad."

Colton's biological father, Billy, had said many times that Colton was welcome to live with him. It was his decision. In Colton's many visits over the years, he'd noted how his dad's household was "normal—very, very normal, the way it's supposed to be."

On May 13, 2009, he traveled from Eufaula to Westport, a small town just outside of Tulsa, to attend a three-day football camp for linemen. He stayed with his dad while there, which infuriated Sherilyn. On the last day, Colton and his mom got into a heated argument over the phone.

"She went berserk on me . . ." Colton said. The final straw was when she said she regretted having him. "After the abuse and her hitting me, something inside me said to go through with it."

So Colton told her: he wasn't coming back after the camp; he was going to live with his dad. Instead of apologizing for her behavior or trying to persuade him to stay, Sherilyn angrily called his bluff and told him he was kicked out anyway.

After he got off the phone, he called Billy, his biological dad, and told him everything that had been happening. His father immediately lawyered up for the impending custody fight.

Meanwhile, Colton's stepfather Bobby was already on his way to pick him up from the camp, unaware of the sea change that had just gone down. When Bobby arrived, Colton was already bawling his eyes out, before he even got out of his truck. Colton explained to Bobby that he wasn't coming home, that he was going to live with his biological dad.

Bobby, the man who had raised Colton and taught him everything he knew, understood the situation better than anyone. He knew why Colton had to go.

Bobby listened and then gave him the biggest hug of his life. "I love you, son," he said.

COLTON RETURNED FOR a visit about a month later in the hope of normalizing relations. It was the first time seeing his mom since the explosive fights that spurred his departure. Despite the rift, he wanted to make an effort to remain in his family's lives.

Things started promisingly: Sherilyn hugged him and apologized. She said she was hurt that he left but that things were getting better around the house.

The facade of goodwill and peace didn't hold for long, though. They ended up getting into another fight, and his mom once again unraveled into a profanity-laced tirade.

He left knowing he'd made the right decision, which became even more clear when Sherilyn refused to hand over his clothes and belongings from the Eufaula house. Colton and Billy had to fight her in court for two months to legally compel their return.

CHAPTER 22

Follow the Money

*... There is no honorable law enforcement authority in
Anglo-American law so ancient as that of the County
Sheriff. And today, as in the past, the County Sheriff is
a peace officer entrusted with the maintenance of law
and order and the preservation of domestic tranquility.
... As Thomas Jefferson wrote in his THE VALUE OF
CONSTITUTIONS, "the Office of Sheriff is the most
important of all the executive offices of the county."*

—LATIMER COUNTY SHERIFF'S OFFICE
OFFICIAL HOMEPAGE

ON DECEMBER 14, 2020, ROUNDING out an otherwise psychotic year in American history, a small podcast published
its twenty-seventh episode, entitled "Israel 'Ish' Beauchamp."

The YouTube video filled my screen with the podcast's watermarked name, *I Don't Drink Coffee*, as well as the former sheriff
himself, looking older but stronger with a thick, partially gray
beard and tattooed muscles bursting like bratwurst out of his
T-shirt. He'd brought two huge guns, which joined him for the
interview alongside a bottle of Gentleman Jack and the two hosts,

who were backdropped by a Michael Myers mask and massive
red KEEP AMERICA GREAT banner.

I cringed but reminded myself that not everyone likes coffee.

When I saw the timestamp, I did a double-take—the video
was twenty-two minutes shy of five hours long, and I learned the
hard way that Beauchamp only discussed the Jamison case for
about fifteen minutes near the end. Much of the time before that
was spent on culture war bravado and punishingly incoherent so-
ciopolitical rants, in between which he described his deployments
and adventures as a mercenary in the Middle East.

The one-time sheriff also discussed his early law enforcement
career, which offered some insightful pretext for the Jamison investigation.

ISRAEL BEAUCHAMP CAME from a family of athletes. Growing
up, he was close to his mom, but not so much to his dad, though
this would change. He joined the military seven months out of
high school because he wanted to be a sniper. Halfway through
his deployment in Kuwait, Beauchamp's mom died, marking a
new phase of his life. On a personal level, he became closer to his
father, with whom he eventually became "best friends."

At his mother's funeral, a local sheriff asked him to consider
law enforcement when he returned from his current deployment.
He did, becoming a deputy and working his way up the ranks
under the administration of Sheriff Wayne Brinkley.

Beauchamp cut his teeth as a deputy during one of the peaks
of the state's multi-decade methamphetamine epidemic, a time
when the rate of meth use among adults between the ages of
twenty-six and thirty-four was eighty percent higher than the national average. In the early 2000s, Oklahoma had one of the worst
meth problems in the country, with then-Governor Frank Keat-
ing designating it "public health enemy Number One."

Every year, law enforcement agencies and departments around
the state busted thousands of meth labs. Working alongside Deputy Adam Woodruff, another future Latimer sheriff, Beauchamp

saw the bust boom firsthand, executing over 200 search warrants—or, in his words, "kicking in a lot of doors."

Oklahoma law enforcement spent so much time targeting meth manufacturers that there was less heat on the mid- and upper-tier sellers, many of whom began trafficking the narcotics coming across the border from Mexican cartels. This realignment would constitute the next phase of Oklahoma's drug war, which saw homegrown labs largely phased out while Mexican cartels monopolized ninety-five percent of the state's meth market.

When Beauchamp took over as sheriff, he had plans to partition parts of Latimer County into a grid so that he could better focus on drug enforcement. But as common as rogue narcotics labs still were in southeast Oklahoma, searching for them in the Sans Bois Mountains was like trying to find the proverbial needle in the haystack.

Beauchamp would experience this plight firsthand.

The Sheriff System

There were three realities that served as an important backdrop to the local law enforcement community during the Jamison investigation. One was the aforementioned meth epidemic.

The second was the sheriff system, the antiquated but deeply ingrained approach to policing and criminal justice that persists in many Southern states.

The Knights Templar–like hagiography of the Anglo-Saxon sheriff that opened this chapter was only an excerpt of a longer edict that delved into the history of the office, tracing its legal, judicial, and correctional origins back over a thousand years to Alfred the Great and even as far back as the Roman occupation of England. Throughout both Anglo-Saxon and Norman rule, English kings appointed representatives to oversee each shire or county. This representative was known as a "reeve," or "shire-reeve." Over time, as the language changed, this became "Sheriff."

"The shire-reeve or Sheriff was the chief law enforcement officer of each county in the year 1000 A.D. He still has the same function in Oklahoma in the year 2000 A.D.," the website stated, adding that the main difference now is that the people choose a sheriff, not a king.

The third reality, which some legal scholars say often directly results from the second (the sheriff system), was the widespread, long-standing, and well-documented corruption exposed in the state's law enforcement communities, which included a string of disgraced and criminally convicted sheriffs in both McIntosh and Latimer County.

Oklahoma's problem with scandal-plagued sheriffs became so infamous that in 2011, *The Oklahoman* published an article with an eye-catching lede: "Does Oklahoma have the most corrupt public officials in the nation?" As if reporting the results of its own case study, five years later, the paper published a "sampling" of the state's long line of "scandal-plagued sheriffs," which included:

+ Love County Sheriff Joe Russell maintained a "drug house" and was arrested and charged with corruption in office, willful neglect of duty, and maladministration.
+ Wagoner County Sheriff Bob Colbert was indicted by a grand jury and charged with bribery and extortion (he had apparently made a habit of shaking down motorists during traffic stops).
+ Tulsa County Sheriff Stanley Glanz was accused of allowing widespread corruption within his department, which was revealed after the sheriff's poorly trained reserve deputy shot and killed a man.
+ Carter County Sheriff Milton Anthony was arrested and pleaded guilty to bribery charges after coercing an employee forty years his junior into having a sexual relationship with him in exchange for Milton hiring her husband as a deputy.
+ Love County Sheriff Wesley Liddell Jr. "found himself in hot water in 1989 when he was indicted for

plotting to kidnap and torture a north Texas drug
dealer, in hopes of locating drug labs inside Oklahoma." He was later acquitted.
+ Former Latimer County Sheriff Melvin Holly was
  convicted of fourteen counts for sexually abusing jail
  inmates and employees, one of whom he took as a
  date to the Oklahoma Sheriff's Association dinner
  and threatened to murder.
+ Former Custer County Sheriff, Mike Burgess, was
  convicted of sex crimes.
+ Former McIntosh County Sheriff Terry Alan Jones
  and Undersheriff Mykol Travis Brookshire were convicted and sentenced to federal prison terms for
  extorting money from highway motorists.

The corruption was not limited to just sheriffs. Oklahoma's
largest public corruption scandal erupted in the early 1980s, when
some 240 county commissioners and suppliers were convicted of,
or pleaded guilty to, kickback-related charges. The statewide
fraud conspiracy enveloped sixty-one of Oklahoma's seventy-
seven counties.

When the US Department of Justice finally collated its public
corruption statistics over a ten-year period, the agency reported that
Oklahoma had 107 public officials convicted of various crimes from
1998 through 2007, kicking off with Eufaula Mayor Joe Johnson,
who was convicted of corruption by a hometown jury in 1998.

In 2015, a State Integrity Investigation gave Oklahoma an F
due to "unchecked cronyism." The next year, more widespread corruption was exposed in the Tulsa Police Department, where
investigators had coerced witnesses, victims, and suspects into giving false statements, resulting in the wrongful convictions of
seven people, including one man, Malcolm Scott, who spent
twenty-two years in prison for a murder he didn't commit.

An investigation into the Tulsa scandal led to the Community
Safety Institute (CSI) issuing a report that concluded: "Oklahoma sheriff's office had a 'system-wide failure' of leadership."

Retired University of Oklahoma professor Harry Holloway, who co-authored the book *Bad Times for Good Ol' Boys: The Oklahoma County Commissioner Scandal,* said that while the corruption seen in Oklahoma was "just as bad throughout the entire South," the structure of county government and the sheriff system played a major role.

US Attorney Sheldon Sperling, who was the prosecuting attorney in many of the state's corruption cases, said the system in Oklahoma placed a dangerous amount of power in the hands of sheriffs who govern rural areas lacking oversight.

"Our system of government should be modernized, but the political reality is that folks want to hang on to their little fiefdoms," Sperling said, referring to the antiquated system that gives each of the state's seventy-seven separate counties its own sheriff, county commission, and local court. "It's crazy that we haven't gone to a regional system."

Criminal justice professor Samuel Walker observed that the county sheriff system had manifested corruption since the earliest "Wild West" days of statehood.

"The sheriff goes back to the founding of the first colonies," he said. "It's really been an endemic problem, because they're independently elected.... They've got a lot of power, a lot of political power, and with power comes corruption."

Southeast Oklahoma has long been acknowledged for its outlaw mentality, even among its local lawmen, who have long defied fealty to federal authority.

As one newspaper stated, "There's two worlds in one state... SE Oklahoma and the rest of Oklahoma... [It's] a place where the law doesn't always apply, where outlaw bikers, meth cookers, and other criminals find refuge from the outside world."

Who Killed the Jamisons?

It took almost four hours for former sheriff Beauchamp's podcast interview to address the Jamison case, but when it did, things moved fast. After they established the initial case facts and some descriptions of the search, Beauchamp said the Jamisons had weighed on him even after he resigned as sheriff.

"It's not what you know, it's what you can prove," Beauchamp said, doggedly. "I know who done it. I know who killed 'em—"

The presumably stunned hosts got twisted up in cross talk.

"A hundred percent they were killed." Beauchamp looked at the camera and whispered furtively into the mic, "The OSBI and the FBI are full of shit. The two parents [Bobby and Sherilyn] were killed; they were shot in the back of the head."

Beauchamp said that Madyson, who was found within a hundred yards of them, wasn't killed.

The host paused for half a beat and asked, "So you think they may have left Madyson alive and then she just died from exposure . . . ?"

"That's what I think, [but] I can't prove that. What I do know for a fact is that at least one of the skulls had a hole in the back of it—a bullet hole. . . . Let's get it out there, because what people feed everybody is bull crap."

"They left it so open-ended . . ." the host, a long-time friend and former colleague of the sheriff, murmured.

"They had to . . . I even had to back then, because it was a public-relations type thing, and I couldn't out the FBI the way that I wanted to—or the OSBI." Beauchamp said there were six FBI agents in the first five days of the search who were "remarkable" and helped build a case profile. "But the next two that took over the case were pieces of crap. They done nothing."

Circling back around to his initial claim, Beauchamp broached the big question: "I can't tell you who done it, because if I do that, they're going to get me for slander because they'll claim that I'm going to ruin their lives," he said. "It's obvious: follow the money, as they say . . . I knew within a month or two who done it, but I can't prove it, so it doesn't matter."

Beauchamp then revealed that in addition to the 32,000 dollars found in the Jamisons' truck, there was an additional 32,000 dollars—Sherilyn's half of the settlement payment—that she brought with her in a brown briefcase-like satchel, which was seen on the security footage being packed into the truck but was later missing from the scene and never recovered. Beauchamp believed this bag was also used to stow her .22 pistol, which "[Sherilyn] carried all the time everywhere she went" but was similarly never found.

He said the 32,000 dollars that *was* found was "hidden underneath the seat, [but] the other one, [Sherilyn's], was in the wide open . . . I think the person that done all this grabbed the money and the missing gun."

Describing the difficulty of the investigation, Beauchamp said, "Their lifestyle made it hard to deal with this case, because they left so many ends open."

"So do you think that this was like, uh, that this person came upon them and saw maybe the money . . ."

"It's pretty simple," Beauchamp interrupted. "This person knew they were going up there. That's all I can say about that—and they either got out by gunpoint or they got out because they knew the person . . ."

Defending his team's efforts from critics—who wonder "how in the world did you not find them?"—Beauchamp said, "Two-point-six miles as a bird flies on Panola Mountain, or the Sans Bois Mountains, is a big deal."

"Sure is." The host, who had grown up in the mountains of southeast Oklahoma, tried to describe how easy it is to get lost there.

Beauchamp was proud of the search they conducted: "No one can tell me we didn't do everything we could. . . . That was the coldest October I can remember."

He praised the various groups who helped, including 4th Street, Troop Z of the Highway Patrol, and other local departments. His highest praise went to the volunteers of Latimer County, who showed up en masse to search a miserable, rain-swept terrain in extremely cold temperatures.

Addressing the accidental death theory, he said: "They did not go out into those woods and expire. [Bobby's] back was basically broke, almost."

So, how did they make it 2.6 miles? The host asked.

"Gunpoint in a vehicle, that's how they made it," Beauchamp declared. "Person drove them out there, then walked them 100 yards off the road..."

According to the former sheriff, the killer didn't spend much time burying Bobby and Sherilyn and didn't have the "gumption" to kill Madyson, who he said was likely left there alone after her parents were killed.

Rounding out the discussion, Beauchamp gave a dismal update.

"In the OSBI, as of right now, the case is closed...which means that no one's working on it...and you and I and a whole bunch of other people [are] very upset with that. Yes, they were absolutely murdered, there's no doubt about it."

The remaining hour or so covered matters not related to the case, but in less than twenty minutes, the former sheriff had revealed new case information and spelled out a theory of the crime. He had even invoked a classic dictum—*cui bono*—follow the money.

Beauchamp also mentioned something interesting about the hunter, Tim Graham, who discovered the remains. If it hadn't been for his quote about the hole in the skull coming out in the paper, the former sheriff claimed, no one would have known about it.

In addition to corroborating my own hubristic hunch that the "Ain't no coyote did that" line was important, it presented a troubling idea, that some entity in the chain of investigatory command would have rather the hole comment not been published. If you think back and remember that article, it immediately struck me as strange the way an OSBI agent tried to overwrite the statement of an eyewitness in the first article published about the remains. It always felt like a "methinks thou doth protest too much" moment.

Beauchamp corroborated a few more suspicions I'd harbored over the years. For one, the Latimer County Sheriff's Office was totally caught off guard by a case of such magnitude and was unprepared for a murder investigation, much less a complicated, high-profile case. Beauchamp admitted this during the podcast, and while part of me respects his honesty, another part of me wonders if perhaps this is also an admission of the limitations of the sheriff system. If local investigators were only capable of doing drug busts and not properly managing a potential triple-homicide case, that's a pretty damning indictment of the system in place.

I also wondered how the animosity between local authorities and state and federal really played out. Based on Beauchamp's invective and his multiple verbal body slams of the OSBI and FBI, it's clear there were some major tensions between departments and investigative bodies. Some weird power dynamics were going on behind the scenes.

One might ask whether it was possible Beauchamp overstated the certainty of his case. After all, there was a predominately empty handle of whiskey on the table in front of him. It's true that he may have absorbed a kind of scenario lock over the years. But it's worth pointing out that it would almost certainly have been easier for Beauchamp to run with the accident narrative—or at least hide behind the safety of uncertainty—than to assert with 100 percent certainty that he presided over a murderer getting away with a triple homicide. Beauchamp still seemed palpably angry about the case, disturbed to his core by the lack of resolution. I just don't see a law enforcement and military veteran harboring such strong conviction fifteen years on without having seen or learned something that strongly suggested foul play.

The former sheriff said he always assumed more evidence would be discovered that could nail the perpetrator. This made me wonder what evidence existed that the public didn't know about.

Beauchamp left the biggest pieces of the puzzle unidentified, but he had revealed, for the first time, the shape of the killer—the perpetrator's character, motive, and likely murder weapon. At a few points, it almost seemed as if he were knowingly dropping breadcrumbs.

Follow the money, he said. *It leads to someone who knew the area, knew the Jamisons were up there, and knew they had a large amount of cash.*

When I talked to Niki about the podcast, I asked her about these breadcrumbs. She had a strong feeling as to whom Beauchamp was referring and proceeded to tell me about her first trip to the mountain. By the end of this voyage, she'd discovered two people she considered suspects, one of whom she spoke to in person.

As I finally moved back to Portland, the next stage of my investigation was clear: if we take Beauchamp at his word and follow the money, where, and to whom, does that lead?

CHAPTER 23

Return to Panola Mountain

"Well, here we go!"
Niki and her cousin Meredith began the eight-mile ascent into the high sticks, where Panola Mountain loomed like Mordor amid the storm clouds on the horizon. Niki glimpsed it through the passenger-side window. They were in its kingdom now, the jurisdiction of the wild—a land untethered from the human grid of utilities and laws.

As they climbed higher and deeper into the great cascading tiers of rock and foliage, the sense of isolation became visceral. The wilderness enfolded a string of remote towns originally built as supply lines for the railroad. When the US government and the "Ironhead" industry monopolized Indian Territory, workers followed the money into the mountains, and every 2.8 miles, a camp arose. These camps became the towns of Sorrels, Smacker, Cavanal, Wister, Fanshawe, Red Oak, Panola, and Wilburton.

A Message from the Dead

Some places have vibes—echoes of the past, information that lingers. Panola's vibe grew stronger the closer they got to the clearing. When they arrived at the Jamisons' last-known point, Niki was immediately hit with an almost mystical sense of déjà vu. It was like the truth behind this torturous mystery lay right before her in every direction, saturating the land and air; the events of that day were still occurring over and over as though trapped in a loop. Yet, she couldn't see any of it. The truth was certain but invisible, suffused just below the surface.

After years of dreaming about and absorbing pictures and stories of the mountain terrain into her mental maps, Panola had turned into a phantom in Niki's mind. It wasn't a land mass or geographic feature anymore—it was a mythic villain. And she was finally facing her nemesis in the flesh; with every step and breath, she drew closer to its black, beating heart.

More viscerally, she was occupying the physical space where her friends disappeared, where Sherilyn had "slipped the surly bonds," where whatever happened, happened. After months of disembodied web sleuthing, she felt a sense of exhilaration to be on the ground, away from screens and messages, physically connected to the last earth on which the Jamisons had stood.

Niki had heard the rumors about this area a hundred times over. She'd been warned several times by both friends and strangers not to come up here. Though she and her cousin were loosely accompanied by deputies, a sense of danger attended their arrival. Panola was an area that attracted people who don't want to be seen, who are in the business of doing things they don't want observed. And she knew that whatever found Sherilyn, Bobby, and Madyson on the mountain could find her (and her cousin, she thought with a pang of guilt).

In the near distance, the junkyard truck came into view, rising from the ground like some abstract art exhibit. She remembered it from the search photographs released by the police. Seeing the thing in person, rendered in all dimensions against the backdrop of this vast environment, unnerved her.

"Look, there's stuff written on it," her cousin observed, pointing.

They parked their car and wandered over to look. Across the rusty, twisted frame of dilapidated alloy, there were gunshot holes and occult inscriptions left by countless drifters.

But, as she looked closer, it appeared someone had come along later and spray-painted over some of the original tags with contravening messages. Something about the style and substance struck her, called to her memory, and she narrowed her eyes to inspect the calligraphic detail.

An indescribable sensation descended upon the clearing, a sublime eeriness, as Niki realized: Sherilyn wrote this.

It wasn't just the phrase, *God loves you*, which had been one of her friend's favorite and most commonly used phrases, it was the penmanship—or, in this case, the spray painting—which Niki had seen for years. No one, not even the police investigators, had noticed this detail during the original search. But she was certain, without a shadow of a doubt, that it was Sherilyn who had overwritten the satanic messages with pious tributes.

The discovery was a gift and a curse, an epiphany so bewildering and painful she didn't know whether to laugh or cry. On one hand, she was grateful for this renewed connection to her friend, who had stood for a time in this exact spot doing what Sherilyn did—trying, however erratically, to spontaneously generate love in the world.

But as surely as encroaching storm clouds, darker thoughts prevailed, for these were also the coordinates where her friend faced the ultimate nightmare: dying alongside her child, unable to protect her.

As if this thought weren't sickening enough, Niki felt another stab of horror as she considered: was it possible Sherilyn had angered someone? It seemed almost silly to imagine a mountain dweller becoming murderously territorial over a hunk of target practice, but this was exactly the type of place where such a deranged mind might dwell.

Later that night, after returning from the mountain, she wrote to her Jamison warriors about the find. It didn't resurface until later in 2011, when Niki received an unexpected message.

A New Suspect

At first, she didn't recognize the name—Michael Taylor—but as the man began to introduce himself, it clicked: this was the father of Ashley Taylor, a young woman from Weleetka, Oklahoma, who had been reported missing earlier that year.

Investigators eventually found her remains on a remote property, where the evidence of her brutal murder had been concealed.

Michael was polite, but his voice contained the raw, broken mien of someone whose every waking moment is haunted by a pain that can never be mended. And the trauma was fresh—Ashley's murder happened only a few months earlier.

Why on Earth is he calling me? Niki thought.

Like virtually everyone else in the state, Michael had heard about the search for the Jamisons. In the aftermath of his own daughter's murder, details from the past began patching through in unexpected ways. Previously arbitrary conversations breached his memory and became salient. Mr. Taylor had information he felt could be relevant, but he couldn't get an audience with law enforcement. When he saw Niki's "Find the Jamisons" page, he decided to contact her.

"I believe it's possible I know the man responsible for whatever's been done to your friends," he said.

"Okay. I'm listening. Who?"

It was the same man, he said, that murdered his daughter.

ASHLEY TAYLOR AND Kevin Joe Sweat both grew up in Weleetka, Oklahoma, only a forty-minute drive from Eufaula. According to friends and family, they were high school outcasts-turned-sweethearts, two "shy and quirky" kids who found a tribe of two. They grew apart after graduation but reunited a few years later after Kevin experienced a life-changing tragedy: his brother overdosed and died, leaving Kevin "broken-hearted" and "isolated."

After moving in together, the two began arguing, and Ashley became withdrawn. Her family and friends blamed it on the noticeably darker and angrier Kevin, who was convinced his brother's death was the result of foul play. When they announced they were engaged, Ashley's family was surprised. Soon thereafter, they left for their honeymoon in Louisiana, and Ashley abruptly stopped answering her phone.

Although her family believed Ashley and Kevin were traveling together, weeks later, they were stunned to learn that Kevin hadn't missed a day of work. They found online pictures of Sweat holding knives and guns and, in one photo, him covered in blood.

Michael and Trish Taylor confronted him and asked where their daughter was. Kevin calmly said that he last saw Ashley when he dropped her off near a bridge after the two got into a relationship-ending argument and scrapped their drive to Louisiana.

"It was shocking," Ashley's mother said. "Right then, I knew something bad had happened. I just didn't know what."

Investigators also found it strange and suspicious that Kevin hadn't gone back to check on his longtime girlfriend or even tried calling or texting her.

Okmulgee Patrol Officer Lyndon Spears, who took Kevin in for questioning, later said, "I've dealt with multiple homicides, drug dealers, gang members, things of that nature. But Kevin is the only person that I was ever in a room with that there was just something unnerving about him, about his aura."

In questioning Sweat, police learned he had already been interviewed by the OSBI about a gun he owned with possible ties to the shocking murder of two young girls, Skyla Whitaker and Taylor Placker. After obtaining a search warrant, investigators found the remains of Ashley Taylor in a fire pit on Kevin's property. Kevin later admitted to cutting her throat and burning her remains.

Investigators also found ballistic matches tying him to the murders of the two girls. In a move that some interpreted as Sweat setting the stage for an insanity defense, he confessed to detectives that he killed the girls because he saw "two monsters" coming toward him. In his head, he claimed, the two little girls on foot posed such a threat to him in his black Chevy Cavalier that he unloaded both his Glock .40 and .22 handguns.

In court, Kevin's lawyer would argue that the suicide/overdose death of his brother had caused such a mental breakdown that the young man experienced hallucinations.

The prosecution argued that Kevin was motivated by a vendetta and killed the girls because he believed their siblings were responsible for his brother's overdose death.

Shortly before murdering Ashley, Kevin confided to her that he had killed Taylor and Skyla prior to their getting back together. Horrified by the revelation, Ashley was going to leave him for good and report him to the police, so he killed her and burned her body.

There was a sense in which Ashley's death directly helped to solve the murders of Taylor and Skyla. But if the girls' case had been solved sooner—or if the OSBI had simply disclosed the contents of its interview with Sweat—Ashley may have lived.

It was a heartbreaking, horrifying case set for adjudication later that year.

Cold Sweat

Having known Kevin for the many years his daughter dated him, in high school and later, Mr. Taylor could recall haunting aspects of the young man's life, as well as conversations with him.

First of all, he told Niki, either his family or his friend's family owned land up on Panola Mountain, and Kevin frequently went four-wheeling up there. He'd even shown Michael the general area on a map.

Kevin told him that there was an abandoned truck on the mountain that he used for shooting practice. One day, Michael remembered, Kevin was furious because he said somebody had defaced the truck, which he considered his property.

Niki felt her blood turn cold...

"You saw my post," was all she could muster.

"I didn't think anything of it when he told me," Michael told her. "But after you said what you saw up there, it all came rushing back. It could be a coincidence, but..."

He didn't need to finish the thought. If Kevin was capable of killing his high school sweetheart and two little girls, who was to say he hadn't done the same to the Jamisons?

Niki imagined it going down. She could see Sweat in his trench coat, fuming as he watched Sherilyn vandalize his property through the crosshairs of his rifle scope. She could see the Jamisons trying to depart the clearing and a vehicle suddenly appearing on the dirt road, blocking their only exit.

Michael shared another unnerving anecdote: while they were dating, Kevin got Ashley a cat, which they named Stormy.

Michael remembered asking about the name. Kevin told him it came from the missing girl, Madyson, whose middle name was Stormy.

Niki befriended Michael and his wife, Fay, Ashley's stepmom, and learned about the bespoke hell they'd been through since their daughter went missing, and earlier when Ashley changed for the worse due to her abusive relationship with Kevin.

Michael must have tortured himself with hypotheticals and an endless cycle of guilt and recrimination. He'd known for so long that Kevin was bad news—but what could he do? It was her choice who she loved. Had she only known the depths of derangement fomenting behind his eyes, she could have escaped.

Niki had felt some of the same pangs of despair about Sherilyn. But her feelings of guilt were more complicated, and she hadn't fully processed them.

As the Taylors awaited Kevin Sweat's trial—where he would be prosecuted for the murders of the two girls, not their daughter—Niki spent more time with them, listening to their stories. The more she heard, the more she was convinced that Sweat was connected to the Jamisons' demise.

The final kicker was when Mr. Taylor showed her images of a quarry where Sweat would go to shoot guns. Niki's jaw dropped when she read its location: Marble City. She recalled the anonymous Topix poster who had claimed the Jamisons were buried under a bridge there.

Once again, an unlikely pattern had materialized in the static—a dubious scrap from an online conspiracy theorist had morphed into a credible lead in her murder investigation.

She dove into Sweat's backstory and sussed out his social media accounts, finding a number of pictures of him donning a dark trench coat in the woods and showing off his guns. She posted a message to the Jamison warriors about her suspicions with a link to Sweat's Deviant Art gallery, which featured an image of him posing with a semiautomatic rifle.

"I believe he had something to do with the Jamison disappearance," she wrote, adding that both she and Mr. Taylor, who she called Mr. X, were ninety-nine percent sure that Sweat was the man in the brown shirt in the surveillance video. At that time, he had the "same height, weight, [and] gait."

After months of procedural delays, Kevin Joe Sweat finally appeared in court for his arraignment. Niki attended the hearing and sat next to the Taylors, who had been among the first people to arrive at the courthouse that morning. As they awaited the judge, the crowded bench seating, packed like a sardine can with family members, friends, court reporters, and media members, felt more like a church pew.

As the judge read the charges, Niki watched Kevin. His appearance had changed. Pictures of a younger Kevin showed him sporting wavy bleached auburn hair, pierced ears, and a cherubic face—a mix of rockstar Scott Weiland and Aurora theater shooter James Holmes. It was yet another reminder as to the infinite gulf between appearance and intent, how behind the face of someone who looks like he could be your local counterculture barista or Apple Store technician can lurk the mind of a deranged killer.

Now, standing before the jurists who would determine whether he lived or died, his head was shaved, his earrings were gone, and he wore glasses. His face was pale and sickly. His orange prison garb looked like there was little more than a skeleton keeping it off the ground.

Her gaze wandered a few yards back to the grim-faced attendees sitting on the benches closest to Kevin and his defense team. She wondered if any of them were Kevin's family.

As if on cue, Fay, who must have caught Niki's glance, casually leaned over to her and whispered, "That's Kevin's brother."

At first, Niki didn't know whom she was talking about—a dozen people sat in that row. But in an instant, it became clear who Fay meant. There was a man who bore a physical resemblance to Kevin.

More importantly, this man was staring directly at her.

Niki stared back, even as part of her hoped he was looking at someone or something else. Suddenly, he nodded with a dour expression that read *I know exactly who you are and why you're here.*

Chills ran up her spine. She wondered if he had seen her post about Kevin.

SWEAT WAS FOUND guilty and sentenced to three lifetime sentences. During the sentencing hearing, he tried to slit his own lawyer's throat with a razor blade.

"The pain is always going to be there, and that's something you can't take away," said Mr. Taylor after the sentencing. As far his daughter's killer: "His reality is starting to come crashing down around him, and he's got to face what the rest of his life is going to be."

CHAPTER 24

The Mountain Man

T HE CLEARING ON WHICH THE Jamisons' truck was found contained a single narrow dirt road that served as its only exit. As they followed this road, Niki watched Sherilyn's final message—the pious tags adorning the junk metal—recede in the rearview mirror and then disappear completely as the thick foliage of the wildwoods enclosed them.

"Where to now?" Niki's cousin asked.

"Just follow this path."

Niki knew exactly where she wanted to go and whom she wanted to see.

According to police, while the Jamisons were on the mountain, they stopped and had a lengthy discussion with a man, D.C., who lived just down the road from the land they wanted to buy. Of course, "just down the road" was a little misleading on a mountain with one road. In reality, the man lived closer to the base of the mountain, but it was a surprisingly short and simple drive from his home to the clearing.

It was October 7, 2009, and this was the last-known conversation anyone would have with the family. D.C. was reportedly outside when their truck drove up on him. From the scant info available that reconstructs the scene, Bobby asked him for directions to their land. This may or may not be true. Peggy, the Panola real estate broker (the Lady on the Mountain), told police in her affidavit that she customarily accompanied prospective land buyers to a particular plot but that Bobby told her he didn't need her help. She said he was polite about it, but that he just needed the coordinates and would find the land himself. Perhaps his GPS device was acting wonky and he really did need directions, or perhaps he stopped just to be friendly, as they apparently discussed life on the mountain.

What also isn't clear is where this encounter happened. Was it near the man's home, closer to the base of the mountain, or was it elsewhere? Did the Jamisons drive onto his property?

Either way, according to reports, he said to them something to the effect of "It's getting dark; you'll never find it this late, you'll need to come back."

They apparently took this advice and left the mountain to drive back to Eufaula before returning the next day—ostensibly their last day—October 8. That was where our knowledge of the Jamisons' timeline came to an end.

D.C.'s NAME HAD been bandied about for years in the online forums. But Niki had never seen his face before. On that day, deputies were conducting another mini-search, for which D.C. was assisting.

As Niki and her cousin joined the small group, she pulled up next to him and smiled. She couldn't get a good look at his facial features, because she was standing to his side, and he seemed resistant to making eye contact.

Eventually, Niki's persistence and social strategy won out, and she was able to strike up a casual conversation with him. She asked what he did for a living.

"I sell bath products," he said.

"Oh, very cool. Like what?"

"Oh, like salts and lotions, bath bombs, that kinda thing."

"Neat! You got a website or business card?"

"Nah," he said, fiddling with something.

"What about a Facebook page?"

"I don't do that."

"You're not selling yourself very well," Niki said with a hammed-up folksy humor. "I'm a woman; I love bath products! You need an Internet presence, pal."

She noticed that he was still avoiding direct eye contact with her. The few times their gazes locked by accident, he would kind of smirk and look away. She had the acute sense that like Kevin Sweat's brother, who gave her a slow and sinister nod in the court-room, D.C. had read about her interviews in the media. He knew who she was and why she was there.

When she asked about the Jamisons, she was surprised by how much he seemed to know about their lives—personal stuff that he could have only gotten from an in-person and fairly inti-mate discussion.

He quickly segued into his life and said he was renovating his property, redoing his house to look like a log cabin. He was build-ing an underground home, he said, with moving containers.

"I'm out of moving containers," he added, sounding excited and genuine for the first time, "but from the inside, it's gonna look like a log cabin."

"That is so cool," Niki forced the words through clenched teeth. Then, drafting in his momentum, she asked, "Would you mind showing us?"

"Maybe when it's further along. I'm, ya know, out of moving containers."

Later, as she and her cousin drove off the mountain, they talked about the encounter. The more she thought about what the man said, the less sense it made to Niki. He ran a bath busi-ness, and a potential customer was excitedly asking about his products, yet he expressed no way to be reached or any indication of online presence.

And who builds an underground "log cabin" out of moving containers?

But what hit her meter more directly was how the man had sponged up so much information about the Jamisons just from

the short conversation he had with them just before their disappearance.

How much time did he spend with them, and how much did
they really tell him? Little details were crucial—say, any instances
in which Bobby or Sherilyn may have casually or inadvertently
mentioned *they meant to buy the land outright with cash.*

Like Colton, Niki had always been skeptical about his claim
that the Jamisons left the mountain on October 7 and returned
the next day. There was no security camera footage of them returning to their Eufaula home, nor were there receipts or any
records of them staying at a hotel. So what did they do that night?
Where did they go?

In her gut, Niki didn't believe the Jamisons went home. She
didn't think they ever left the mountain that day—or ever again.

After the debriefing, she and her cousin descended the rest of
the mountain in darkness and silence. She desperately wanted to
learn more about D.C. but, for the time being, there wasn't a lot
she could do.

Niki was utterly drained of energy, and when she got home,
she posted about her discovery of Sherilyn's messages on the
mountain and her conversation with D.C. Then she went right
to bed and slept for days.

Reade's Encounter

I came across Reade Hogan's name while reading through newspaper articles about the case. The first time we talked, Reade said
he had been a US Marshal at the time of the investigation. This,
it turned out, wasn't exactly true but was truth-adjacent enough—
Reade worked for the tribal agency, which had a cross-agreement
with the US Marshal's office, so he did technically work *with* the
marshals. Reade had taken the initiative to spearhead this collaboration and was trained in investigative tactics.

He was a young man at the time, full of piss and vinegar. After
he got the call from Panola, he made the two-hour drive in less

than sixty minutes, blaring the emergency sirens for much of the way. But when he got to the clearing, he realized right away that the Latimer County Sheriff's Office was in over its head.

"It was terrible. It was cold, kinda blustery, windy, we had had rain, and it was still raining—cold rain—a real nightmare just getting up there.... Everyone was working as hard as they could to do the right thing and help that family but to no avail. It was wet, and the dogs were having a hell of a time catching a scent and staying on it. Perfect recipe for not being able to find someone."

After his rig setup failed to be useful, Reade helped in whatever way he could. He assisted the K9 team and scoured the mountain.

Later in the day, he volunteered to accompany Sheriff Beauchamp and another deputy, who were tackling a new chunk of the grid slightly down the mountain from the clearing.

That's when the encounter took place.

"There was a pretty shady character," Reade told me within a couple minutes. "Up there on top of the mountain."

Because of his "scraggly," rustic appearance, Reade called him the "Mountain Man." In the haze of his memory—clogged with over a decade of formative life experiences—the details of how the encounter began weren't clear. The Mountain Man just kind of materialized—not in a paranormal sense, but in the way one's dreams and memories might cross-pollinate over the years as one tries to reconstruct the timeline of a disquieting event.

Reade recalled how he felt more so than what he saw, and the overwhelming impression was that the encounter hadn't been by chance. Their paths didn't cross naturally or by accident; the man probably spotted their approach from afar and intercepted them.

The Mountain Man had some kind of residence there on the mountain, though its exact appearance was concealed in the background of Reade's mind by shadowy thickets. Reade could see glimpses, which he described as a kind of shack or small cabin.

Reade was almost certain *he* approached *them* first. "Like he was trying to 'get ahead of it' and keep us away from his property."

"Seemed like the backwoods type," Reade said. "He struck me as odd, shady, one of those guys who wouldn't look you in the eye."

I practically begged Reade for conversation specifics—who spoke first, what did the deputies ask him, what were his responses. But after more than a decade, only a gestalt of the experience remained committed to his memory.

However, there was one detail that Reade readily recalled: the guy was building something on the property and had recently laid wet foundation.

A Suspect Arrested

By 2017, Niki had stepped back from the case to take a long, much-needed break. She was having a particularly good week when an article came to her attention with the title "'Glad it's over': California murder suspect arrested in Oklahoma."

As she read the article, her skin began to tingle, and the sleeping monster awakened.

The article stated: "It's been 10 years since [D.C.'s alias] moved to Okay, settling in with a woman who knew little about his past. Now he's taken up residence in the Wagoner County jail, awaiting the next steps in the murder case against a man named [D.C.]."

A man with the same name as D.C. was accused of killing his boss, a sixty-eight-year-old man named David MacLeod, who was found dead at his ranch in Kettenpom in 1997. D.C. had been running from law enforcement for the last twenty years and was even profiled on *America's Most Wanted*.

"This is the same man I spoke to on the mountain," Niki said to me a few years later, after messaging me a link to the article. "I knew he was off. You just get a sense of people."

Putatively, this was the same man who was the last person to speak with or see the Jamisons alive.

Niki posted the article for her Jamison warriors, who, after all these years, still eagerly anticipated case updates. She also posted a video that featured dashcam footage of someone driving the short route from D.C.'s residence to the clearing. The drive—a single circuitous path with no turns—takes less than two and a half minutes.

On a lark, I texted Reade the article Niki sent me. At the top was D.C.'s 2017 mug shot, which showed a hard-set symmetrical face with a strong jawline, whitish-gray beard stubble and hair, plump cheeks, a broad forehead, and piercing eyes. An age-progressed artist's rendition depicted an older D.C., who shared a resemblance to actor Ron Perlman.

"Is this the 'Mountain Man' you saw?" I asked Reade.

"Holy shit!" He wrote back. "That's him—spot-on . . . almost one hundred percent sure . . . maybe he was paranoid that the family recognized him and silenced them. Just a theory. Plus, what a fantastic hiding place."

So now two different people were telling me about unsettling encounters with the last person to speak with the Jamisons who, at the time, may have been an outlaw running from a two-decade-old murder charge. *Could this be the guy?* I thought, a chill passing through me. Was this the face in Beauchamp's mind when he said he knew who the killer was? When he followed the money, was this where it led?

Perhaps, this was why Beauchamp seemed somewhat resigned to knowing the killer's identity but not having enough evidence to make an arrest—he knew that US Marshals already had the guy in custody.

Though I was intrigued, I was also a little worried. For one, I still couldn't confirm that the Mountain Man that Reade encountered was the same D.C. that Niki met, and if that was really the same person to whom police were referring when they discussed the Panola neighbor who was the last to speak to the Jamisons. What started out as a simple unnamed witness in the paper had turned into an accumulating snowball of identities and innuendo.

Secondly, and more importantly, these suspicions were still based on circumstantial evidence at best. Remembering Ron Erwin's story, it struck me as dangerous to start calling someone a murder suspect without more information. Multiple people had already been posed as the potential killers in this case, with little to no evidence connecting them.

I looked up court records and was able to find the Oklahoma extradition order for D.C., which remanded him to the custody of Trinity County, California, to face homicide charges. But when I entered his case number in the California court system, nothing came up. I tried looking up his arrest, indictment, trial, etc., and in both Oklahoma and California. The case does not seem to exist. Does that mean he took a plea? I looked him up in several prison inmate databases. Still nothing.

When I searched for his name as a resident of Oklahoma, there was a D.C. with a PO box in Panola. It's hard to imagine there being two people with the same first and last name with an address in this tiny mountain community in southeast Oklahoma, but it still wasn't fully adding up.

However, for the first time, I felt like there was a non-zero chance of solving the Jamison case. I would need to go to Oklahoma and get more sources.

I would come to find myself speaking with two sleuths who had gained access to law enforcement and local informants during the original investigation. From there, they had followed the money to wildly different destinations.

PART IV

Last Days

"*The apparition of these faces in the crowd;*
Petals on a wet, black bough."
—EZRA POUND, "IN A STATION OF THE METRO"

"*And we'll now and then take*
To Eufaula Lake,
From our cabin
On the backside of wild."
—MEL STITES, FROM "BLACKJACK SHADE"

AS A SEVENTH-DAY ADVENTIST, Pastor Alonso was taught to
think that every crisis was a portent of the End Time. Wars, fam-
ine, earthquakes, and economic collapse were merely the birth
pains of the next age.

During the last meetup of the summer, he told his new Eufaula flock that the persecution, pain, and suffering to come will
make even the most pious concerned for their salvation. Which

is why they must be ready, for return of the Son of Man will come at an hour they do not expect.

There can be no Restoration without End Times, so embrace the hope contained in God's plan and develop your own plan that is Biblical and God-inspired.

ALL MISSING-PERSON cases are tragic and terrifying, but there is something particularly disturbing about the disappearance of a family. As a unit, the family represents the most primeval and universal of collectives, a protective cocoon in a hostile universe. When a whole family disappears, the public's alarum grows in orders of magnitude, breaching our faith in the guardrails of organized society.

So inverted, safety in numbers becomes a mass vanishing.

We like to imagine being with our loved ones when our time comes, trusting that bond will provide solace. As a child, I was terrified my family and I would be abducted from our home in the middle of the night and had recurring nightmares about it. I morbidly wondered if when a family disappears together, each member's individual fear multiplies exponentially as they see it reflected in the eyes of their loved ones. The fear of children who suddenly realize their parents cannot make the nightmare go away; the fear of parents who suddenly realize they are powerless to protect their children from the monsters they swore weren't real.

There can't be many terrors worse than this.

THE CASES OF the McStay family and the Jamison family, which had so eerily mirrored each other, shared yet another serendipitous connection. After years of the two families having seemingly vanished into thin air, the remains of both were discovered during the same week in November 2013.

The McStays were found in California, and from that point on, the investigation of their disappearance took a very different route, unraveling a brutally violent murder conspiracy that ended with a homicide conviction.

The Jamison family case received no such resolution. The truth of their final hours remained cloaked in mystery.

After over two years of digging into the case, I entered the final months of my research. I had learned a considerable amount about what the family's lives were like leading up to that trip, but the portrait that emerged was just as mysterious to me as their cause of death.

I was, however, finally finding some convergence points, patterns in the static. It was leading me closer, I hoped, to who the Jamisons were and what really happened on the mountain.

But as I began laying the groundwork for a "boots-on-the-ground," fact-finding mission in southeast Oklahoma, things were about to get even stranger.

For most of the time I was researching and interviewing people for this book, I actively tried to avoid forming any conclusions that might bias me and distort my perspective. This was easy at first, because all the theories seemed to merge together into a morass of uncertainty.

However, the speculation turned alarmingly specific and accusatory when I began speaking to two independent sources who had been associated with the early investigation. These two—a missing-persons investigator and a blogger—had access to key witnesses and informants, including D.C., during the first two years of the Jamison case.

The conclusions these sleuths reached were very different, but they both involved fiery allegations against Jamison family, and each of them was aggressively certain that their theory was correct.

Making the dynamic even stranger, the two had both initially worked with Niki to try and solve the case before having fallouts, which Niki described to me and posted about in the most vehement of terms online.

Fifteen years after the Jamisons went missing, fractious rifts still remained.

CHAPTER 25

The Cartel

D URING THE FIRST FEW YEARS of the investigation, Brett Faulds occupied an unexpectedly influential position in the true-crime blogosphere. His site *Keep the Search Alive* ruled the early search engine results of the case, funneling a steady flow of traffic and tips from all types of people—acquaintances of the Jamisons, locals from the Red Oak/Panola Mountain area, informants, private investigators, and even law enforcement agents.

Having originally pursued a career in acting and entertainment, Brett had no formal training in journalism or criminal justice. He was drawn to the Jamison family case because at the time the initial search took place, his daughter was the same age as Madyson. Every time he saw the photo of her, he imagined the horror of such a loss. Brett parlayed his fascination with the case into blog posts that he hoped would drum up enough interest to generate new info or leads, even if by sheer dumb luck.

Brett published a controversial and ultimately inaccurate post in which he claimed to have evidence that the Jamisons were still alive and had "walked away" from the mountain. I was curious what his thoughts were on the case over a decade later.

"I wanted that girl to be found," he told me early in our conversation. "I was insanely optimistic that these people would be found alive, because I really thought there was a very high probability that they left town—because of what they were involved in."

"What they were involved in . . ." I repeated.

"You can tackle this case from a number of angles, and that's what makes it tricky—there was a lot of static, there's a lot of interesting circumstances. But when you look at what really happened . . . not one time in the media, except for Sheriff Brooks, did someone come out and say what these people were really involved with."

Now Brett had me spooked. I had a vague notion of the direction we were headed but could have never guessed the final destination.

Some of his sources in the Latimer County law enforcement community, he claimed, included PIs, sheriffs, sheriff deputies, and undercover narcotics agents, who contacted him first after seeing his posts.

"It's something that happens quite frequently in every town across the country," Brett continued with a Pennsylvanian accent. "Whether they go missing and are later found dead in the water or in the woods: in the majority of the cases, they have died an accidental death due to drugs or alcohol."

The Caretaker and the Enforcer

Brett said that at the beginning of the Jamison investigation, there was speculation about the Jamisons' Realtor, Peggy. I asked him why that was, and he blamed the Investigation Discovery show, which cast her in a suspicious light.

"I can tell you with one hundred percent certainty," Brett said, "not only did the Realtor not do it, but the Realtor was very upset. She thought about the Jamisons every day; she was very distraught that these people were missing. She was the 'Lady on the Mountain,' and that was her mountain, and she didn't want anything like that to happen up there. She went out there searching for weeks; she looked for buzzards for weeks, thought maybe if she saw buzzards, they would lead her to the dead. But she never saw them."

"And [Peggy] talked to the person who lived on the mountain the longest—the oldest resident of the mountain—who told her: 'Nobody on this mountain did anything to them people. Whatever happened to them happened on their own.'"

She described the people living on the mountain as basically being outlaws—people who want to be off the grid, and usually not for particularly good reasons.

"The guy who lives at the bottom of the mountain saw the Jamisons' truck that day . . . he saw their truck go up the mountain. He indicated there was not anyone behind them."

"Are you talking about D.C.?"

"At the time I spoke to her, I think it was D.C. and one other person, and the other person was never there. They used it as a hunting cabin . . . it's mostly vacant lots for sale; what happens is people wander onto this land and try to squat on it . . ."

Brett characterized Peggy and D.C. as having a sort of caretaker-enforcer relationship. Peggy was "the caretaker of the mountain," the gatekeeper who managed the inflow of new residents to their remote community, while D.C. was the enforcer who helped her lay down the law by chasing squatters off the mountain, by force if necessary.

The reason D.C. originally seemed sketchy, Brett said, was because he was into "big-time criminal activity" himself.

"I'm sure you've heard of bath salts. Are you aware that in certain parts of the country at that time, bath salt was being manufactured, and it was being used as a methamphetamine [replacement]?"

I remembered some of those bath salt cases. There was a brief period when bath salts were feared to cause cannibalistic street predators. I remember a flurry of sensational news headlines, including a picture of a mostly naked man on his hands and knees who looked like one of the infected in 28 Days Later.

"People would smoke it, they would snort it. D.C. was involved in making bath salts. The reason D.C. didn't wanna talk to anybody—the reason he seemed sketchy and standoffish—is be-cause he himself was involved in criminal activity. Now he claimed to me he had no idea who the hell the Jamisons were, and had never met them before."

This was interesting.

"Well, D.C. supposedly was one of the last people to talk to them, so are you sure he said that he'd never met them?"

The Realtor reportedly spoke to D.C. multiple times, point-blank asking him what he knew about the Jamisons' disappearance. He said that he saw the truck drive up that day but didn't see anyone following them and didn't speak with Bobby or Sherilyn.

The only way this could make sense was if the original report-ing about the Jamisons' time on the mountain was inaccurate. Brett said D.C. had a property at the very bottom of the moun-tain and didn't see any other vehicle coming up the mountain until a day and a half later, when the "gas guy" arrived. The gas guy was the witness who saw the Jamisons' truck and reported it to the authorities.

"The gas guy?" Once again, I was confused. "The reporting says that a deer hunter saw the truck and then went to a landowner to report it."

"Well, that sounds like D.C. That would lead me to believe they're talking about D.C."

I was having trouble distinguishing between the (first) deer hunter, the gas man, the man at the bottom of the mountain, and D.C. More and more, this guy resembled the shapeshifting El Cuco in Stephen King's *The Outsider*.

Law enforcement looked closely at D.C. early on in the homi-cide investigation. Evidently, they couldn't connect him to the disappearance.

Armed Guards

Like many people, Brett at one point believed the Jamisons had been murdered. But then he was contacted by a series of sources who painted a very different portrait of what was going on in the weeks, months, and years before the disappearance.

Sheriff's deputies reportedly met Sherilyn's mother Connie at the Jamisons' lakefront home, finding that "the condition of the house was deplorable." She was frantically cleaning up because bags of trash were stacked to the ceiling.

Brett told me one of his "oh shit" moments in the case came from the gas guy, a source courtesy of Heather, the missing-persons investigator who appeared in the ID special.

Bob Sr. owned several properties around town, Brett explained, and one of them contained "pole barns." I had no idea what a pole barn was; Brett explained that it was basically East Coast slang for a garage. Bob Sr. supposedly had two pole barns on a property that he rented to people as storage units. The gas company approached him about renting these spaces, and they made an agreement.

Subsequent to the Jamisons' disappearance, the gas guy saw Brett's posts, contacted him, and they spoke for an hour about what he saw on Bob Sr.'s property.

Brett said: "[The gas company employee told me] they took their equipment out there and were scared to death, because in the adjacent pole barn, there were 'Mexican cartel guards with automatic weapons' guarding it. He said, 'Buddy, we were so scared, we packed up all our stuff and got the hell out of there.' There were literally drug cartel members with automatic weapons walking around there twenty-four-seven. 'Every time we came to get our stuff, we saw them,' he said."

"You're saying the Jamisons weren't just using drugs, they had an entire operation going on?"

"Absolutely. The ID show painted these people as a nice, warm, loving family who were involved in the paranormal and disappeared; they made it mysterious. [But the Jamisons] were known to law enforcement. And I was told—and you can go back and find it in the old newspapers—that there was an undercover drug operation going on in the area, and the Jamisons were known to them for dealing with drugs and methamphetamines . . ."

"Are you talking about trafficking?"

"I'm talking about, they would go to Mexico, pick up methamphetamines, store it in their garages, and distribute it in the area. That's how they had that lakefront house. Look at their finances—they didn't have jobs, he was disabled. Look at that brand-new truck they had. Look at their finances; if they were on disability, where the hell did they get the money to pay taxes on this house, live in it, [and then] they have other properties, a truck, other vehicles, a boat, a jet ski—and they're caring for a child—where do you get the money for that if you're not working?"

Then he brought up the shipping container, about which I've always had a strange feeling.

"They weren't going to live there. They were looking for a secluded place to start their drug operation, because that's the only way they were able to afford their life. Their drug operation got burned to the ground a few months before. One of the Bob Sr. properties—I think the one with the pole barns—had a fire."

This made me think of former Sheriff Brooks's statement about cartel members burning down one of Bob Sr.'s businesses. I mentioned this to him.

"That's the fifty-million-dollar question," Brett said. "The real reason Bobby was suing his father was because he got cut out of the business deal that was run through that garage, and it got burned down, and he was left with nothing. . . . Why do you think Bobby wanted that land? It was cheap and in the middle of nowhere because it was basically uninhabitable."

I'd heard other statements from investigators that there was no electricity or plumbing on the mountain, except for whatever generators or systems were self-installed.

"But you gotta keep in mind the mental state these people were in when they entered these woods. You're talking about one adult in this case who had bipolar disorder, and if she's also on methamphetamines in a wooded area, now think about that for a minute. Now look at the other adult in this case: he was heavily on meth, and he took painkillers because he was [injured]."

"So you're in the Sheriff Brooks camp?"

"I was glad to hear Sheriff Brooks come out and say what he said, because he was one hundred percent accurate. All this portrayal of them being a good Christian family—not only did they do meth every day, but they sold meth every day . . . traveling back and forth to Mexico."

"Who were they selling to?"

"I would say these people were keepers of drugs. Okay, the cartels move the drugs from Mexico to Oklahoma; they sit in Oklahoma, and then they go to wherever after that."

Brett would mention the Mexico connection several times, and it reminded me of what Mrs. Hurst told me, that the Jamisons "had property in Cancun and would go and stay in Mexico for days or weeks at a time." She wasn't the only person who had referenced the Jamisons staying in Mexico.

The Jamisons were an upper-level hub on the chain of operations, but then they made a big mistake, Brett said.

"They tried making it themselves. . . . That's when things fell apart."

Going Rogue

Brett spoke more about the federal meth investigation, which I'd already marked as my first fact-checking item. Bobby had allegedly believed that one of their neighbors was tipping off the feds, which, along with their personal drug use, forced their operation to abruptly shutter.

"This isn't something they suddenly got involved in. It was a prolonged period of time they were doing it."

He characterized the operation as intergenerational. Bobby inherited it from his father and then ran it into the ground.

"That's why Dad didn't want to support his butt anymore. The media made them seem like victims, and that's completely the opposite of what happened. . . . If you got a hundred-something thousand lakefront house and you're packing the trash in your house, you're on drugs. You're talking about people with mental illness, with chronic diseases and medication, and then you add meth on top . . ."

Things fell apart, and Brett's guess was that Bobby and Sherilyn consumed too much of their own supply and stopped making money for the top dogs.

"That's when bad things happen," Brett said.

"Sounds like the kind of thing people get killed for," I observed with an unspoken *hint, hint.*

"Maybe it was homicide," Brett hedged again. "If D.C. had said, 'Look bud, they were followed up that mountain by someone,' I would say it was homicide. But no one saw anyone else up there with them; they were alone."

I wasn't sure how D.C. could say with certainty that no other vehicle went up unless he sat at his window and watched the road for twenty-four straight hours. Additionally, when the police reportedly interviewed D.C., he told them the Jamisons left the mountain to return home on the 6th before returning the next day.

"Nobody saw them come down, nobody saw them go up. This area is full of criminals. It's a bad area. It may be beautiful, but the people are bad, and they rat on each other, but no one has come forward saying the Jamisons were killed."

Brett said that the year the Jamisons disappeared was the year Bobby tried to start his own meth operation on the mountain.

"And so that's what they were gonna do with that moving container?"

"Well, they sure as hell weren't gonna live in it. Anybody who says that doesn't know what the hell they're talking about. They're not gonna live in a shipping container on the side of a mountain. That's where they're gonna make the meth."

"How did you find out they were making it?" I asked, trying to learn as much about his sources as I could without being annoying.

Brett again described the influx of messages he got from Latimer County locals and neighbors, who repeatedly described the Jamisons as drug addicts.

"They couldn't believe [Child Protective Services] didn't take their kid away. They couldn't believe they existed for as long as they did without something bad happening...if they had been found, someone would have taken that daughter away."

THE CARTEL 225

One of Brett's law enforcement sources had evidently told him that the CPS checked on the Jamisons' Eufaula home several times due to reports of drug use and an unhealthy environment. I recalled that in Okiegranny's timeline, she wrote that Jack Jamison and Bob Sr. filed a report with DHS concerning this same issue.

We discussed the possibility that the Jamisons were on the run and, fearing they were going to lose Madyson, took extreme measures.

I asked about Niki's theories and his relationship with her. After initially working together and speaking on the phone several times, they had a falling out, after which Niki wrote a scathing post about him. Brett said that as soon as he began asking her about drugs, she shut down. She believed—or perhaps wanted to believe—that the Jamisons used in the past but had gotten clean.

"She basically said she would never speak to me again . . . and that's what everyone does [in these situations]. . . . When people find their missing loved ones deceased in the woods, a hundred percent of the time, they think it's a homicide. . . . When the family knows about bad behavior, they don't tell you about it. But generally, that bad behavior is connected to why they went missing."

Finally, I asked Brett about the elephant in the room, the albatross around his neck, which was the bold theory he trumpeted that turned out to be wrong. Brett had published blog posts declaring that the Jamisons were still alive and had "walked away" from the mountain.

"I really thought they left that mountain with somebody else," Brett said, "maybe part of the drug cartel. They parked their car, they jetted because there was heat on them. And people who do methamphetamines behave in a very paranoid manner. So I thought there was a good chance they got off that mountain and were at some other location."

"Did you get flak for that? Were people mad at you?"

"Oh, people were mad at me, and I didn't give two shits," Brett said. "They wanted me to come out there, and I said well, I can come out there, but what am I coming out there for . . . ? To access information on the ground there? Because I've already done that. I talked to enough people that I know exactly what was going on with these folks..."

He added that contrary to Niki's online claims, he never asked for money to help investigate and never earned a penny researching the case. I'll note further that, unlike the vast majority of YouTube channels and other content creators who have published material about the Jamison case, Brett's blog wasn't monetized to earn ad revenue.

As my first conversation with Brett drew to a close, we circled back around finally to the central question of what happened on the mountain. While I would need time to process his claims, I was curious why he was so convinced their deaths were an accident.

It seemed to me that his theory, which posited that the Jamisons were chronic meth users and up to their necks in shady dealings, wouldn't preclude the possibility of foul play. Drug dealers, much less drug cartel members, are not known to take kindly to the kinds of rogue behavior Brett was attributing to Bobby; his own father, who Brett characterized as a mid-level kingpin, threatened to kill him less than a year earlier. Why was homicide so less likely to him than getting lost?

While the accident theory was totally possible, I explained, I leaned more toward foul play. This was when the conversation got a bit more heated, and we had some animated cross talk as Brett grilled me about the lack of evidence.

"If they were shot," he said, "they would have found a bullet, the coroner would have found something."

"I talked to the guy who found the remains, and he swore it looked like a gunshot hole. His claim hasn't changed in ten years. Beauchamp publicly stated it was a gunshot hole and said they were murdered. I'm just assuming he has more info than we do."

"The cops didn't find any bullets; they didn't find any evidence that they were executed together. I think they were found together because they didn't have any coats, and they probably covered themselves in leaves."

"Fair enough," I said, as this image seared itself into my brain.

I asked him about one of his sources, Heather, with whom I was trying to arrange an interview.

"Heather believes they were murdered; she's believed they were murdered from day one." Brett then tripled down, saying there was zero doubt in his mind that Bobby and Sherilyn were not only on drugs but seriously involved in selling and transporting them. "If you look at the facts, there's no other rational explanation."

Brett closed our conversation with a corruption rabbit hole.

I told him I felt Beauchamp had done the best he could with the search but that his investigative experience was limited to drug busts.

"Well, that's because there's a lot of drugs there. Are you familiar with the sheriff before him? The drug dealers out there [in southeast Oklahoma] buy the sheriffs new boats every year—they buy them all new fast boats. It's indicative of what's been going on out there for years..." Brett said, laughing.

"You're saying the cartels buy off local law enforcement with kickbacks."

"I'm laughing, but it really does happen. I mean, the sheriff before Beauchamp, he got caught; the sheriff before him—I think it dates back four sheriffs in a row that were caught taking money from drug dealers."

Mules of Eufaula

In reviewing Brett's claims, I started with a big one that would be fairly simple to fact-check: was there a major federal meth bust in Eufaula shortly before the Jamisons went missing?

It didn't take much of a search to find the answer.

Sure enough, in the spring of 2008, roughly six months before the Jamisons' disappearance, feds descended upon Eufaula, arresting and charging fourteen people with criminal conspiracy to traffic meth, cocaine, and crack. The bust was the culmination of an extensive undercover operation undertaken by a trifecta of local, state, and federal law enforcement agencies.

Sheldon J. Sperling, US attorney for the Eastern District of Oklahoma, said the indictments were the fruit of a five-year "collective" investigation by the Oklahoma Bureau of Narcotics (OBN), the Bureau of Alcohol, Tobacco, Firearms and Explosives (ATF), the Federal Bureau of Investigation (FBI), the Eufaula Police Department, the Checotah Police Department, and the Muskogee Police Department.

"'Mules' were engaged to transport the drugs."

News on 6 broke the story with additional context on the extent of the criminal enterprise: "Federal prosecutors round[ed] up a fourteen-member drug ring that was supplying half of the state of Oklahoma. Hundreds of pounds of meth, marijuana, cocaine, and crack were all being pumped through one place.... Many would be shocked to learn that Eufaula, the home of the Ironheads, would be home to one of the largest drug rings in the eastern half of the state."

The ringleader, according to federal authorities, was a man named Johnny "The Tick" Smith, who allegedly ran his operation like a business and gave incentive trips to his foot soldiers that included resort vacations in Cancun.

In a particularly creepy line, the article stated: "... Smith didn't just lavish his employees with gifts in life.... Assistant US Attorney Rob Wallace said, '... Those are honorifics who died, in their way of looking at it, in the line of duty.'"

For over five years, undercover agents worked with local informants to infiltrate Smith's "inner circle."

So not only was there a huge meth bust in Eufaula, the lifecycle of the investigation was almost perfectly contemporaneous with the Jamisons' timeline: it started in 2003, the same year they moved to Eufaula, and wrapped up in 2009, the year of their disappearance.

As for the rest of Brett's claims . . .

I wasn't sure yet. I needed to talk to at least one of his sources. His theory surprised me only in its simple logic. Previously, he had pursued a complicated conspiratorial explanation that involved the Jamisons in witness protection or otherwise authoring their own vanishing act. Now he believed one of the most practical narratives, accidental death, but it was still wrapped in conspiracy gossamer.

In some ways, this theory was not shocking. There was nothing new or controversial to his belief that the family's deaths were accidents due to getting lost. And the allegations of the Jamisons using meth were present from the very beginning of the case, pushed by none other than the sheriffs themselves—first Beauchamp, who took a more speculative stance, and then Brooks, who had stated with certainty that Bobby and Sherilyn were daily users.

In other ways, of course, Brett's theory was undeniably wild. The Jamisons weren't just meth users, Brett believed. They were upper-level "mules" in an intergenerational, cross-border drug trafficking operation responsible for supplying narcotics to the eastern half of Oklahoma. Near the end, Bobby decided to go rogue and start making his own meth in his own moving container on his own land on the mountain.

And yet, as intense as this sounded, it was nothing compared to what Heather the PI was about to tell me.

CHAPTER 26

The Residue of His Estate

A 2014 EDITION OF *PEOPLE* devoted a feature story to Heather Holland, crediting her with helping nine different families learn the fates of their missing loved ones.

Detective Sarah Krebs of the Michigan State Police said, "To have somebody like Heather who will do [independent online research] for us and give us the tips that make a match. It's like they hand us the case on a silver platter."

Krebs recalled that in 1992, Heather helped solve the identity of a missing man by working with his family as a liaison and securing his medical records, which led to a positive ID.

"[She]'s a great asset to law enforcement. It's another weapon we can give the families of missing people in their search."

A similarly glowing *USA Today* article profiled Heather's collaboration with Carolyn Spires in the search for her missing stepdaughter Kristen, who vanished in 2010. Heather and Carolyn's quest took them across four counties together and in April 2011, the two women were traversing the frozen tundra of Big Rapids, Michigan, when something caught their attention. It appeared to be a small hollow of disturbed ground—a location in the ice that wasn't icy.

Carolyn grabbed a scraper and began carving into the cold land, eventually unearthing a bone and then a whole gravesite.

She had found the remains of her stepdaughter.

The discovery allowed Kristen's parents to bring their daughter home, and it gave investigators a fighting chance to pursue her killer.

"If it wasn't for Heather, I don't think we ever would have ever found her," Carolyn said.

Mecosta County Sheriff's Office Detective Sgt. Casey Nemeth characterized the discovery as "borderline divine intervention."

Mtrooper Unmasked

Prior to speaking with Heather, she mentioned that I could find some of her thoughts on the case on *Websleuths*, where she used the name Mtrooper. This was a big revelation. I had known Mtrooper was a real investigator, but I didn't know who it was.

This made Heather additionally interesting to me, because there aren't many professional investigators who publish case info on message boards. Heather's early posts about the case as Mtrooper centered on a series of financial anomalies, and it was easy to see where Brett's sources impacted her thinking and vice versa. She openly speculated about whether the family's disappearance was connected to Bob Sr.'s ties to the Mexican mafia, which she claimed were factual.

Heather also confirmed that the money the Jamisons had on them came from the settlement in Bobby's lawsuit against his father.

In another post, Heather (Mtrooper) asserted a number of case facts that were previously unknown to the public:

+ There was a reward offering for information on the Jamison disappearances, but it was not posted by the family.
+ In discussing the possibility that a local killed the Jamisons, Peggy (the Lady on the Mountain) had talked

about a guy living in Red Oak who used to work for
the Jamisons (not K.B.).

+ The infamous last picture of Madyson was taken at
the property (presumably the one they wanted to
buy), which would seem to disprove the theory that
they got lost trying to find the place, though it could
have happened as they returned.

Through her avatar Mtrooper, Heather had been vocally critical of the family's response. Early on, she focused on their failure
to and seeming disinterest in providing reward money, but over
time, it intensified.

After months of researching the case from the sidelines, in mid-
May of 2010, Heather cold-called the Latimer County Sheriff's
Office and pitched her investigative services to Beauchamp himself.

"I called and said this is who I am, this is what I do, I can get
a dog down there, and he opened his sheriff's department to me.
I've never met a sheriff that was more inviting with open arms. I
mean, I'm from Michigan—I'm not from OK, nobody knows me.
But he sent me a copy of everything he had, we drove around, he
took me up there ... I went hard."

Like many other investigators and searchers who worked on
the case, Heather got swept up in the mission, becoming personally attached to the outcome.

"I got into this business to find missing people, not to solve
murders ... this one bothered me because of Madyson.... My dog
is named Madyson," she said near the beginning of our first call.
"Like you wanna talk about a girl that captured my heart? I have
one cadaver dog and I named her after Madyson."

Heather spoke like she was in a perpetual state of multitasking,
a rapid-fire, no-fluff info dump that was hard to keep up with at
times. In my first real question, I asked her about the various
theories posited in the case.

She managed to dismiss two right off the bat: "I don't buy the
murder-suicide thing. If you're going to walk somewhere for that,
I think you would have followed a road. I don't think you're gonna

do a two-point-seven-mile trek through the woods only to end up, not even a hundred yards from the road. People were like, 'They were lost.' No, there's a road right there . . ." Echoing the Grahams, she said, "There were helicopters in the air within days after they were declared missing. [They weren't even] on the property they were looking at."

"So why do you think the search didn't find them?"

"I think they were probably dumped later. I mean, this is all speculation . . . but I don't think they were killed there, I don't think [Smokestack Hollow] was the crime scene . . ."

Heather then hit me with her first uppercut.

"I think Madyson Jamison was worth a lot, worth more dead than alive," she said, "and I think it had something to do with the uncle. It had something to do with all the bad things they had going on between money and drugs."

The Creepiest Little Clause

As she said this, a leaf blower started up outside my window, and my dog Bella, who is unyieldingly observant in between naps, jumped to the window, pushing up the blinds with her snout so she could behold the displacement of the leaves.

"Let me get my head around this," I said, feeling unwell from sleep deprivation. "So, for starters, you think they were murdered."

"Absolutely."

A second leaf blower started revving its engine outside, further confounding Bella and making it difficult for me to hear or concentrate.

Pressing my left ear to try to mute the noise, I asked Heather an obtuse question: "And you think it had something to do with money."

"Have you looked at [Bob Sr.'s] will?"

"Somewhat," I said, escaping to quieter room.

"So I turned over the divorce records to the OSBI, because they had no idea how much Madyson Jamison was worth dead. And there's the creepiest little clause in there . . . it's called the simultaneous death clause, which is not the craziest thing in a husband-wife scenario. Never have I ever seen it between an old man and a child ... if she dies, everything goes to who? Jack Jamison."

I recalled this from the forums but was stunned that fifteen years later, she believed it just as adamantly as she had then.

"If you are unable to determine who dies first," she continued, "Madyson Jamison or [Bob] Jamison Senior, then everything would go to the brother Jack. . . . When that simultaneous death clause went in there, it put a bounty on Madyson's head."

I'm not sure which came first: my thoughts blurring into confusion or the convergence of the dueling leaf blowers right outside the window. I was shocked to hear such a highly praised and accredited source making such an incendiary allegation.

Heather believed Bob Sr.'s death was the "catalyst" leading to Madyson's death.

"Listen to this ..."

She recounted a brief timeline of events: Bob Sr. filed for divorce in 2008; he rewrote his will Oct. 27, 2008; divorce was granted in August 2009; Bob Sr. was admitted to hospice care the next month; the family went missing the following month; Bob Sr. died on 12/9/09 (Heather mentioned rumors that he overdosed on meds, which makes sense, she said, "because this whole thing only makes sense if they both die"); and Starlet filed for probate on 12/16/09 and then filed for the estate of her ex-husband, thinking it was still in her name.

"She didn't realize that the will had been changed. The only one who knew it had been changed was Jack."

Concluding the timeline, she said: "Jack challenges Star's claim to the estate on 12/18/09."

They were essentially fighting over Madyson's estate while she was still missing. Bad optics, no doubt, but I was still struggling with her premise.

"So you're certain that Jack's getting the money depended on Madyson dying?"

"Positive. Simultaneous death clause ..." she read from the actual court document, which I'd perused a few times, "... 'Such that it is impossible to determine who died first.' That's the sentence right there that makes you go ..."

"If Bob wanted the money to go to Jack, why didn't he just leave it to Jack?"

"He didn't want the money to go to Jack; he wanted the money to go to Madyson."

"Oh ... OHHH ..." The full weight of the scenario hit me. "So you're saying Jack's the *only one who knew about this*, of course, because he's the executor of the will now."

"Right ..."

She continued: "I don't think Bob Sr. was in his right state of mind when he was updating his will, and he might have had help. My understanding is he had dementia."

"So you think Jack coerced him?"

"Yeah. Bob Sr. loved Madyson. He wanted everything to go to that little girl. I don't think he was in on this plan. I don't think he had anything to do with their disappearance. That was all Jack, who proved they were missing under questionable circumstances. Any other place in the United States of America—Michigan, Ohio, etc.,—if somebody goes missing, how long do you have to wait to have them declared deceased?"

"I don't know."

"Seven years if I remember correctly. However, [Jack] managed to totally circumvent having them declared legally deceased. It is troubling to me that this went down before they were found and were known to be dead—and it was only because there was that questionable circumstance. No other judge—" Heather went on a slight tangent railing against the idiosyncrasies of the Oklahoman judicial system. "I literally almost didn't take the case because it is so janky down there. But I'm like ninety-eight-percent sure that Bob Sr.'s death was connected with this, and I'm definite Israel [Beauchamp] is probably right on the same page with me. Just follow the money."

There's that phrase again.

After closing my window to reduce the leaf blower noise, I was dizzy, sweaty, and somewhat irritable.

"So you don't think there's any chance it was a coincidence?"

"It was an eight-hundred-thousand-dollar coincidence...that's a conservative estimate."

"Jesus." I sighed in despair. "Definitely seems like a strange thing to add in—why would anyone anticipate the possibility of a child's death?"

"Exactly. Simultaneous death clauses are usually for husbands and wives." Sensing I was overwhelmed, she said, "I know. This case has more red herrings than any I've ever dealt with, and I've seen a lot of cases..."

Amazing People

I needed a break from hearing the phrase *simultaneous death clause*, so I asked her about Brett's claims of a family drug operation. She said there was "crooked" activity going on and, echoing some of early claims by law enforcement, included a variety of scams through insurance and drugs. But she thought of Bobby as more of a drug user than a seller.

I asked her about Peggy the Realtor (the Lady on the Mountain) and D.C. the neighbor (the Mountain Man), who had garnered the suspicions of Niki and Reade.

"I met with Peggy; amazing person. I met her several times, just a sweet, sweet lady. She was almost in tears the whole time. She said she talked to Star and that she was very cold, and she didn't shed a tear. D.C., amazing people."

"You had good interactions with D.C.?"

"Nice guy."

Wild—this was the same guy Niki believed might be the killer. I told her about the article Niki sent me about a D.C. arrested for murder and extradited from Oklahoma. After we got off the phone, I sent her the article.

Heather called me the next morning and the first thing she said was: "That's not D.C."

Now I was super confused, because there seemed to be two different D.C.s living on Panola Mountain. But whichever one Heather was talking about, she had questioned in person.

"My spidey senses are pretty good in fifteen years. Every time I talked to D.C., he was pretty open and upfront with me ... he said, 'Do you wanna search my place?' several times. He was super nice, very forthcoming, and seemed like he wanted answers, too."

I told her about Niki's and Reade's encounters.

"He wasn't living in a shed or anything, he had his own business."

"The bath salts?"

"He wasn't a bath salts kind of guy. He was doing something with baths but I think it was bath products, like bath bombs, homemade stuff."

"So you're saying D.C. was on the up and up, but was law enforcement not investigating him at one point?"

"Well, the sheriff didn't want me talking to him, because anything he told me would be inadmissible in court, so I didn't know what to do about that. I guess he poured a concrete slab for his house while the Jamisons were missing, which makes me wonder."

You're not the only one, I thought. Reade had mentioned seeing fresh foundation on the mountain when we spoke about his encounter. This was the first strong link suggesting that D.C. was the Mountain Man.

I asked why she thought the perpetrator would have left the truck behind. She didn't believe the Jamisons were killed right there on the clearing but were dumped in Smokestack Hollow later. Madyson, she suggested, wasn't killed the same way as her parents and probably had her neck broken. This made me recall Beauchamp saying something almost identical (minus the specificity of the broken neck) on the podcast.

"There were quite a few assets that changed hands prior to Bob Sr.'s death. But he hated Bobby. Cut him out of the will, sold the gas station that Bobby was supposed to get half of. And when he screwed him out of it, he reneged on the deal ..."

Heather dropped some more details. She said that Bobby and Sherilyn were definitely getting a divorce, or had at least told the people around them that it was in the cards. She mentioned that, like Beauchamp, she'd received a call about the gunshot hole in one of the skulls. She also described the pictures from inside the truck as "haunting," including some strange items, such as "a life-sized Barbie" and bunch of big rocks and boulders in the flatbed.

There was something that was bugging me, and I finally articulated it in a question. I asked her if there was more evidence connecting Jack. She had built a compelling motive, but I still didn't see anything close to proof that Bobby's uncle arranged for the three Jamisons to be killed in order to collect his brother's fortune.

"We don't have proof of it," she admitted. "If we did, this would be a different story. We know that they met someone up there because of the way the truck was parked. They were blocked in. I think they got forced out at gunpoint. And I think someone knew they were going to be up there.... There was bad blood between Jack and Bobby. Ask Jack what his relationship with Bobby was."

I remembered the second time I spoke to Jack, he surprised me with several bitter swipes at his nephew Bobby, whom he characterized as a mooch. Coming from a man who spoke so plainly and neutrally about everything else, it was a noticeable departure from "speak no ill toward the dead."

Jack, according to Heather, had means, motive, and opportunity. She didn't think he did it himself. More likely, he hired someone. But she didn't have evidence of that, either.

Just as I thought the conversation was winding down, she hit me with another uppercut.

"And Bobby was an informant for the FBI at one point...I couldn't get any more info on it, but I'm gonna guess it was about his father."

She read from an email she'd received that was passed along from an unnamed sheriff: "'There were some guys who were released from prison that Bobby had been an informant on.' Bobby informed for the FBI, so God knows..."

Heather said that she had additionally heard from people in town that Bobby was flashing cash around in Red Oak. Apparently, there were locals who believed someone followed the Jamisons to the mountain for the purpose of robbing them. She'd also looked into a Red Oak-based former co-worker with whom Bobby had a falling out, but the lead dead-ended.

"Too many motives ... I've always been a big fan of following the money—and it almost always leads back to family."

AFTERWARD, I WAS stupefied. I wondered about Heather's belief that Beauchamp viewed Jack the same way as she did. When Beauchamp said, "Follow the money," Niki, like most people, assumed this meant the cash the Jamisons had on them. But Heather had followed the money to a completely different destination.

Over the course of our talks, I noticed that she had mentioned several times how kind, receptive, and "super awesome" the sheriff had been to her. The last time she brought it up, though, it had taken a slightly different turn.

Beauchamp hadn't responded to any of her recent messages.

When I looked back through my Mtrooper notes, I found a Websleuths post from fifteen years earlier that was similar, with Heather writing that after she'd passed along her notes on the probate war and Jack Jamison, Beauchamp wasn't returning her calls. She expressed concern that he was angry with her.

I don't know if that was her last correspondence with Beauchamp, but it sounds like he broke off contact with her. One explanation is that the stress and burnout caused him to cut off all channels to the case, including Heather. Another explanation is that he didn't like her investigative direction and/or her posting online about it.

The Banality of Evil

I'd be lying if I said there wasn't a part of me that wanted to believe Heather after that first night we talked. I considered her a credible source with years of experience working cases. She had bona fide plaudits and law enforcement-endorsed skills in missing-person investigations. And the simultaneous death clause was definitely a strange detail that caught the eye and was hard to explain.

Her narrative was the banality of evil incarnate.

As with Brett's meth syndicate and Niki's rotating cast of murder suspects, there was a certain appeal to grand theories that solved the puzzle once and for all, and familicide-for-hire certainly fit the bill.

The only real thread I had to work with was this supposed simultaneous death clause. Above the exclusion clause that cut Bobby and Starlet out of Bob Sr.'s will, Article IV of the document named Jack as the trustee of the estate, charged with overseeing and dispensing it to Madyson until she reached the age of twenty-one, at which point she assumed control.

The next subsection stated that in the event that Bob Sr.'s granddaughter, Madyson, does not survive him, all "residue" of his estate goes to Jack and Amos Jamison (Bob's other closest male sibling).

Below the exclusion clause, Article V gave us the simultaneous death clause, which stated: "In the event that any beneficiary hereof and I both shall die in a common accident or disaster, or under such circumstances as make it impossible or difficult to determine who died first, then it shall be conclusively deemed that such beneficiary did not survive me."

So following Heather's line of logic, Jack coerced his brother to add this clause and then fought to legally determine that Madyson had not survived Bob Sr. because she died when the family went missing in October 2009, three months prior to Bob Sr.'s passing. The problem is, no one should have known for sure that Madyson was dead at this time, as her remains had not yet been found. It was an insidious line of thought. But I would need to reach out to a lawyer friend to know how unusual it was, or if there was a more logical explanation for the cryptic legalese.

While I was intrigued, and part of me wanted to trust Heather, another part of me had a hard time believing this theory. There was no evidence besides motive, and it wasn't a particularly solid motive given that Jack couldn't have known that he would prevail in the effort to have Madyson declared dead. More importantly, *cui bono*—the Latin phrase meaning *for whom does it benefit*, commonly reduced to "follow the money"—doesn't necessarily prove anything in and of itself. Anytime someone dies mysteriously, there are going to be family members who stand to gain from the death a sudden financial largesse, but that's not evidence they committed murder. If and when evidence arises connecting the decedent's death to a suspect, you then seek to answer the question of why, and it is then that a monetary motive could be highly relevant.

Heather's theory of malice aforethought was provocative, but she may have put the cart before the horse. I'm not sure she had enough evidence to justify being certain of it, much less publishing the claims online.

"Ask Jack ..."

If I believed there was enough evidence to reasonably suspect Jack Jamison, I probably would have called him a third time. But I didn't, and, generally speaking, I'm reluctant to call senior citizens with accusations of contract killing.

Okiegranny later wrote a post on *Websleuths* saying that the estate money was evenly divided among the Jamison siblings, which Jack's daughter Dana corroborated.

As for the simultaneous death clause, I contacted a college friend who is a no-nonsense attorney with knowledge of probate law. I asked him specifically about simultaneous death clauses and whether the appearance of one in the Jamison will raised an eyebrow.

"The whole point of the provision," he replied, "is to override state laws that require an heir to survive the testator by a certain period (one hundred and twenty hours, for example). Married couples use such clauses because they die together a surprising amount of the time. But having a simultaneous death clause between an old man and a young child is bizarre on its face. I don't understand the utility."

I didn't understand it either, but by this point, I was starting to feel like I didn't understand anything.

After over a year of taking dump truck–sized amounts of kratom, I found that without it, I exhibited all the symptoms of restless leg syndrome (RLS). Having never experienced the condition before, I had no idea how wretchedly uncomfortable it was.

And to be clear, it's not just in the leg—it's an unceasing, full-body quiver of squirming, restless spasms that make it impossible to lie still or relax or do much of anything but hold yourself and shudder. And, of course, it rendered sleep impossible. As soon as I took kratom, it would go away. But without it, I quite literally could not fall asleep.

At one point, I went seven straight days without any powder, determined to buck it. Even after taking dozens of melatonin, Tylenol PM, sleeping pills, trying alcohol to see if it helped it all—nothing worked.

My miracle cure for chronic pain had turned into a physical addiction—to an obscure plant harvested mainly in Malaysia, which was under threat of FDA regulations. And in addition to chronic leg pain, I now had chronic restless leg, a disorder that combined spasming, convulsing, and the feeling that subcutaneous colonies of ants were crawling through my arms and legs.

CHAPTER 27

The Pattern

FAYE OWNED THE HAIR SALON in Oklahoma City where Sherilyn and Chrissie worked. She was soft-spoken, direct, and non-dramatic—no embellishment or speculation. She had known Bobby's father's family and recalled seeing Bobby as a kid working at the tree farm with his dad.

Faye told me she had suspected Sherilyn was on drugs at work on some occasions. When Faye came in to have her hair done by Sherilyn, she saw it up close—a hyperactive way of talking and moving that suggested the use of stimulants.

When I heard this, part of me wondered if this was just Sherilyn's hypomania combined with what Chrissie Palmore described as her ADD-like behavior. I can say from firsthand experience with hypomania, ADD, and stimulants that there can definitely be a cross-over of symptoms.

But if Faye's first anecdote didn't convince me, her second was hard to ignore.

She recalled that for a brief period during their time in Oklahoma City, Bobby and Sherilyn lived in the basement of one of their parents' homes. At some point, Sherilyn took in a friend of hers who was addicted to meth. According to Faye,

Sherilyn let the friend live with them so that she could focus on getting clean.

By the time the living arrangement ended, however, the friend was still hooked, and Sherilyn and Bobby were both using as well.

Faye's account was light on details, and she didn't say how she knew about this meth origin story, but she struck me as credible.

Bleach

Chrissie Palmore spent much of the interview defending Sherilyn from spurious rumors, describing her as a hardworking mother who loved her kids. She had a few hilarious observations about the absurd coverage of the case on social media. Specifically, she was flabbergasted by the analysis of the surveillance tape that is rampant in dozens of YouTube videos.

"That was the stupidest thing I've ever seen," she said. "I don't stop and chat with my husband when we're loading up the car."

This made me laugh.

She described the rumors and conspiracy theories in the case as "a giant snowball that kept rolling and getting bigger. Once people said certain things, they became true through repetition ... and it's so sad, a whole family was taken out and there's nothing—no resolution, no clues, no leads."

As far as the plan to live on Panola Mountain, Chrissie said that Bobby and Sherilyn had always wanted to go off-grid and have their own land—Bobby especially, and eventually Sherilyn, too.

"But those mountains—oh my God, you could give me a million dollars and some land out there and I wouldn't take it. There is some weird shit up there, some bad, bad stuff goes on."

Regarding drugs, Chrissie said, "I worked with her for two or three years and I never saw her doing drugs or talking about them. She was a normal person, like the rest of us, working hard and trying to figure out her way. . . . I know her, I knew her."

By the end, though, she admitted to having moments in which she wondered about Sherilyn. Chrissie said that her husband had regularly speculated about whether she was using meth. Chrissie hoped it wasn't true, but she couldn't help but notice that her friend, at roughly 5'7" and maybe 105 pounds, was rail-thin. After Sherilyn gave birth to Madyson, she dropped the pregnancy weight and was back to a size double-zero in less than a month. For most women, such post-pregnancy weight loss takes six months to a year.

Chrissie had been gutted by Madyson's picture in the missing poster. When she was able to get over the shock of it, she noticed that the girl's hair was completely bleached blond, which troubled her. It had never been that color when the Jamisons lived in Oklahoma City.

"It still troubles me," she said to me over the phone. "You don't do that. You don't put bleach on a child's scalp like that."

The Monster and the Genius

Speculation over the Jamisons' drug use started early on in the investigation and never let up.

In an interview with family members, Starlet and Connie were directly asked about the Jamisons' potential meth use. They denied any knowledge but discussed the reputation of the remote mountains in southeast Oklahoma, which were characterized as a "haven for meth labs, where criminals cooked up the drug miles from prying eyes."

"There are lots of them up there," Star said. "It is well known. Maybe they stumbled across one of them when they were there and someone came after them?"

One might be disinclined to believe Brett's decades-old claims about an intergenerational family meth operation. But if you strip away the ephemera in this case and focus on the right clues, an undeniable pattern emerges and it tells a story.

First, let's look back at one of Niki's interviews. Though she denied knowing anything about the Jamisons using or selling drugs, at one point she stated:

"Prior to [Colton moving out], they had been getting child-support payments, but they lost those, so they were struggling to keep up with the repayments on the house. It's possible they thought they would do some kind of one-off deal to get them back on track and maybe that's what they were doing up there."

Second, in another article, Connie recalled a comment Bobby made the summer before the family's disappearance that struck her as "strange."

She said that at the time, "They were having financial trouble" and "Bobby told Sherilyn, 'I know where I can get the money, but I won't involve you.'"

Third, after their disappearance, police divulged a few excerpts from Sherilyn's "hate letter" to Bobby, in which she wrote:

"You are a very toxic person. You need to find happiness. You contaminate everything you're around, it breaks my heart." The next part is what caught my eye: "It saddens my soul that *you have turned into the monster you are. I would not wish my daughter raised in foster care because her father is in prison and her mother murdered.*" [emphasis mine]

A few days before the disappearance, Sherilyn's tone toward Bobby dramatically changed and she wrote, "Bobby Jamison is a genius, a man with special gifts ..."

Fourth, let's review a statement I found buried midway through a *Daily Mail* article in which Connie said:

"I don't know all the details, but I can tell you Bobby had recently gone to police to report someone in the local area for running a meth lab. Obviously that person is going to be very upset."

This aligned with what a sheriff told Heather, which was that Bobby had at some point been a federal informant. But who was he informing on? A single local dealer doesn't motivate the involvement of federal investigators unless it's part of something bigger.

It turns out there was something bigger, much bigger, in the works—the massive federal drug bust that had zeroed in on the tiny town of Eufaula and brought down a fourteen-person cross-border meth operation.

Fifth, in the same email in which a sheriff discussed Bobby with Heather, he said, "There were some guys who were released from prison that Bobby had been an informant on."

So, based on these five clues, let's curate what we know about the Jamisons based on their own words, the interviews of the people closest to the family, and the investigators' public admissions: Bobby, acting out of some level of financial desperation, did something that put himself at risk of imprisonment and Sherilyn at risk of murder; whatever this was coincided with his reporting a meth lab to the police, which itself coincided with a huge narcotics bust in Eufaula, after which two prison inmates said Bobby had narced on them. Shortly thereafter, Bobby and his family vacated their home in Eufaula without telling anyone where they were going, and brought over 60,000 dollars in cash to buy land on which they planned to live in a moving container.

When we arrange the pieces of the puzzle like this, it looks more like the Jamisons were scared for their lives and hiding.

The Informant

The idea of Bobby as an informant cast the case in a new light for me. For one, it would help explain the strange but persistent ambiguity and silence with regard to basic details. The FBI is notoriously secretive and possessive when it comes to asserting its authority over local investigations. If one of the agency's field assets is the victim of a murder or becomes ensnared in a local case, they go to great lengths to keep that information from the public for fear it could jeopardize not only future federal prosecutions but the anonymity and safety of their intelligence and law enforcement assets (the five-year meth bust in Eufaula, for example, would have required enormous resources and years of covert undercover work).

Bobby as a government informant would also explain the fallout between him and Bob Sr. If the FBI leveraged Bobby to get info about his father's operation, as Brett overtly suggested, and

Bob Sr. became aware of this, their sudden and violent rift suddenly makes more sense.

Let's remember that Dana described Bob as tough but loving and said that he had always taken care of Bobby financially. Writing your only child completely out of your will is a big-time move—a Shakespearean level of f-you, as is, in a markedly less Shakespearean way, reneging on a verbal promise of ownership shares in his gas station.

Previously, it's been difficult for me to imagine how their relationship deteriorated so rapidly, how Bob Sr. went from always providing for his son—who had cancer twice, battled chronic pain from a car accident, and seemingly had no other real source of income—to cutting him off and excommunicating him entirely. I don't see that level of response coming about unless it was in reaction to an equally dramatic perceived transgression. Snitching to the feds would certainly constitute such a transgression. That's the kind of betrayal that would inspire acts like writing your only son out of your will and then threatening to kill him.

The witness protection theory never made much sense. The FBI wouldn't allow so much money, resources, and time to be wasted on a manhunt for a family that wasn't actually missing. What makes more sense is that Bobby was an informant (perhaps after cutting an immunity deal), and the FBI muddled the case so that an asset of a larger operation wasn't foiled.

Bobby as an informant also begs a reevaluation of our central question: what happened to the Jamisons? Looking objectively at the circumstances, Bobby was behaving in a paranoid, erratic fashion and was attempting to move his family to a secluded mountain to live in a shipping container. If you add to that equation that he was an informant whose assistance had helped secure convictions against some criminal acquaintances, the picture shifts. It begins to look an awful lot like the Jamisons were afraid for their lives and looking for a hideout, which may explain Madyson's bleached hair and absence from school.

Why else would Sherilyn write to Bobby about Madyson's
mom being killed and her dad going to prison? Why else would
Bobby be so afraid that he would file a court petition stating he
feared Bob Sr. was involved with "gangs and meth" and would kill
him and his family?

Maybe they were paranoid; or maybe there were folks who
wanted them dead. The truth is usually somewhere in the middle—and the extremes inform the means. I'm not in agreement
with Brett and Heather on all their beliefs, but I'm inclined to believe aspects of what they're saying. When you add to it the
pattern of five clues, the puzzle doesn't yet fully fit, but an image
starts to emerge. It tells a story of escalating risk and desperation.

And it begins to look less like the Jamisons disappeared and
more like they were *disappeared.*

IT'S TEMPTING TO reduce complex mysteries down to a single
simple truth. But more often than not, human reality is determined by a plurality of causes and forces that interact and evolve
in a chain reaction of largely unpredictable events.

There is an allure to Brett's meth trafficking theory. It explains
some of the case's anomalies and the bizarre, delusional behavior
of the Jamison family. The moving-container-on-the-mountain
story makes more sense as a cover for illicit activity and subterfuge. For purposes of establishing the Jamisons' true motivations
for going to the mountain, it is easier to believe the *Breaking Bad*–
like meth narrative.

So too is there an allure to Heather's theory of a nefarious plot
by Uncle Jack.

We instinctively want a logical explanation for how a family
could disappear and then reappear as partial skeletons four years
later. Evil makes a better villain than chaos; flesh-and-blood vil-
lains can be punished.

But when we become too attached to how certain narratives
fit together, it's easy to over-connect the dots—to find patterns
that aren't there—and lose the thread entirely.

I was alarmed by the external threats that faced the Jamisons, but I was just as, if not more, alarmed by the evidence of convergent mental health crises. The more I learned about the unsettling final weeks and months of the Jamisons' lives, the more I felt that what happened on the mountain couldn't be explained with a single reductive explanation.

CHAPTER 28

Dark Tourism

As I CONTENDED WITH CHRONIC leg pain and the kratom/RLS predicament, smoke from the wildfires rendered the sky an ominous wash of gray and orange; it kind of felt like the end of days.

But though I had my physical maladies and it seemed like human society was collapsing, I had never been happier.

A little more than a year earlier, I was a lonely, bitter, bedridden hermit crawling into his forties. I woke up one day in 2020 and realized I had everything I needed in life, including love.

I met Laura during the pandemic, and we quarantined and spoke via phone and video chat for almost ten days before our first in-person date, which was a walk around a rainy cemetery. The topic of conversation was whether Mary Shelley's books were considered science fiction; Laura said she had invented the genre, and she was right.

We connected on just about every level, and within a matter of days, we were both terrified and enraptured by the magnitude of love we felt. Laura just so happened also to be a bona fide bookworm and a true-crime maven, a veritable encyclopedia of case history and podcasts.

We got a great apartment together and adopted an incredible puppy dog. I was content and at peace for the first time in a long while.

But as we planned a fact-finding mission to Oklahoma, it never left my mind how precipitously chaos can reassert its dominion, ensnaring one like a drop net in the jungle. Perhaps that's why I'm drawn to true crime and dark lore. A sense of the sublime—cosmic horror—lures me to study how the artifice of order and control can collapse.

When I was a child, I had a brief spell of night terrors that rendered me in a sleepwalking state. I knew I was asleep, but I was sealed off in some oneiric panic room. It was as if the nightmare realm had hooked onto the fender of my unconscious mind and been dragged back with me into waking life. But this was no normal nightmare or terror—it was an overwhelming, incapacitating sensation of such vast, crushing enormity and hopelessness that I've never been able to summon an adequate description.

The only way I can frame it is to imagine that one has been charged with a time-sensitive job of reverse engineering and documenting every particle interaction in the history of the universe, a comprehensive audit of everything that has ever happened. I wasn't so much thinking this as feeling it, visceral shivers of nausea at the tolling of an ancient clock. Petrified, I would stagger around the house with my hands on the side of my head, moaning that it didn't make sense, that it was impossible—*it couldn't be done.* Fortunately, these dream incidents went away. The only concrete image I ever recalled from one of the episodes was a battalion of soldiers crossing a small drawbridge.

Some thirty years later, I suspect the nightmare was my unconscious mind grappling with chaos. Growing up, the only real exposure I had to the chaos theory was the book *Jurassic Park* and, later, the scene in the movie adaptation in which Jeff Goldblum caresses the hand of Laura Dern and uses a drop of water to illustrate that the universe is fundamentally unpredictable.

Small variations at the beginning of a system lead to big variations at the end.

But there are patterns in the chaos. Scientists say that within the phase space of the universe's paradoxically deterministic unpredictability, you can find "a peculiar kind of order," what they call *strange attractors*, mysterious fractal-like structures that tilt the odds toward a preferred state.

Cryptid Country

As Laura and I entered "Little Dixie," we started seeing Bigfoot statues and Sasquatch iconography festooning the small-town streets and business marquees.

Like the Pacific Northwest, southeast Oklahoma is cryptid country. Bipedal hirsute beast-men are not just part of the area's local folklore and historical heritage, they're an integral part of its culture and economy. Just as Eufaula's major source of revenue became lake tourism, a number of the small towns orbiting it rely on a similar but slightly tweaked model: "dark tourism," towns which are known for some sensational myth or tragedy and lean into it.

Dark tourism can include familiar classics like cryptids, UFOs, haunted buildings, cursed wells, mystery spots, and vortexes, as well as more ghoulish attractions like infamous murder sites, witch hangings, serial killers' childhood homes, and assassination coordinates.

Given all the strange theories in the case, it shouldn't have surprised me to learn that there was a fringe but vocal contingent of conspiracists who believed cryptids were involved in the Jamison disappearance.

High Strangeness

I first learned about the cryptid angle while reading one of Brett's posts, under which a commenter wrote there was a high probability that the Jamisons fell victim to "predation by something other than humans or a known apex predator."

He added: "Sometimes the mere simple facts of a case can lead us to a conclusion far outside our comfort zone . . ."

Then I found the *Appalachian Intelligence* podcast, which made an episode entitled "Missing 411 and the Jamison Family Case." The three hosts, whose Appalachian dialect stretched vowels to their breaking point, discussed whether the family's disappearance was connected to the nearby "Sasquatch Wars" in the Kiamichis, home of the alleged fifteen-inch footprint. In recent years, local residents of Smithville have apparently been calling state forest rangers about sightings so often that they had to hold a town meeting.

A new generation of quasi-cryptid conspiracies, exemplified by "Skinwalker Ranch" and the *Missing 411* series, have rebranded by integrating other unexplained phenomena into a more diffuse, unspecific mystery—a hybrid of the paranormal, extraterrestrial, and conspiratorial realms that is sometimes referred to as *high strangeness*. The holistic spookiness that results often includes true-crime cases.

David Paulides, for example, started his *Missing 411* book series as a compendium of the hundreds of unsolved missing-person cases from national parks. He's careful to not overtly reference or suggest cryptids, but he ran a Bigfoot hunting website earlier in his career and regularly gives speeches at conventions about anomalous activity. The suggestion he ultimately makes is that something is happening to people in the national parks that can't be explained by accidents, weather, or conventional animal predators, something that his readers and supporters characterize almost as a higher intelligence running some kind of secret paranormal experiment.

His self-published books have spawned an Amazon Prime show and a veritable movement online, where countless Twitter threads and Reddit groups obsessively pore over these cases. The books have expanded to include missing persons in urban environments, such as Elisa Lam in downtown Los Angeles (the subject of my first book), and a wide variety of cases in which the victims' bodies are found in strange or previously searched locations.

The Jamison case lent itself perfectly to this lore because of suspicious circumstances of how, when, and where their remains were found combined with the pre-existing Bigfoot mythology of this area.

THE NAMES HAVE varied from your standard Bigfoot and Sasquatch to more local fare like the Boggy Bottom Monster. Some just call it "the creature." Just north of Latimer in McCurtain County, the state's major hub of reported Bigfoot activity, locals have spoken about a "man-beast" since the 1970s, and the folklore stretched back much further. According to Choctaw legend, the name of the man-beast is *Hattak Lusa Chito*. The man-beast first appeared in the early 1830s after it was removed from a Mississippi swamp by a great witch, *hatukchaya*, and relocated to McCurtain County, where the man-beast servant was ordered to terrorize families. Interestingly, the legend states that when the man-beast scares people, he senses their fear and becomes fearful himself, often running away. After its master, the great witch, was killed by humans, the man-beast was liberated from servitude, but it's said that he will serve as master to the next person who shows him no fear. Fragments of this legend were published in the July 9, 1978, edition of the *McCurtain Sunday Gazette*, in an article entitled, "McCurtain Has a 'Man Beast.'"

In 1849, a settler named Bertrand Tonihkah wrote in his diary of a creature called the "One-Eyed Bascomb," known to locals as an elusive hunter and trapper. Tonihkah saw this creature in a swamp and wrote that it had long arms, a stooped posture, and a "strangely loping gait."

More sightings and stories followed, with one ending in the suspicious death of a man who had previously told his wife about encountering a "fellow [who] wasn't wearing any clothes, was hairy all over, and was the biggest man he had ever seen." Another story told of some hunters camped along the Mountain Fork River who saw a hairy ape man fleeing them. One of the hunter's hound dogs supposedly gave chase and was later found torn in two.

Such apocryphal stories originate from oral histories and retellings of both real and imagined events—frightening, unexplained incidents in which humans confronted a natural world filled with mortal dangers and terrifying unknowns. In 1855, before electricity, motorized transportation, and most medical science, a person who was alone in the woods at night could be expected to come home talking about an anomalous monster.

For towns like Honobia, Smithville, Battiest, Octavia, and Hochatown, the "dark tourism" generated by hirsute beasts is just part of city planning. Hochatown grew from timber town to "the moonshine capital of Oklahoma" in the 1930s. In recent decades, the town was little more than an isolated backwoods until a group of business owners began leaning into the Bigfoot mythology to draw tourists to its beautiful green mountains, trout fishing in Broken Bow Lake, and the nearby Beavers Bend State Park.

Despite being unincorporated even today, Hochatown has boomed into a "funky hamlet" of cryptid culture.

"Bigfoot's been very good to me. I cannot complain," said Janet Cress, a Hochatown gift shop owner, whose gift shop Janet's Treasure Chest sells "Bigfoot coasters, Bigfoot stickers, Bigfoot pamphlets, Bigfoot T-shirts, Bigfoot hats."

Another local town tried to establish its own congressionally ratified Bigfoot hunting commission with a sizable cash bounty.

THE ONLINE CONTENT generated by the Jamison family case on YouTube falls into a variety of "dark tourism" buckets. The thumbnail pic for one video showed three robed and masked figures wearing deer antler headdresses and performing some occult ceremony in a field. The juxtaposed text read: "Cult Killed Family?" The title of the video, which had 2.8 million views, was: "The DISTURBING final moments of the Jamison Family."

I clicked on one video because the show's host was a counselor with a PhD whose area of specialties included mental health. I suppose I should have known what to expect when the title of the video was "Roof Demon Killers? | Jamison Family Deaths

Case Analysis," but I can forgive a clickbait-y title if the content makes up for it. Unfortunately, it became clear pretty quickly that the counselor was just recycling the same case descriptions and details and adding in psychiatric platitudes.

Other video titles include "Jamison family: A disappearance in the name of the Devil" and "The Unsolved Mysterious and Paranormal Murder of the Jamison Family."

It's a case that invoked folk-horror themes of evil in the remote backwoods countryside, ancestral pagan archetypes that still lurk in the shadows of modern society. The Jamison story tapped into a collective and longstanding fear of satanism and witchcraft in America's forgotten heartland.

Terminus Town

I expected Eufaula to be small, but it felt even smaller. We drove in from northwest Arkansas, where I had visited some childhood friends. The state border with Oklahoma was cushioned with hundreds of miles of bucolic, rural hills and woodlands, making the entry to Eufaula seem like a passageway into a secret frontier civilization.

I had always heard that Oklahoma wasn't as flat as is commonly perceived. And though I grew up right next door in Little Rock, Arkansas, my only previous time in the Sooner State was when our family had visited cousins in Tulsa. I'd never been to southeast Oklahoma, nor did I know that it is vastly different physiographically, geologically, and, in key ways, historically and culturally from the rest of the state.

There's a reason why southeast Oklahoma became treated as its own separate fiefdom within the state. This is "outlaw country," and the history of violence and extremism dates from the earliest days of the republic.

After the creation of the new Eufaula, its emigrants from North Fork Town a couple miles over had a short honeymoon in their newly chosen home. Because the buildings were hastily assembled with wood, Eufaula burned down again in 1872, less than a year after the relocation.

They rebuilt yet again, but the new residents had already learned that Eufaula—or "Eufoley," as some called it—was a railroad terminus town, the end of the line, where outlaws, thieves, and hucksters thrived. Katy railroad officials requested federal help to protect their assets; Uncle Sam, seeking to protect its own lucrative railroad investments, sent Secretary of the Interior Cox to investigate the troubles while he officiated the opening of the Canadian River bridge. He was able to do both immediately, as upon arriving in Eufaula, four "terminal toughs" robbed a passing stranger of eighty dollars in gold.

The bridge opening went smoothly, but that night, gunfire was heard intermittently throughout the town. The next day, as Secretary Cox "made an inspection of the dives and brothels called Eufaula," he saw the body of a man who had been murdered the night before, "still lay[ing] in the tent where he fell."

While in town, Cox was approached by a scrappy crew of the town's most prolific criminals—murderers, gangsters, and robbers—who told the Secretary in so many words that they wouldn't leave Creek Nation and wouldn't stop killing and robbing if it pleased them.

Back at his train car, Cox tried to address a crowd but was interrupted by a gunshot that missed the Secretary by only three feet. After diving into the next carriage, he sent a telegram to military officials in Washington, DC, stating that "neither life nor property was safe in the Territory" and requesting military assistance. Washington dispatched the Tenth Cavalry, known as the Buffalo Soldiers, to impose law and order (at least temporarily) on the town.

The next crucible in the history of Eufaula was the McIntosh County seat war of 1908. Infuriated after losing a pair of contested elections that bestowed county seat status on the town of Checotah, the people of Eufaula withheld the county records and the official county seal. This infuriated the citizens of Checotah, who had been dancing in the streets beneath ringing church bells while shopkeepers passed out cigars. They decided they would take the records and seal by force.

One of the early editors for the *Indian Journal*, Hugh M. Riddle, described what happened next, recalling that on a "quiet Sunday afternoon … [a chartered train] loaded with riflemen made up of farmers and businessmen" creeped at a calm walking pace down the tracks southbound from Checotah into Eufaula. Word of the sneak attack had gotten out, though, and when they opened the compartment doors, Eufaula's own gunmen were waiting, and a hail of bullets rained. The train reversed its drift back the way it came as Checotah's militia retreated.

AT THE TURN of the twentieth century, Eufaula was a cotton town with five gins running. A major center for crop farming and trade, Eufaula received visits from presidents, including Harry Truman during his whistle-stop campaign, and presidential hopefuls, who swung through to court voters at the two-story Tully Opera House.

In the late 1920s and early 1930s, the petroleum boom hit Oklahoma, eventually making gas and oil the state's largest private industry. By the 1960s, around the time Eufaula got its first FM radio station, KCES, cotton was no longer king. Beef cattle, livestock, and dairy farming became the new primary economic activity.

The final—and most dangerous crucible—was the creation of Eufaula Lake itself. The controversial proposal was vehemently debated with nothing less than the soul and future of Eufaula at stake. Dire economic warnings came from both sides. Ultimately, the project was approved, old Eufaula was flooded and submerged, and the one-time terminus town was transformed into a crown jewel of recreation and tourism.

This comprehensive shift in culture came just in time to converge with the meth and narcotics epidemic, which became both a public health crisis and a black-market bonanza that thrived in small rural communities like McIntosh and Latimer County.

THE HISTORY OF Eufaula is embossed with nostalgia—stories of hill-country music, frontier justice, endless fields of corn, cotton, and black-eyed peas, and makeshift boats that ferried families and farm animals across the flooded brown-and-red water of the North Canadian River.

Local histories of the time are full of wistful memories of carrier paperboys and the *Indian Journal*'s new Linotype machine, the Mills family farm and Tom Watson's watermelons, the town's children selling scrap metal after Pearl Harbor, antique emporiums filled with needlework and handmade lace; Ironhead football and summer conditioning in the hay fields, the Miss Eufaula pageant (themed on "Somewhere Over the Rainbow" and "Daddy's Little Girl") and its coveted rhinestone crown; the First Baptist Funeral Quartet, Brother Belvin's Bible drills, the magic of family movie night at the Palace.

But underneath this curated history, there's a dark undercurrent with memories of a different variety, a legacy that still shapes and poisons the soul of Oklahoma—the "separate but equal" policies that conferred second-class citizenship on Eufaula's black community and relegated non-white families to the town's east side, which white residents called "Sandtown."

This history remembers the heinous betrayal of the Creek Indians—with whose blessing and assistance Eufaula was founded—when 60,000 members of the Cherokee, Creek, Seminole, Chickasaw, and Choctaw nations were forcibly removed from their ancestral homelands.

Eufaula was a violent terminus town that transformed into a crop farming center, but like Red Oak, Panola, Wilburton, and all the towns and cities of Oklahoma, it was forged in the genocidal fires of manifest destiny. The state is forever haunted by the Civil War, the Trail of Tears, the Tulsa Race Massacre, and the burning of prosperous black neighborhoods, the Reign of Terror in Osage County, where white lawmen conspired to murder over sixty full-blood Osage Indians and embezzle their fortunes via marriage and violent coercion.

This dark legacy persists in the present-day indifference of law enforcement to hundreds of missing or murdered indigenous women. Oklahoma has historical amnesia, but behind the nostalgic veneer of frontier justice and "outlaw country," you can track the genesis of moral rot that has resulted in a perpetual crisis of corruption among the state's public officials and law enforcement.

If there is a "Line of Tragedy," it is this.

THE JAMISONS MOVED to Eufaula amid the first or second generation that experienced an entirely different local economic philosophy from anything the town had ever known: a tourism-based economy, built almost singularly around the town's behemoth man-made lake, with its 800 miles of shoreline, over which the Jamisons' home looked.

While tourism is a powerful development engine, it also changes the culture and character of a place, further dividing its social and ethnic classes. And when a tourist town experiences a twenty-year meth and opioid epidemic, you get mental health crises and corruption. The Jamisons belonged to a region and demographic with some of the highest levels of poverty and substance abuse and one of the country's weakest records on mental health services.

The reclusive family lived in a town that was both 100 percent financially dependent on a culture of tourism and responsible for trafficking a bulk of the meth reaching eastern Oklahoma. Long severed from a time when residents took pride in heritage and the production of locally manufactured exports, contemporary Eufaula felt like a town lost in time.

WE STARTED OUR first day there happy we didn't have bedbugs and brewed some coffee in the motel coffee maker. It was undrinkable and, unfortunately, no restaurant or coffee shop was open in Eufaula from Sunday–Tuesday, except for a smaller diner.

Inside, there was a table of elderly folks who looked like they might be local. Laura recommended I ask if they'd heard of the Jamison case, and I did. Unfortunately, they were from North

262   THE VANISHING AT SMOKESTACK HOLLOW

Dakota or something like that. They didn't know about the case and didn't even seem certain that I was human.

Fortunately, our waitress had heard of the case. She didn't know much about it, but she brought out a cook from the back who had lived in the area for a while and whose family had hunted on Panola Mountain.

It was a dangerous area, the cook lady said, a consistent refrain we heard from other southeast Oklahomans. Lots of people go missing, she added, especially in the mountains.

Both women had way more to say about the Peggy McGuire case, which had rattled Eufaula residents.

Queen of Diamonds

Subsequent to the Jamison family's disappearance, two more people went missing in Eufaula in separate but similar incidents.

In 2013, Tommy Eastep vanished while visiting Eufaula. Police found his locked, abandoned truck on a secluded backwoods road—circumstances weirdly similar to the Jamison case. A decade later, his mom told me there had been no progress in her son's case.

Two years later, Peggy McGuire also went missing in Eufaula, and after hearing from the cook lady and the waitress, I looked at her case more closely. The OSBI gave twenty-eight-year-old Ms. McGuire the "Queen of Diamonds" card from their weird-ass digital missing-person deck, stating that she was last seen on November 16, 2015, dropping her son off at school, outside Eufaula, OK. McGuire had spoken to her stepfather while on her way to the home she shared with her son and his father.

She had not been seen or heard from since. Her Toyota truck was recovered on November 18, 2015, from the parking lot of TJ's Ice House Bar in rural McIntosh County.

As in the Jamison case, investigators conducting the search for Ms. McGuire were baffled by a lack of initial clues. Sheriff Ledbetter said he was dealing with a 350-plus square-mile area without a definitive starting point.

Her case also featured an ominous piece of surveillance video. Investigators found grainy footage that showed McGuire's truck being parked at a remote bar on Highway 9 at 5:00 A.M., at which point a dark, unknown figure got out of the vehicle and walked down the highway as a lightning storm started.

She was a licensed practical nurse who had only recently passed her boards at the time of her disappearance. Family members said she loved animals and cared for over 150 head of cattle. Her son was her life; nearly everyone who knew her said she would have never willingly abandoned him.

The one person who disagreed with that characterization was the boy's father, Thomas McIntosh, who told local outlets he believed Peggy was still alive and had run off. After her disappearance, Thomas took custody of the child and banned Peggy's mother from seeing him.

In 2016, the OSBI revealed the discovery of new evidence taken from Peggy McGuire's home, where Thomas and her children still live, and the eighty acres of land on the property. The released court records detailed some disturbing forensic evidence that was recovered: swabs of bloodstains located on the couch and back porch, as well as swabs from a stain discovered in a "bucket of the front-loading tractor." They also confiscated from Thomas's truck a leather glove with "red stains."

As incriminating as it sounded, seven years passed without any charges or arrests in connection to McGuire's disappearance. It sounded like one of the many cases of "no body, no prosecution."

Sheriff Ledbetter

With bellies full of pancakes, eggs, and coffee, we made our way to the McIntosh County Sheriff's Office, which was located in what would turn out to be an impressive building for the area's law enforcement facilities. It looked like a mix of a public library and one of those info centers at rest areas off the freeway.

My expectations of Sheriff Ledbetter matched the reality: he was a nice and responsive man, with a soft, slightly distracted disposition. He was in constant motion the whole time as we stood in the lobby. He made it clear pretty quickly that he didn't know much about the case, but he kept returning from other rooms and hallways to renew the discussion. McIntosh County was where the Jamisons had lived, he said, but Latimer County (and, according to him, Leflore County) were the jurisdictions that had investigated, along with the OSBI.

I was hoping he might have some kind of case file or at least some info on the family. If they really were reported to CPS, for example, it's possible such information would be on hand. But he didn't, and it wasn't. He did, however, share a surprisingly apropos anecdote with us.

In the context of how very strange circumstances can look almost certainly like foul play but are really just messy human error, he told us about the local case of a man who was found with a gunshot wound to his leg, sitting upright in a car. Investigators spent weeks assuming foul play was involved only to learn the man had accidentally shot himself.

Mona the Drug Counselor

As we had waited for Ledbetter, Laura looked up the distance to Latimer County, and it was only an hour. We decided to check it out, though we had already agreed there was no way in hell we were going to Panola Mountain.

We arrived in the town of Wilburton, home of the Latimer County Sheriff's Office, and went to the county courthouse, erroneously believing it to be the location of the sheriff's office. In timing that can only be described as staggeringly serendipitous, we almost immediately crossed paths with someone who had been directly involved with the Jamison case.

In search of the sheriff's office, Laura and I wandered into a big gray building that sort of looked like a courthouse and a mailroom conflated into one. There was a woman in the hallway, and I asked her, "Excuse me, ma'am, is the sheriff's office here?"

"No, this is the government office," she said, with a clipped humble accent. Heading out the door with us, she pointed: "Sheriff's is just around the corner on Central."

"Thank you," we said.

As we walked the sidewalk alongside her, under the shade of some old-growth trees, she introduced herself as Mona. I asked if she lived in Wilburton.

"I've lived here since 1953," she said, adjusting her glasses as though challenged to a riddle.

"Cool. Do you work in the government office?"

Mona fiddled with some of the papers she was holding. "No, I came up here to get my marriage license because I'm going on a trip without my husband, and I already sent for a passport but it hasn't arrived, so now I have to drive to Hot Springs."

I grew up only an hour's drive from Hot Springs. My family and friends and I used to go there sometimes on the weekend to hear the jazz and drink thermal rainwater from the time of the Great Pyramids. Hot Springs was also where Bobby and Sherilyn Jamison got married.

"We're researching a case that went down here in 2009—the Jamison family, do you recall hearing about that?"

"Oh, yes." She gave the first inkling of a smile. "You could say I heard a bit about that one. I consulted on it."

"Whoa." I was so surprised that I forgot to ask what she meant by 'consulting on it,' and asked the second most logical follow-up question. "What do you think happened?"

"Personally? I think it was a drug deal gone bad."

"And that's something that's known to happen up there, drug deals?"

Mona laughed derisively. Laura and I looked at each other and laughed along with her.

"Dumb question, I reckon?"

"Yeah. You don't wanna go up there." Mona didn't make a lot of eye contact, but she had plenty to say. "This is what happened, or this is what I can tell you that I do know for sure. When Sheriff Beauchamp was in the midst of his investigation, he needed an extra set of eyes to watch all of the video of the people who were killed . . . and he brought it to me."

"I'm sorry, why did he bring it to you?"

"Because I'm a drug counselor."

My mouth dropped. "Oh my God, are you the psychologist Beauchamp consulted about the security camera footage?"

"Can you wrap your head around that?" Mona didn't fully smile, but she pursed her lips in a show of solidarity.

Laura and I beamed at each other, and I'm pretty sure we both said the word "exciting" at the same time.

"Okay, well . . . what did it look like to you? What did you see on the video?"

"I saw people who were tweaking really bad. There were several different cameras; if you've ever been around people on methamphetamines and their train of thought—they would go in and change their clothes, and then they would do something around the vehicle, and then go back into the house and change clothes again. They were definitely on drugs."

Mona said that she viewed at least thirty minutes of video, as opposed to the few minutes released to the public.

"Can you elaborate on how they were acting 'tweaky'?"

"If you've ever lived with someone who is on meth a lot . . . they will start one project and then stop and start another."

As she said this, I recalled Niki's description of Sherilyn's hypomanic behavior.

Mona's next line sounded like it could have been right out of the movie *Fargo:* "I questioned [Beauchamp] about it, I said, 'What do you think?' And he said, 'I don't know, what do you think?' And I said, 'Well, I think they're doin' drugs. They're doin' meth.'"

Mona said it was definitely foul play but that people go missing in the area so often that no one even bats an eye anymore.

I was surprised by this, and Mona gave me another *Duh, don't you know anything?* look. We all laughed again.

"Why are you sure it was foul play?"

"I don't know, but I think it was foul play." She paused for a moment, and then seemed to finally relinquish something a bit deeper. "This is what it seems like to me, and this is what I told Israel: it's like someone took their truck and laid it down on this pad, [the clearing], and then dropped 'em and left 'em. My guess is they went up there for a drug deal."

"Why do you think they brought their daughter to a drug deal?" Laura asked.

"I don't know, that's the scary part." Mona paused and then asked, "Where are you from?"

We said Oregon, adding that Laura's from Minnesota originally, and I'm from Arkansas.

Mona seemed like she really wanted to make something clear. "Well, there's parts of the mountains here you don't want to go to."

We thanked Mona profusely, wished her a wonderful trip, and shoved off down the sidewalk. She waved politely and then got distracted by something on her sleeve.

"I think I washed my top with something that was purple," I heard her mutter.

Sheriff Woodruff

> *The Office of Sheriff is one of antiquity. Man learned quite early that all is not orderly in the universe. . . . As such, man's quest for equity and order gave birth to the Office of Sheriff, the history of which begins in the Old Testament and continues through the annals of Judeo-Christian tradition.*
>
> —LATIMER COUNTY SHERIFF'S
> OFFICE HOMEPAGE

Prior to the trip, I'd researched Sheriff Adam Woodruff, the author of the imperium written on the LCSO homepage. I already knew from his social media posts that he could be aggressively ideological. But I was fairly surprised by one line in particular, which served as the tip of the spear:

"The Office of Sheriff is the most important of all the executive offices of the county," Woodruff wrote.

Despite the noble lineage of the Anglo-American sheriff, the Latimer County Sheriff's Office was located in an inauspicious trailer that reminded me of the temporary classrooms my junior high school used. It was a bit galling to realize how small and underfunded the police force was that handled those crucial first forty-eight hours on the Jamison crime scene.

I suppose there was a redeeming humility to it after the lecture on Judeo-Christian policing traditions, a touch of antiquity to whatever funding misappropriation or budget shortfall had consigned the rural county's entire sheriff's department to a space the size of an urban studio apartment.

As we parked, I was nervous and physically uncomfortable. The searing, throbbing pain in my right leg had gotten worse and now encompassed the entire appendage—radiating from the hip to the thigh, knee, calf, shin, and ankle. Even my right buttock muscle was in pain. Only the toes were spared.

It wasn't severe every moment of the day, but when it was bad, it left me in a state of perma-writhing. The limp in my walking had worsened, too, and there were days I simply couldn't do it. On those days—such as the present—I used a cane. It was either that or greet the sheriff with various grimaces, grunts, and dramatic shudders.

Here comes Old Man Anderson, I thought to myself, as we approached the sheriff's trailer.

I had to get over some jitters of self-consciousness at first, but I'd grown to love the cane, and I loved Laura for recommending and encouraging it. The gradual dawning of the reality that I had chronic pain and a potentially long-term physical disability wasn't the lonely, existential row it could have been because

I had love and companionship in my life, which was both healing and energizing.

It's astonishing the degree to which perspective and mood can
modify the experience of physical discomfort. Scientists believe
there are strong correlations between chronic pain and mental illness, and I'm a (gingerly) walking case study.

INSIDE, I ASKED if Sheriff Woodruff had time for a brief interview. After a short wait in the lobby, during which I hobble-paced,
the sheriff came out and invited us back to his office.

Woodruff was just how he looked in his Facebook pictures, tall
with shaved hair and goatee. He didn't have an imposing physical
presence per se, but there was a gleam of intensity in his bespectacled eyes that made me feel he had anticipated this conversation.

A story Beauchamp told of a younger Deputy Woodruff had
stuck with me. Apparently, Adam responded to the scene of a horrifying car accident where the wife of a wasted-drunk driver had
her arm ripped off and was bleeding out right there on the road.
Woodruff apparently waited there with her, helping the woman
until the end.

He took a seat behind his desk, and we sat on a couch on the
other side of the room. I started by confirming that the OSBI and
FBI ruled the Jamison family's deaths were accidental and probably exposure-related.

"Has your opinion on it changed? Where do you currently stand?"

Sheriff Woodruff's voice and speech rhythm is similar to Beauchamp's and Mona's, a version of the laconic Southern drawl
inflected with a calm Dixie pitch.

"Sheriffs before me certainly have their opinions, you know,
Beauchamp did his interview and said what he said. I will say, it's
odd. But I have faith in the OSBI. Israel—we go back and forth
on this still—either way, it was tragic."

"So you and Beauchamp talk about it still?"

"Yeah. Well, we worked the case day and night for months. We
covered at least ten miles, maybe more. We were using remote-
control drones before they were popular."

As he continued, the sheriff dropped an interesting hint:

"Me and Israel went back and forth when the remains were found. They were in a kind of a ditch area and *we both were almost sure we searched that area.* But they could have died somewhere else and been dragged there." [emphasis mine]

I told the sheriff about my conversation with the Grahams and asked him about the infamous hole-in-the-skull.

"There was a hole," Woodruff replied, "and from what I remember, they believed it was left by a hog or something."

"A hog?"

"Like, wild hogs."

I probably should have understood him quicker, given that I grew up the next state over, where the most popular sports team, the Arkansas Razorbacks, are named after the colloquial term for feral pigs. I remember going to games as a kid and observing in mild horror the pre-game ritual in which tens of thousands of fans collectively call the players to the field with a series of gradually intensifying "pig sooie" chants.

Returning to Israel's claims, Woodruff discussed their diverging views diplomatically.

"Israel's got his opinions, and they're valid. He knows a lot more of the inside stuff from the investigation like suspects and motives. And if you focus on that, then yeah, you're gonna think they were murdered. I'm not saying Israel's wrong, because he could be right. A part of me agrees with what he's saying, a part of me doesn't. If you're working a case for that long, you hate for it to just be an accident."

I decided to get a bit more direct. "Beauchamp says the murderer was a specific person. Do you know who that person is?"

"I don't."

"Has he said the person's name to you?"

"Uhhhh, he said several people's names, but we hadn't really talked about it much since the end of the case. He works for me part-time, so he is my deputy, but he's working mostly drug cases."

This surprised me a bit.

"Has he pursued working more on the Jamison case since re-turning as a part-time deputy?"

"No."

"It seems a little strange that he would say it was a hundred percent murder and that he knows who did it but not continue investigating. Is it just a lack of evidence, or is there some bigger reason?"

"It's more that the OSBI and FBI ruled the case closed. And it's hard once you have two big agencies like that calling it closed—it's hard for a small sheriff's office to open it back up and get traction. I can tell you, we want the facts, we want to know what happened. But it can be an uphill battle."

"It seems like you guys did everything you could think of to solve this." After the slight dig, I felt a bit of toadyism was in order.

Woodruff described arriving to the mountain on the second day with an abscessed tooth and encountering constant mud, rain, and cold for weeks. He said he felt like he was freezing to death. The searchers got several fires roaring to keep people warm and avoid hypothermia and frostbite.

"It was a very frustrating experience. For months and months, we worked on it to get closure for the family. There are some cases that really get to ya in this profession. Many of us have kids, and with Maddy, you know, we still just don't know."

At the mention of Madyson, Woodruff appeared to get misty-eyed for a moment.

Then he dropped another small and somewhat confusing breadcrumb as to his private investigative thinking: "They may have died of exposure, but were they there against their will?"

Woodruff said that the number of people that go missing every year in Latimer County was "outrageous" and "amazing." The residents in the area believe there is a serial killer. Woodruff explains to them that disappearances happen everywhere all the time, and it's not always criminal.

"Sometimes people get lost in the woods ... and a good hard rain can wash away everything."

I asked Woodruff about all the conspiracies and different suspects in the case from TV and Internet exposure, and he told me that after the ID episode, the LCSO got hundreds of calls from people in every state claiming to have sighted the Jamisons.

"One of the first calls came from the edge of Alaska. People were seeing them everywhere. The episode was good ... but it made our jobs that much harder, because we spent a lot of time following dead leads. We spent a lot of time on the video footage. In hindsight, maybe we should have searched a little more up there ..."

Woodruff said most of the people who worked on the case probably wouldn't talk to me because they were so scarred by it. This included Sheriff Beauchamp.

"That's why he resigned. It ate him alive."

After a pause, Woodruff suddenly asked, "Were you the one who messaged him?"

"Probably."

"Yeah, he called me and said, 'I'm gonna tell him when you're coming home so he can talk to you.'"

Woodruff offered to try getting me the case file. I doubted it would happen, and it didn't. But when I think about the "very thick" case file described by former Sheriff James, I salivate.

AFTERWARD, LAURA AND I continued the ongoing search for coffee and discussed our reactions.

I had often wondered what Beauchamp and other searchers and deputies thought when they learned the location of the remains. Woodruff saying that both he and Beauchamp felt they had thoroughly searched Smokestack Hollow and not found the Jamisons' bodies was one of the diamonds in the rough. It was an implicit suggestion that the remains could have been deposited there later.

But what was Woodruff not telling me? Had he really not discussed with Beauchamp the identity of the person he believed killed the Jamisons? Was Beauchamp really working for him part-time on drug cases but not investigating the Jamison family killer? What did that mean? Was the killer dead or already in prison?

Laura has an intuitive sense of whether someone is trustworthy. She's naturally dialed in to how others emote, the flow of micro-expressions and when they read as dishonest or deceptive. It's partly from years of having to be cautious and extra vigilant of the people in her environment—or the everyday reality of being a woman, as she described it.

But Laura assumes the best in people. She instinctively wants to give strangers the benefit of the doubt and not assume malicious intent. So if she senses a sketchy vibe from someone, I take it seriously.

She felt law enforcement wasn't being entirely honest in the Jamison case, or, at the very least, they were withholding information from the public.

THAT NIGHT, WHEN we returned to our motel room, I received a text from Reade, who had messaged me frequently since our phone conversation.

The text read:

"I truly believe I know what happened.... Maybe I'm wrong bro, but shady shit is shady shit."

CHAPTER 29

Check That Foundation

I HAD AWAKENED A BEAST in Reade. The week we were in Oklahoma, he sent me a series of increasingly intense texts that started with a short but cryptic message:

"The more I've thought about this, the more the memories return . . ."

Our conversation appeared to have triggered a flood of memories from his time on the mountain, which he was reliving—both visceral impressions of what he saw and experienced, as well as the guilt he repressed afterward. He put it out of his mind, but he'd never quite been the same. Now, as he reconciled his memories, some aspects of the narrative changed while new details trickled in.

The core of his beliefs remained the same: Reade was convinced the Jamisons' killer, or someone who knew of the killers, was on the mountain during that first day of the search and that he'd come face-to-face with him—the Mountain Man.

The more he thought about it, the angrier he got. In his mind, a triple-murderer waltzed out from under their eyes, smiling, bullshitting, and getting away relatively unscathed. Reade started calling him "Suspect #1" because as he remembered details of how the encounter went down, he felt that the man had been asking questions to probe the sheriff's knowledge, to see how much law enforcement knew.

Reade was reasonably sure the guy had been a dope cooker, which made the way he was treated—with wide latitude and kid's gloves—all the more strange.

Shady Shit

Hanlon's razor states to never attribute to malice what can be adequately explained by ineptitude.

When Reade thought back on how the search and investigation was handled, he was fairly sure the case was botched by local law enforcement. He also sensed the trappings of a small-town coverup. But more than anything, he wanted to find the rest of the Jamisons' remains.

In one text, Reade wrote: "Guarantee you this: if you gave me two weeks with the right crew and equipment, I'd put a GPR on a certain location and find another graveyard."

This confused me, because the Jamisons' remains were already found. But Reade believed there were more Jamison bones and artifacts buried under the foundation.

"I'm incredibly suspicious of those 'remains,' man," he wrote. "I believe it was a solution to a community that was outraged."

In other words, the bones that were found represented a sampling of the family's remains, but the rest were still concealed in a second gravesite. Reade was so revved up that he pushed for us to drive to Panola together and make a documentary about it.

Between our first and second calls, Reade flip-flopped on a few things. The first time around, he said Beauchamp and company did a decent job; subsequently, after more thought, he said the investigation was botched.

It was a strange time, he said. Their agency was getting its federal jurisdiction, and his boss didn't want him stepping on anyone's toes. Additionally, at the time of the search, Reade said there was a transition of power going on inside the Latimer

County Sheriff's Office. Beauchamp was already on his way out the door.

Reade clarified his role and job. He wasn't an official US Marshal, but he established the cross-agreement between the tribal agency and the marshals. He told me that when the Jamisons went missing, the 2006 Adam Walsh Act was starting to go into effect, and the tribal agency needed to register a large number of sex offenders. Reade helped establish that process, which included DNA collections.

He also tried to assure they would have backup. If he was headed out into a fifteen-county jurisdiction to hunt down absconding sex offenders, he wanted armed reinforcements on call.

The most significant change regarded the picture of D.C. arrested for murder: Reade no longer felt this was the same person as the Mountain Man he saw that day.

Other elements of his description remained unchanged. He remembered that the Jamisons' truck was pointed uphill; the tracking dog had followed a scent from the passenger side of the vehicle 400–500 feet up the hill to the bluff, where it abruptly terminated.

Because this was the approximate location where a child's footprints were found, Reade believed the canine had been following Madyson's scent. And he believed the scent's termination point marked the spot where Madyson was snatched by the perpetrator and carried back down the hill.

Something Sinister

After his provocative texts, I called Reade from our Eufaula motel. He answered the phone and launched right in.

"The more you probed and the more questions you asked, the more I realized ... I started to think about things, you know."

He said that just before I called, he had been telling his mother about what he saw and sensed while on the mountain in 2009. His mom asked if he was sure he was right, and he said he was.

"The truck looked like someone had walked them out at gunpoint and executed them," Reade said, and then switched lanes to discuss the Mountain Man. "They let [the only person on the scene] walk on back to his hovel. They didn't even go in there, once. It was 600 meters down to his gate [from where the Jamisons' truck was abandoned]. It was really strange, dude; this is a potential triple-murder, and the way the investigation was conducted was just sloppy."

Perhaps his most salient critique referred to how the evidence—particularly the victims' truck—was handled. According to Reade, deputies were inside and all over the truck, badly contaminating the crime scene right from the start. Reade was young, right out of college, and not a seasoned investigator, but he knew the basic protocols for what was and wasn't supposed to happen at beginning of a missing-persons case. They brought in the standard search and rescue teams and cadaver dogs, but there was seemingly no effort to preserve the inside of the truck so that prints or forensic evidence could be lifted.

"It was a shit show . . . nobody was in charge. Hell, I was in charge. I just drove two and a half hours, and I'm the guy in charge?"

"What do you mean, you were in charge?"

"I was telling 'em where to look—'look here, look there.' I asked, 'Has anybody tried lifting fingerprints off this truck?' I walked down with the sheriff and undersheriff, and I'm the one that initiated that. I asked, 'Do we have people that are close?' And they were like, 'Uh, I dunno about that—you mean like people who live here?' And I was like 'Yeah.'"

Reade said this in a way that made me laugh.

But the worst part was approaching the little shanty on a steep hill with a sign that Reade characterized as basically saying "Fuck Off." It was there that the Mountain Man intercepted them.

"He walks out of that gate, walks up to us, and is like, 'What's going on?'" Reade guffawed. "*What's going on? I think you know what's going on.*"

His nose prickled at what he perceived to clearly be the fumes of meth production. Additionally, he could see in the background that there was wet, recently poured concrete foundation—a 1,000 feet of it—occupying a space bigger than the actual living quarters.

Reade remembered him—Suspect #1, the Mountain Man, whose face he has seen many times in his dreams.

"As your paths crossed, who spoke to him first? Was it Beauchamp?"

Reade paused for a moment and then said, "Now don't get me wrong, but I'm just gonna say, it's almost like the sheriff knew the guy. It was weird. And so I said, 'Where have you been the last twenty-four hours?'"

Reade said he received a turn-around death stare from Beauchamp. It wasn't his jurisdiction, and he didn't want to step on toes, so he let it go for the moment. But when they got back up the hill, he said, "He's dirty! He knows more than what he just told us!"

He spent the rest of the day telling anyone who would listen: "You need to check that foundation."

Reade no longer believed this was the same guy as the D.C. arrested for murder. He wasn't even sure the Mountain Man lived on the mountain. More likely, he was just a guy cooking dope.

"You ever smelled meth? You can smell that shit in the air. I said to the sheriff, 'These guys are cooking dope.'"

"Do you think it's possible the sheriff was hesitant to go on the property without a search warrant and probable cause?"

"No, I think ..."

Reade presented a controversial theory that was unproven but which has turned out to be the case in many small towns plagued by cartel drugs. He wasn't pulling any punches. He told me he ran this idea by his uncle, a local judge, who said, "Good luck proving that."

As for motive, Reade suspected the Jamisons were killed after driving up the wrong road or walking onto someone's property and witnessing a drug loading or transportation operation.

WHEN READE LEFT the search that day, he left law enforcement for good. He joined the Navy and was a Corpsman attached to the US Marines stationed in Pendleton, near San Diego.

He was jaded by his experience on the Jamison case and left with the feeling that "something pretty sinister had happened."

The main reason he departed from the tribal agency was the rotten nature of the job itself.

"The recidivism rate is like ninety-one percent," Reade said. "And it's hard to know that you're checking in on someone who is probably going to do something terrible to another person. It starts to really wear on you, especially when ninety percent of my cases were against individuals age twelve or younger."

He still questions his decision to walk out on the Jamison search, but he said he began to fear for his safety, and his then-supervisor told him he was spinning his wheels.

At the end of our call, Reade said, "I still wake up at night and wonder, if they had just looked in the right places, they may have found something that was pretty sinister."

Undersheriff Bohn

Beauchamp had long rebuffed my attempts at an interview, as he had others. According to a number of people to whom I spoke, he, Starlet, and Connie were done talking about the case. I certainly don't blame them, although in Beauchamp's case, Colton might be owed some answers.

But I was still hoping to "follow the money." Did it refer to a stranger on the mountain or someone the Jamisons knew?

Matt Bohn was a deputy with the Latimer County Sheriff's Office from January 2004 to August 2011. During the Jamison investigation, he was the undersheriff and worked closely with Beauchamp and Woodruff.

I contacted Bohn through Facebook Messenger about asking him some questions.

"Ask away, sir," he wrote.

It took a few weeks to get the responses, but Bohn was patient and true to his word, seemingly answering my questions to the best of his ability.

The Jamisons' deaths, he believed, were the result of homicide but, surprisingly, he was evenly split between foul play from a third party and murder-suicide.

"I went back and forth between M/S and robbery a million times," Bohn wrote.

I asked him about suspects, listing the different theories, including the suspicions over D.C. Bohn confirmed D.C. was likely the last person to see or speak with the family, adding that investigators interviewed him as a suspect several times.

Bohn also said there were discoveries made during the investigation that weren't revealed to the public "in case more evidence came to light." This is a standard practice among law enforcement, and given Beauchamp's certainty over the killer, it made sense.

The former undersheriff shot down some theories, too. He didn't think the Jamisons died during a drug deal gone wrong and said he'd never heard anything about Bobby being an informant. Bohn seemed to dismiss out of hand the premise of the family's involvement in a meth operation and expressed choice words for people such as former Sheriff Brooks, who had pushed the drug narrative without sufficient evidence.

I asked him about whether there was friction between the Latimer County Sheriff's Office and the OSBI/FBI, which Beauchamp outright stated in his interview. Bohn didn't say much about this except that the OSBI was running the show once the remains were found. I couldn't help but wonder about this. It strikes me as strange that virtually all local law enforcement believes foul play was involved, while the state and federal agencies maintain they got lost and died from exposure.

I tried to push a little harder on the identity of the killer. Bohn said he wouldn't give me a name, but he sketched a scene similar to what Beauchamp described on the podcast.

"Someone up there knew they had money on them, in Sherilyn's bag."

THERE WAS A common refrain among the searchers and law enforcement personnel when it came to the psychological toll the

Jamison case took. The search was grueling physically and emotionally on volunteers and veterans alike, and the inability to save Madyson devastated them. On the investigative side, the endless rabbit holes and red herrings had baffled and frustrated everyone involved.

I remembered that when I was speaking to Reade, he'd mentioned how the K9 handler said the scent path was the most bizarre she'd ever seen, as though someone sprinkled raft particles randomly all around the mountain to confuse the dogs. It almost felt like the same had happened with the case itself—reality scattered fragments of the truth around in every direction, confounding anyone who dared try to make sense of it.

In the years that followed the closing of the case, Beauchamp, Woodruff, Bohn, and Reade all experienced extreme frustration and trauma over not being able to solve the mystery and bring closure to the family.

Beauchamp went on to have a successful career as a state department instructor for "tactical solutions" and private security detail. But the former sheriff, whose daughter was the same age as Madyson at the time of the search, still seemed haunted by the case.

So, too, did Bohn, whose youngest child just reached Madyson's age.

"It still weighs on my brain," he wrote in our final exchange. "You can't always get peace even if you know the answer."

CHAPTER 30

The Remnant

F ROM THE EARLIEST DAYS OF reporting about the Jamison family disappearance, a constellation of almost mythic story-lines threaded through the narrative. It's one of the traits that made the case both excruciating and fascinating.

One of the most bizarre—and enduring—storylines was that in their final weeks, Bobby and Sherilyn repeatedly contacted a spiritual advisor, Gary Brandon, about demonic visitations at their home.

For many years, I'd wanted more info about this aspect of the story, ideally from Mr. Brandon himself. Why had the Jamisons come to him? What was their relationship? Did we know the full context of their statements?

I'd always felt there had to have been a pretty compelling reason why the FBI pursued this lead so early and vigorously.

But there was no additional reporting about the story after the initial flurry. And Brandon himself was never even interviewed by a newspaper or media source: the FBI spoke with him over the phone as part of the case profile they developed, and this was shared with local law enforcement and subsequently leaked to the media. But the person at the center of the action—who supposedly met face-to-face with the Jamisons at a restaurant only a few days before their disappearance—didn't once publicly address or acknowledge whether the accounts were true. He never confirmed, denied, or commented in any way.

According to Niki, Gary Brandon was originally scheduled to be interviewed for the ID show but abruptly dropped out shortly before filming and subsequently went off the radar. He'd been radio silent ever since.

LIKE OTHERS, I'D tried reaching him for several years, sending countless unreciprocated messages into the void. I even tried messaging his wife on Facebook, but received no reply.

In the homestretch of writing the book, I finally pierced a corner of the veil concealing the Gary Brandon story. I didn't get to talk to *him*, but as with the other white whales—K.B., D.C., etc.— I was able to reach someone who knew him and, more importantly, was with him at church events attended by the Jamisons.

The information he provided me was surprising. It didn't solve anything necessarily, but it had an unexpectedly chilling effect on me.

Pastor Alonso

Geraldo Alonso is the pastor at the Lubbock, Texas, Seventh-day Adventist ministry, his fourth career pastorate. One of his duties is running the Junior Academy, whose stated goal is to "prepare children for eternity" and "take them to their Savior."

Pastor Alonso is a portly man with black-rimmed spectacles and a slight perma-grin. He has described his cultural origins as "a combination of legal and undocumented immigration," writing on his blog that he feels "homegrown in a place that is foreign to [his] eyes."

One of the pastor's earliest memories is getting sick as a child and his grandmother Ita laying him down and performing her "*curandera* duties." In traditional Latin American culture, a *curandera's*

rituals can involve everything from herbalism, bodywork, and coun-
seling to sweat lodges, midwifery, and trance creation.

For young Geraldo, it was "a cold egg and almost wordless but
fervent prayers that somehow sounded like chanting."

He remembered crying and screaming "with every ounce of
[his] soul" as his mother held him down so that Ita could rub the
cold egg "in rhythmic motions" all over his body.

Elsewhere in his blog, he wrote about overcoming his social
media addiction and applying the lessons and wisdom of the
Bible to the modern world.

It took a minute to get a phone interview with Pastor Geraldo
Alonso. After responding favorably to my first email, I didn't hear
from him for six months before he finally rewarded my persistence and arranged a time for us to speak.

Alonso told me that back in 2009, he was the pastor at the Muskogee Seventh-day Adventist Church, which organized a series of
"meetups" at the McIntosh County Fairgrounds in Eufaula. These
weren't official services, like the ones they held at their church. The
meetups were part of a special "evangelical outreach program" targeting small towns in the immediate region such as Eufaula and
Lubbock, Texas, where up to 100 people attended on any given evening. The program sponsored these multi-purpose recruitment
drives to help the SDA organization sign up new parishioners,
share the gospel, and lay the foundation for future church locations.

When I asked about Gary Brandon, who was described in at
least one article as a pastor, Alonso corrected the record.

"Just to be clear, Gary Brandon wasn't a pastor. I was a pastor
at the time. He was one of our local elders who participated in
the evangelic meetings—special Bible prophecy meetings. He and
another guy, can't remember who he was . . ."

"Was it Ken Reeves?"

He paused for a moment, as though surprised I knew his
name, and then said, "Yeah, it could have been Ken Reeves."

Alonso characterized Brandon and Reeves as evangelists and
teachers who operated more in an upfront capacity, whereas
Alonso himself was more "behind the scenes."

Pastor Alonso said they held about fifteen weekly meetings in
Eufaula. Brandon, he said, introduced him to Bobby, Sherilyn,
and Madyson, whom he personally met with four or five times.

"They seemed really interested in the message that was being
shared on Bible Prophecy. And I do remember them having questions about a demonic presence, or some supernatural force in
their home."

At the end, the Jamisons expressed interest in staying connected with the church and keeping the lines of communication
open. And apparently, they did stay in contact with Gary Brandon, sending him notes, calling him, and even meeting with him
at a restaurant to discuss the demonic presence in their home. Unfortunately, Alonso said he didn't know anything more specific
about these discussions and couldn't shed any new light on them.
Unlike Brandon and Reeves, he was never contacted by law enforcement after the disappearance. In fact, he said he wasn't even
aware Brandon and Reeves had been interviewed by the FBI until
I told him.

"Not long after that," he said, "they went missing... there were
lots of conversations about how the wild hogs out in that area are
very vicious."

The wild hogs again. Previously, I'd seen some online chatter
about this angle, but with first Woodruff and now Alonso, it appeared it was a real theory.

But I was actually more interested in the meetups—what kinds
of stuff did they talk about; was it different than your usual service?

"One of the things we emphasize is Last Days prophecy. It
doesn't matter how bad the world may be falling apart, God's
going to help us through.... We focus a lot on the Book of Daniel,
chronicling the Bible's predictions for how the end of the world
may occur. So that's what we focus on. Giving people hope that
no matter how bad life gets, Jesus can help them."

"For my own edification, can you tell me more about the Last
Days message that you discussed?"

"I don't remember exactly, but we try to stick as close to the
Bible as possible."

"Sola Scriptura, right?"

"Yes, exactly. So we usually start the meetings in the Book of Daniel. I don't know how familiar you are with the Bible ..."

"Well, I'm Jewish and essentially areligious, so assume not very."

"Okay, no worries. So I'll give you a thirty-thousand-foot view. We usually start the meetings asking people, 'Do you ever ...'" Alonso paused here, seeming to stop himself short, and then continued. "We usually ask questions that are more personal, like what's going on in the world. Inflation, war ... do you ever have doubts? Do you ever worry about what the future may hold? Something like that, just to make it relevant in real time ..."

Pastor Alonso gave me a disjointed crash course in Seventh-day Adventism. He mentioned the Babylonian empire and some dream about a statue of the world's superpower emperor made of different metals—a head of gold, arms of silver, legs of iron, etc.

"Tyrants come and tyrants go, empires come and empires go, but the one true thing throughout is that God is in control."

In subsequent research, I learned that Seventh-day Adventists believe the Book of Daniel contains crucial prophecies that are relevant to the end times and the Second Coming of Jesus Christ. They interpret the prophetic passages in Daniel as providing a framework for understanding historical and future events. The resulting eschatology is epic, presenting a sequence of prophetic eras and signs that culminate in the end times, a period of unprecedented turmoil and upheaval commonly referred to as the Great Controversy—a final clash between the forces of good and evil, with Satan making his last desperate attempt to deceive and destroy humanity.

Seventh-day Adventists believe the signs are already unfolding all around us and that they indicate the nearness of Christ's return.

One central event in Seventh-day Adventist canon is the concept of the Investigative Judgment, which they believe began in 1844. As a true-crime fan, I found this to be particularly interesting, because the way it's described sounds like an actual trial taking place in a metaphysical courtroom where the defendant is your soul. During the Investigative Judgment, Jesus Christ Himself examines the lives and characters of believers to determine their fitness for eternal life. This judgment is seen as part of God's process of vindicating His character and His people in the face of Satan's accusations.

The Investigative Judgment was in progress in 2009, when the Jamisons were learning more about it, and it's still in progress now, according to SDA. During these trials, a small group of faithful individuals, 144,000 strong, will be alive just before the Second Coming of Jesus Christ. This group, the "remnant church" of the faithful, plays a crucial role in proclaiming the three angels' messages, which are the final call to worship the true God, uphold His commandments, and reject the false religious systems of the end times.

The sealing of the 144,000 is seen as a mark of God's ownership and protection, a work of the Holy Spirit, transforming and equipping these individuals to stand firm in their faith amid the intense spiritual and earthly battles that will occur during the Last Days, when the Antichrist and the final world religious system—Babylon, or the Beast—exerts global influence and enforces false worship.

The Second Coming of Jesus Christ will be a visible, literal event. The sun and moon will darken, and the stars will fall from the sky. The dead in Christ will be resurrected, and together with the living believers, they will be called up to meet the Lord in the empyrean.

The culmination of the End Times will bring about God's final victory over evil and the ultimate fulfillment of His plan for humanity.

Pastor Alonso ended with a quick nod to the practice of Sabbath and then summed up his pitch.

"In these meetings, we're giving these promises and telling people how to live by the principle of the Bible, but we're also asking them to join our church. So it's about the Bible, but it's also an invitation."

Apocalypse Literature

When I told Laura about my conversation with Pastor Alonso, she suggested I look into the Lori Daybell case. In the news headlines, Lori Daybell was described as the "doomsday mom," her family a "doomsday cult." Lori and Chad Daybell, who ran a religious self-publishing company devoted to end-times literature, were first arrested in Hawaii on February 20, 2020, on charges of desertion and nonsupport of dependent children, as well as obstructing a criminal investigation.

After being extradited to Idaho, Lori and Chad faced additional charges related to the disappearance and deaths of their children, J.J. and Tylee. The indictments alleged that Lori and Chad had conspired to kill both J.J. and Tylee because they believed that the children were "zombies" and were possessed by evil spirits. According to the indictment, Lori and Chad believed that killing the children would "free" them from the evil spirits and allow their souls to ascend to Heaven.

Court records detailed Lori's belief that she was a god preparing for Christ's second coming in July 2020, "receiving spiritual revelations and visions to help her gather and prepare those chosen to live in the New Jerusalem after the Great War as prophesied in the Book of Revelations." Lori also told her ex-husband that she was a "translated being who cannot taste death sent by God to lead the 144,000 into the Millennium."

All of this matches the apocalypse narrative preached to the Jamisons by Pastor Alonso, and the doppelgänger "zombie" delusion matches Sherilyn's belief of demons inhabiting her husband and taking the form of various children.

There are significant differences between the Jamison and the Daybell cases, not the least of which is the fact that the Jamisons were not charged with any crime, much less murder. But some of their more radical spiritual beliefs align. While their central theological orientations were not the same—the Daybells practiced Mormonism/LDS, while the Jamisons were dabbling with Seventh-day Adventism—they both adhered to the more extreme beliefs of evangelical Christian apocalyptism. Moreover, they both had become obsessed with fringe ideas about demon possession, spirit doppelgängers, and their own special abilities ("charismatic gifts").

I HAD A strange feeling after talking to Pastor Alonso. He's a nice man, and I appreciated his candor. But in truth, I was stunned to learn the Jamisons had been regularly attending End Times Bible prophecy meetings in the lead-up to their disappearance.

I was also a little unnerved at the way the pastor described the apocalypse as a message of hope.

I thought of Bobby and Sherilyn, long past the end of their tether—two people on the brink of total meltdown in every measurable way, ground down to the raw nubs of their minds by an endless torrent of pain, grief, conflict, trauma, and loss—stumbling upon Alonso's revival tent at the fairgrounds like the proverbial oasis in the desert, "Brother Love's Traveling Salvation Show." A family that already believed it was under all-out attack in a spiritual war with demons—a family whose life was imploding—might hear such a message and take comfort that what's happening to them will soon happen to everyone, that this pain and confusion is part and parcel of a cosmic war between good and evil. Their suffering is the natural course of God's law restoring justice to the universe.

We don't know the extent to which Bobby and Sherilyn believed all the tenets of Seventh-day Adventism, but based on their stories of spiritual warfare on the shores of Eufaula Lake and the repeated attempts they made pressing their spiritual elder for specific advice in the battle against demons, it's certainly possible they heard the three angels' warning about the imminent destruction of the world by Satan's minions and took it literally. When you consider Sherilyn's fervent conviction in her and Madyson's spiritual abilities—their special indigo destinies—it makes sense that she would be attracted to the narrative of the remnant, the 144,000 who must withstand the tyranny of the Beast in those final dark years of doubt and chaos before the Lord's return.

Perhaps these thoughts played a role in their plan to move to Panola Mountain. Maybe the message of the remnant was the final voice of authority convincing Bobby and Sherilyn that the demons on the roof were part of something bigger—something for which they needed to be prepared.

When I asked Niki about Bobby's purported interest in special bullets that kill demons, she side-stepped a bit and suggested he had asked about it in a more sarcastic sense. But I think if he was kidding, he was kidding on the square. He was joking about something serious.

As I read more of the apocalypse literature contained on SDA websites, I noticed a persistent theme of being ready and having a blueprint for the end—planning you and your family's exit.

I'm sure most of the world's twenty million adherents aren't actively planning their families' deaths. But you can't predict how a message of restorative destruction will affect people who have gone off the rails. It's a form of indoctrination that both attracts and perpetuates radicalism.

Here I'd spent all this time debunking the satanic/occult and white nationalist conspiracy theories, and it turned out, there was cult activity in the Jamison case, after all.

CHAPTER 31

Folie à Famille

I N ADDITION TO REVEALING THE family's involvement with an End Days religious sect, Pastor Alonso's story helps corroborate the Jamisons' demon delusions and gives us more of a timetable of how long they were having these experiences. They don't appear to have been a few ephemeral episodes: it was an ongoing sequence of experiences that played out over at least fifteen weeks with the last-known conversation between Bobby and Gary Brandon taking place on October 3rd, only three days from their first drive to Panola Mountain.

Previously, we assessed research on how trauma can produce delusions and disassociations that are conducive to parapsychological experiences. But when two adults and a child share the same delusion continuously for months or longer, we have to at least consider the possibility of "shared psychosis," or induced delusional disorder. The condition is popularly known by its French translation, *folie à famille*, though French psychologists prefer to call it *folie communiqué*, "a communicated psychosis."

This is a complex, poorly understood psychological phenomenon with several variations on a theme. In shared psychosis, one individual, known as the primary case, has a pre-existing mental illness that includes delusions, hallucinations, or other forms of psychosis; the secondary cases, usually close family members or friends, develop the same delusions or beliefs as the primary case. The secondary cases usually lack a pre-existing mental illness; the delusions arise due to the influence of the primary case.

There are many contemporary examples of family murder-suicides that involved some degree of *folie à famille*—the Crowleys and the Harts, for example. The one that disturbed me more than any other was a lesser-known case in Pennsylvania—the Decree family.

In February 2019, a social worker with Children and Youth Services arrived at the Decrees' small apartment in Morrisville, Pennsylvania, for an unannounced welfare check. When no one answered the door, a maintenance worker let the representative inside. She found broken furniture and dead bodies strewn across the floor, as well as two disoriented but living family members, Shana Decree and her daughter Dominique, who were both lying in bed, unresponsive.

The victims included two of Shana's children, Naa'Irah Smith, twenty-five, and Damon Decree Jr., thirteen, as well as her sister, Jamilla Campbell, forty-two, and Campbell's nine-year-old twin daughters, Imani and Erika Allen. The bodies were found in various rooms of the apartment. All had been strangled or suffocated.

According to the police affidavit, authorities went to the hospital and interviewed the nineteen-year-old Dominique, who had visible injuries to her neck. She asked if her family was alive, and then kept repeating that she wanted to die.

Shana and Dominique were arrested, and as the investigation unfolded, it became clear that the Decree family had become a completely secluded, cultlike environment of extreme delusions. According to reports, Shana and Dominique Decree believed that they were receiving messages from the afterworld and that their family members were possessed by demons. They believed that killing their family members would allow the demons to escape their bodies and free their souls.

The Decree family's religious beliefs were so extreme that they had been asked to leave a local church due to their erratic behavior and strange statements. They reportedly moved to Morrisville, a borough in Bucks County, Pennsylvania, to be closer to a spiritual leader who they believed had the ability to communicate with the spiritual realm.

Shana had a history of mental illness and had been hospitalized for psychiatric treatment in the past. Dominique had also been hospitalized for psychiatric issues and had reportedly been diagnosed with schizophrenia.

The affidavit states that in early February 2019, Shana withdrew Damon from school, planning to homeschool him. Shana later told police "that everyone in the apartment, including the nine-year-olds and the thirteen-year-old, wanted to die." They were fully convinced that the world was ending and that demons were all around them.

Dyad

I don't think murder-suicide is the most likely scenario with the Jamison family, but I do think they were experiencing something in the ballpark of "shared psychosis." The primary case appeared to be Sherilyn, who had long struggled with bipolar disorder and had a history of fervent spiritual beliefs regarding demons and spirits, which darkly intensified after the traumatic loss of her sister. Bobby, who had developed depression after his back injury, was the secondary case, gradually assimilating the more extreme symptoms of Sherilyn's delusions and hallucinations. Madyson, who was almost certainly traumatized by her parents' fighting and bizarre behavior, may have been mimicking them and/or experiencing a secondary case, as well.

But the Jamisons' *folie à famille* seems to have had a twist. If you remember, Niki told of Sherilyn being attacked and almost knocked down the stairs by a black-eyed Bobby, who she feared was a demon, or under the control of a demon. Incidents like this may point to the primary case losing and/or relinquishing control of the narrative to the secondary. Bobby seems to have been passive and deferential to Sherilyn on most matters, but he'd long pushed for isolation and living in remote, secluded environments. Sherilyn stated this outright in her letter when she called him a "monster" that had turned the family into "hermits."

The two were a dyad of warring delusions in a fluctuating power dynamic. While Sherilyn introduced Bobby to demons and spiritual warfare, he drew her into a secluded and presumably dangerous off-grid existence, with one serving as justification for the other.

Murder-Suicide

What's unusual in considering the possibility of murder-suicide in this case is that there's no clear candidate for who the perpetrator would have been or if it could have involved each of the parents. Both had been exhibiting the same warning signs and had been subjected to many of the same stressors. Perhaps it was a shared decision within the shared psychosis.

The Latimer County Sheriff's Office initially considered the possibility of murder-suicide after learning that Sherilyn owned a gun and had written a "hate letter" to Bobby. When the family's home was searched, police discovered an additional troubling letter. It's not fully known what was contained in either of these documents, but they were morbid enough that Beauchamp told the press, "They were certainly a family obsessed with death."

According to data compiled by the Violence Policy Center, the majority of murder-suicides involve domestic partners or family members, with over ninety percent of perpetrators being male. Firearms are the most commonly used method of murder-suicide, with seventy-seven percent of incidents involving a gun.

In an interview with *Wired*, Professor David Wilson, Director of the Centre of Applied Criminology at Birmingham City Uni-

versity, discussed his study of the phenomenon, entitled "Characteristics of Family Killers Revealed by First Taxonomy Study."
Wilson analyzed cases from 1980 to 2012 and found that over half
of the murder-suicides took place more recently in the first decade of the twenty-first century.

"Family break-up—including related issues, such as access to
children—was the most common cause of family murders," Wilson told *Wired*, "followed by financial troubles, honor killings,
and mental illness."

Wilson identified four types (common motives) of the so-
called "family annihilators":

- "Self-righteous killers" hold the mother or father of
  their children responsible for the breakdown of the
  family. They sometimes contact or meet with them
  beforehand to explain what they are about to do.
- "Disappointed killers" believe their family has let
  them down and must be destroyed out of shame.
  They're often provoked by major acts of disrespect,
  such as the children rejecting their authority or refus-
  ing to observe the same religious customs.
- "Anomic killers" see their family as a symbol of their
  own financial, social, or career failures—bankruptcy,
  for example—and believe they're stained for life and
  must be eliminated.
- "Paranoid killers" are often motivated by a desire to
  protect their family from a real threat, such as having
  children taken away by social services, or a delusional or hallucinated threat, such as demons or the
  Illuminati.

Among contemporary cases, self-righteous and anomic are the
most commonly seen murder-suicide motives, usually involving
fathers who have developed warped or radicalized beliefs about
the role of the woman in a family and the shattered identity of
the man as head of the household.

In the Jamison case, I believe we can safely rule out one of the two most common motives. Bobby, from all accounts, was the opposite of self-righteous and did not overtly view Sherilyn as responsible for the breakdown of the family. In fact, there's fairly good anecdotal evidence that it was flipped in the Jamisons' house, that Sherilyn blamed Bobby for the family's hermetic state.

None of the four buckets fully captures the psychological dynamic between Bobby and Sherilyn. Number four, the paranoid killer, comes the closest, but in many ways, the Jamisons were an anomaly.

I originally put very little stock in the murder-suicide theory, largely because I felt that many characterizations of the Jamisons had been unfair. While I still believe these characterizations should not have colored the early investigation in such a stigmatizing way, it's no longer possible to ignore the evidence that the Jamisons were deeply troubled and possibly a threat to themselves.

Psychologists say "family annihilations" can rarely be predicted, but there is a list of warning signs and stressors commonly present in documented cases. Let's assess what we know about the Jamisons with regard to these nine variables:

1. Mental illness: Both the Jamison adults had experienced mental illness: Sherilyn was diagnosed with bipolar disorder (and her episodes grew worse after her sister died and her son moved out). According to family and friends, Bobby fell into a deep depression after his back injury and was potentially experiencing severe anxiety after his father disinherited him and threatened to kill his family.

2. Financial stress: The Jamisons struggled financially for several years. Not only were both Bobby and Sherilyn reliant on disability insurance, Colton moving out deprived them of needed child support payments. According to family members and Sheri-

lyn's handwritten notes, Bobby took on an unknown, dangerous task to relieve their financial concerns.

3. Grief/trauma: We know that the sudden death of Sherilyn's sister Marla was a significant event in the decline of the Jamison family's stability. Death threats from Bobby's father may have served as an additional source of trauma.

4. Domestic violence: This one is less clear in the Jamisons' case, but based on anecdotal evidence, both Bobby and Sherilyn were involved in instances of domestic violence in the year before their disappearance. Sherilyn was accused of verbal, emotional, and physical violence against Colton and Bobby, and Bobby was accused of pushing Sherilyn on the stairs.

5. Divorce: According to many sources, Bobby and Sherilyn's marriage had been in decline for some time and had, at the time of their disappearance, collapsed. They were both speaking openly about divorce, which appeared to be imminent.

6. Substance abuse: Bobby took opioids after his car accident, and, according to Colton, Sherilyn began to abuse both the pills and patches to the extent that she overdosed and Bobby had to hide them from her. Colton also said his mom was "pilled out" on Xanax. According to other sources, Bobby and Sherilyn used meth, too. Sherilyn's former boss said they got hooked on it while in Oklahoma City. Sheriff Brooks claimed they were daily meth users.

7. Possession of a gun: The presence of a gun in the home significantly increases the risk of a family murder-suicide. This may be particularly true if the individual has a history of violence or mental health challenges. Sherilyn owned a .22 pistol that was never recovered from the family's home, truck, or the location where their remains were found. Sherilyn was

known to keep this gun near her and had fired it at
someone in anger.

8. Extremism: Bobby, Sherilyn, and Madyson attended
End Days bible prophecy meetings extensively before
their disappearance. We don't know if, or the extent
to which, this community of adherents factored into
the Jamisons' plans, but it's relevant to a discussion
about extremism and suicidal ideation. Additionally,
we know that the Jamisons had often talked about
wanting to live off-grid and apparently had plans to
homeschool Madyson and live inside a moving pod
in the mountains.

9. Legal/custody problems: In the year before their disappearance, Sherilyn lost custody of her son Colton,
who moved out to live with his biological dad. Sherilyn waged a bitter, lengthy legal fight but lost him and
the child support she'd depended on for many years.
There were additional rumors that Bobby and Sherilyn had been reported to and investigated by Child
Support Services for having a potentially unsafe or
unhealthy living environment. A few sources claimed
they believed they were at risk of losing Madyson.

The Jamisons hit every bucket on the murder-suicide checklist.
That doesn't mean it happened, of course. But it would be impru-
dent to ignore the reality that literally every stressor—every single
warning sign commonly found to precipitate murder-suicide—
was present in their lives.

Psychologists say that anniversaries of traumatic events and
deaths can act as additional triggers. When I read this, I immediately looked up the date of Marla's passing, which was Sept. 25,
2007. The Jamisons disappeared on October 7, 2009, less than
two weeks after the third anniversary of Sherilyn's sister's death,
which was a source of endless torment for her. So the family actually matched ten warning signs.

The frequency of these incidents in the United States has been on the rise in recent years. And while they are rightly viewed as a form of domestic violence between intimate partners, it is important to note that children are often the victims of family murder-suicides. In fact, a study conducted by the Violence Policy Center found that children under the age of eighteen were present in over half of all family murder-suicides that occurred between 2014 and 2019.

If for a moment we forget everything we know about the case and just consider the facts—two parents on the verge of a divorce, both taking large amounts of painkillers, experiencing sustained demonic delusions, and attending Last Days meetings, took their six-year-old into the mountains to live in a moving container and then vanished without any rations or supplies save for a pistol—it looks pretty galling.

CHAPTER 32

The Last Visit

As I moved into the endgame, I was disappointed in my-self for not having discovered more evidence—the definitive missing pieces of the puzzle.

I knew it was absurdly naïve, but there was still a part of me that felt the truth was sitting right there in front of me, just slightly out of focus, waiting to materialize. I wanted to believe there was one final pattern—a theory of everything—that could explain the truth of what happened.

At some point, I realized that the truth isn't always reducible to a single cause or simple answer. Sometimes events are shaped by a plurality of influences and factors that cross-pollinate and blur together.

In the Jamison case, there were actually two different mysteries. There was what happened to the family on the day they went miss-ing, and then was what happened to them in the years, months, and days leading up to their disappearance. The two may be connected, or they may not be. But part of me felt that neither could be fully understood in isolation.

In my final conversations with Niki and Colton, I edged a little closer to understanding this.

Giving Up the Ghost

The last time Niki saw Sherilyn was around September 1, 2009, just over a month before the family disappeared. This was the day she showed up on her doorstep with a briefcase of money—her half of the settlement money Bobby received from his father after suing him for back interest on the gas company.

"I'm leaving Bobby; we're done," she muttered, before asking if she could crash for a few days. "I can sleep on our bowling couch."

Niki knew what she meant—the ancient couch they upcycled from the bowling alley during their earliest days together. An era from a long-lost time when they were younger versions of themselves. It was a kind of golden age—but you never know what these are until they're gone.

Back then, before her mind was eroded, Sherilyn wouldn't have even needed to verbalize a request to sleep over, because consent would have been a foregone conclusion. But it had reached a point where it was difficult to see the line between a natural human reaction to grief and a destructive pathology. Things had gone from bad to worse between Sherilyn and Bobby, and they got even uglier after Colton moved out.

Making the present scenario trickier, however, was a recent unexpected rift between Sherilyn and Niki's husband Wayne. Six months earlier, during a dark hypomanic episode, Sherilyn had said and done things that Wayne wasn't getting over. The feud would likely have been resolved eventually, but for the moment, the feelings were still raw.

Niki was caught in an impossible situation: Wayne had made it clear that a break from Sherilyn was in order; if he came home from a long day of work to find her camped out on the couch, there was going to be trouble. At the very least, Niki needed to talk to him about it first before she could say yes to Sherilyn.

She tried to spontaneously generate order, hoping she could explain the situation in a way that wouldn't send Sherilyn into a rage. But she knew as soon as she started—it couldn't be done.

The woman before her, the friend she loved more than any other, could not withstand one more corpuscle of rejection or abandonment. She was maxed out.

Niki didn't even need to say anything. Sherilyn could see the pained reluctance on her face and instantly interpreted it as dead-to-rights evidence of betrayal.

"Okay, fine," she said with icy indifference, cutting off any direct eye contact with her.

Sherilyn told Niki she had to take Madyson back to Eufaula so she didn't miss school.

"I'll call you," Niki yelled out as Sherilyn slammed the door.

She went to check on Ronnie's temperature. Then she headed out to do errands. The last stop was Walgreens, where she bought the items on her list, including cold medicine, cough syrup, and ice cream.

She was just getting ready to check out when Bobby called. Niki answered and immediately heard Sherilyn in the background slamming doors and cursing. Niki's heart sank.

"Sherilyn is really—uh," Bobby stammered, struggling to play intermediary, "upset with ya. Felt like you let 'er down. Were you supposed to call her or sumpthin'?"

Niki explained that she was waiting for Wayne to get home and that her daughter was sick. Bobby repeated what Niki said to Sherilyn.

He didn't repeat Sherilyn's replies. But Niki could hear her seething hatred through the phone. When she got like this, Niki pretended it wasn't Sherilyn—and, in a way, it wasn't.

"It's okay, Bobby." Niki felt worse for him than for herself.

"Yeah."

"Tell her I'll call her back."

As she was about to hang up, Sherilyn snatched the phone from Bobby and continued cursing her, closer and louder. There was no escaping her wrath now.

"*OUR FRIENDSHIP IS OVER!*" She screamed before hanging up.

"Ma'am . . . ma'am?"

Niki looked up to see the cashier calling for her. Paralyzed by her friend's words, she hadn't moved up in line, and people were waiting on her, some of them irritably.

When she got home, Niki sat in her car in the driveway and cried. She couldn't believe it had come to this—over a decade of friendship, imploding. There was a sickening irony in the remembrance of their first conversation—about feng shui and the balance of positive energy—versus the reality of what Sherilyn's life had become. But more than anything, she was worried for her friend's welfare and, it turned out, for good reason.

That was the last time Niki talked to Sherilyn.

A couple of months later, when she learned they were missing, she had a realization that flashed within her like lightning on a pitch-black horizon: she knew how Sherilyn felt when she suddenly lost her sister in the midst of a feud. Marla died before they could reconcile, and it left a sense of irreversible loss—guilt worse than death, regret more haunting than any ghost.

Warning Shots

"Well, here we go," Niki said, smiling.

She got only silence from the driver.

For her second trip to the mountain, Niki had a different co-pilot: her husband. Wayne had been patient and supportive for the last few years as she transformed into a citizen sleuth. He'd accepted that there was a force compelling his wife to find the truth, and that part of that meant her staying up all night messaging weirdos and going down Internet rabbit holes. But the strain and fatigue had gradually, incrementally, taken a toll, and it was beginning to show.

Perhaps it was because the search—Niki's independent investigation—was no longer confined to the Internet and phone. She had gone to the actual crime scene, a creepy and notoriously dangerous and remote location. And now he was going with her.

He didn't seem nervous or frightened, more disappointed. For years on end now, she had put every scrap of energy she had into solving the case. The Jamison case had taken over her mind, poisoned her, and it was bleeding into everything else. She knew it. She could feel the bolts and screws of her life rattling, the infrastructure weakening, destabilizing. Demons she put down ages ago were returning, and they were infinitely more terrifying now because she had so much more to lose.

When they pulled off the narrow road and drove onto the well pad, the clearing gradually came into view.

The junkyard target practice truck was still there, tagged with Sherilyn's last message to the world: "God loves you."

Niki smiled.

Then, out of the corner of her eye, something framed in Wayne's driver's-side window drew her attention, and her smile dropped into the pit of her stomach.

On the far side of the clearing, lined up on the road by the bluff, were half a dozen parked trucks and SUVs. They were essentially blocking the only road that exits in the clearing—the same egress where the Jamison truck was found.

"What the hell?"

Wayne did a double-take out his window, pursed his lip for a moment, and then grumbled: "Prolly hunters."

They parked and looked around on foot. Niki showed him the sights and sounds of the mountain crime scene—the junkyard exhibit whose creepiness never failed to impress, the bluff where Madyson was likely last photographed, and, of course, the last-known point of the Jamisons.

The truck was no longer there, of course. But in its place were the six new ones sporting Texas license plates. No matter how they tried to ignore it, the presence of these vehicles never left their minds.

"The only property around here belongs to D.C.," Niki announced in her confusion, more to herself than anything. "So I don't know why the parade is in town."

"Belongs to who?"

"The last person to talk to 'em—he lives, like, a fourth of a mile down that road..."

As she pointed to the area beyond the clearing, Niki heard something, the soft but unmistakable sound of laughter coming from the tree line. As she stopped and listened, the sound of an indeterminate number of male voices traveled like binaural phantoms, their source close enough to see, yet invisible.

There was another short burst of laughter. Then there was silence.

Niki looked at Wayne and waited, but the voices didn't repeat. They both shrugged and started toward the trail.

Niki was thinking about how to lighten the mood when suddenly, a gunshot filled the air, followed by a second and then a third, each a blast of white-hot panic that reverberated through their musculature and ricocheted off the clearing.

Petrified, Niki looked at Wayne, whose normally staid face was somehow both flushed and pale.

"Okay, let's load up and go," he said.

Niki was frightened and confused, but the thought of leaving didn't make sense to her.

"We've only been here an hour, now you want to—"

"You don't understand," Wayne interrupted, his voice rising and softening at once, "*those were warning shots*, Niki. We need to leave. Now—please."

They walked swiftly back to their ride, packed up, and hauled ass off the clearing.

Glaring at the trucks in the rearview mirror, Niki wondered if their giggling, trigger-happy owners were friends of D.C. trying to intimidate her. She'd advertised her trips to the mountain on Facebook, so it wasn't impossible that someone organized there in advance to send her a message.

She would never stop believing D.C. was involved in the Jamisons' death. And if there was one undeniable truth she'd gleaned from her years of hunting the truth, it was that some kind of network existed there. The closer she'd gotten to putting the pieces together, the more unsafe she felt. Even though she lived three hours from Panola and Red Oak, she feared it—now more than ever. She wasn't sure if it was a "good ol' boys" type of small-town corruption with drug running and local police on the take, but there were multiple people involved, and they controlled the mountain.

Everybody knew, but nobody talked—they took it to the grave. What happens in Panola, gets buried in Panola.

NIGHT FELL AS they drove home. Niki, who had been staring out the window in deep contemplation, looked at Wayne as he drove through the blackness in silence. He had finally seen the case's dark synchronicity in person. He had the same spooked demeanor as the night of his out-of-body experience at the Jamisons' house.

Niki almost said, "Talk to me," as she had then, but she already knew what he had to say.

It wasn't just about the gunshots. The imbroglio on the clearing had just opened her eyes, making her see for the first time that this quest for the truth had become self-destructive. After years of reading Sherilyn's journal, talking to her in dreams and memories, praying for her, reaching out to her through psychic mediums, Niki realized she was channeling her, though not so much her spirit as her despair. She was no longer meaningfully advancing toward the truth of her friend's death as much as she was mirroring the downward spiral at the end of her life.

Perhaps she wanted to feel closer to her, or suffer in solidarity. No matter the reason, she knew she would have to stop investigating. Only then would she be able to get into a healthy enough headspace to reconcile the way things had ended between Sherilyn and her. Until then, the quest for truth and justice, no matter how justified, would only deepen the wounds.

I'M GRATEFUL TO Niki for revisiting her painful memories with me. Though she has stopped trying to solve the case, it's obvious she still has a burning desire to know what happened. And she still harbors frustration about the search and investigation. Her main criticism—which is shared by Reade and myself—concerns

how long it took for the truck to be treated as a crime scene. By
the time anyone thought to lift prints or look for forensic evidence, the inside of the truck had been touched, altered, and
contaminated.

She was also dismayed by how the Jamisons were treated by
the media and general public.

"One thing I learned from this case is that if you are not perfect," Niki wrote to me, "if you have mental illness, if you deal with
your issues in unconventional ways, then you do not get the same
kindness and compassion as others do—even when you need it
the most."

In prayer, she still talks to Sherilyn, or a composite of the Sherilyn she once knew, carrying her memory into the future.

She still has the vintage couch they salvaged together at the
bowling alley all those years ago. The threadbare heirloom lives
in her garage, collecting dust and raft particles, motes of the past
suspended in the late afternoon sunlight.

From time to time, Niki sits there and visits her friend.

"One of these days," she promises, "I'm going to have it reup-
holstered."

Hesitation Marks

In early September, right around the time of Colton's sixteenth
birthday, Bobby called him and said that his mom had been admitted to St. Anthony's Hospital in Oklahoma City.

Colton went to visit her at the state's oldest hospital, which
was founded in 1898 by the Sisters of St. Francis. He navigated
to the psychiatric wing, where he found that Sherilyn was responsive and happy to see him. Whatever medications they dispensed
had at least temporarily stabilized her.

"What happened, Mom?" Colton asked after sitting down beside her.

Sherilyn held up her forearms with a look of shame. The cuts,
which looked like cat scratches, were superficial "hesitation marks."

Approximately fifty percent of people with bipolar disorder attempt suicide, as compared to one in twelve people in the general population. Twenty percent eventually succeed.

Sherilyn seemed to like the treatment and therapy she was receiving.

"It's silly, but it's helping," she said, recounting the different exercises, which included coming up with five reasons why she was there, qualities she liked about herself, qualities she didn't, etc.—prosaic stuff that allowed the staff to get a baseline read on her psychological state.

THAT WAS THE last time Colton saw his mom. Sherilyn was released from St. Anthony's on September 10, and just under a month later, she, Bobby, and Madyson vanished in the high-elevation woods.

Feeling that we had developed some trust, I finally asked Colton a question that I had put off for a while, largely because I'd never given much credence to the underlying premise. He'd already told me foul play was his best guess for what happened to his family, but he didn't seem wholly convinced.

I asked him about the murder-suicide theory. Was it out of the question, or could he imagine something like that having happened?

"Honestly," he said, "it's not impossible."

Up and Up

Colton wanted to know what happened to his family on the mountain, but I got the sense that, over the years, what had really eaten him up inside had less to do with what happened on the mountain and more to do with what happened in the years before. He didn't seem haunted by uncertainty over the cause of death, and I realized that's because there was no solving the case for Colton.

Closure wasn't possible.

The most punishing unsolved mystery wasn't a question of murder but the severed love of a son for his mother. Whether his family's demise was due to hypothermia or foul play, there was no conclusion that could answer the more painful question of why his mom abandoned him, turned against him with such spiteful hostility as she spiraled into darkness.

He knew that the answer was pain itself—Sherilyn's pain after the sudden death of her sister and the subsequent inflammation of grief, trauma, and mental illness. Could things have changed with more time; could he have come to terms with his mom? This question can never be answered.

"I'd still like to pick Beauchamp's brain at some point," he said at the end of our final conversation.

"You deserve that."

"It's almost like he knows what happened, and someone else knows, too, but he was powerless."

Then Colton surprised me.

"This was kind of healing in a way," he said. "And, honestly, I'm probably doing better now than I ever have. I'm on the up and up. You can't sit back and dwell—I got two kids of my own, I'm married, and I gotta build stuff up for them, you know?"

After his family's disappearance, Colton came of age participating in gang-like activity and struggling with drug and alcohol abuse. But he'd passed through the eye of the storm, threading the needle, and came out on the other side. Now he had his own family and was starting a landscaping company.

He was also back in school again, studying theology.

"I would like to go into ministry," he said. "I have a calling to help other people."

CHAPTER 33

It Found Them

I SPENT COUNTLESS HOURS TRYING to imagine what happened
to the Jamisons, considering every imaginable configuration of
events. When I clear the static and train my thoughts only on the
thorniest, most stubborn facts, Sherilyn's briefcase appears, containing her pistol and a large amount of cash, and I consider the
fact that it was never found. Ironic, the biggest pieces of evidence
for foul play are missing pieces of evidence, but their absence is
hard to ignore.

I also think about the strange condition in which their truck
was left and the fearsome reputation of the area, known for its
drug deals, meth labs, and territorial, well-armed landowners. I
think about the gunshot hole in one of the skulls and Beauchamp's adamant claims that the Jamisons were killed by
someone on the mountain who knew they had money. I think
about the family's history of conflict and death threats, and the
ominous pattern of statements suggesting Bobby played a game
of brinkmanship with drug lords.

When I consider these data points, I lean toward foul play—
most likely an opportunistic crime by someone who was familiar
with the area and found out the family was going off-grid with a

significant amount of cash. Bobby was reported to have been telling strangers about their plans in Red Oak and on the mountain.
A local with intimate knowledge of the area who was upwind of
the Jamisons' money and destination plans and realized it was an
easy mark.

Like Colton, I get an undeniable feeling that the Jamisons
were followed to the mountain.

Perhaps this was the scenario underlying Beauchamp's suppo-
sition that the perpetrator killed Bobby and Sherilyn but not
Madyson. A perp making a quick money grab might have decided
child homicide was above his pay grade. Or perhaps that's giving
a murderer too much credit. Maybe Madyson ran away, and he
decided not to pursue her. After hours of hiding, she returned to
lie beside her slain parents and there succumbed to the elements.

It's also possible they witnessed a drug deal or meth lab and
were chased down and removed from their vehicle. Or, perhaps
they stumbled upon someone's home or property and were shot
as trespassers.

While the meth explanation would plug many of the case's
holes, it is still not wholly corroborated, especially the trafficking
accusations. And in some ways, meth is unnecessary to understanding Bobby's and Sherilyn's psychology. They were already
both chronic opioid users, but more importantly, years of pain,
grief, disappointment, stress, trauma, and mental illness had taken
both Jamison adults to the brink of a meltdown and dissolution.
Meth intoxication makes sense in that context as an additional
stressor, but it's not a required variable.

One of my biggest questions pertains to the moving container.
I had long been suspicious of the narrative portrayed on the ID
episode, that the Jamisons were planning to live in the moving
container so they could start a new life on the mountain. Talking
to Brett fanned the flames of this suspicion, because his counter-
narrative, that Bobby was using the moving container to start his
own meth operation, seemed more logical given the reputation
of the area and his vociferous claims of a Jamison drug-trafficking
operation.

However, given what I had learned about the family's last years, months, and days, it was not difficult to imagine Bobby and Sherilyn trying to live off the grid in a moving container. There's a whole movement of modular living enthusiasts who convert abandoned pods into tiny homes. In Oklahoma, which was hardest hit by the Great Recession in 2009, the movement was fueled partly by local economic distress and the meth epidemic, creating a fertile setting for off-grid living.

I once slept in a cot in my employer's office building for six months because I couldn't deal with reality. If I'd been in the Jamisons' shoes, I might have viewed Panola as my ticket to freedom, too.

And though I was finally able to beat the kratom addiction and restless leg using a medicine, I still have chronic pain—and bipolar, of course—and it's not hard for me to imagine how the cycle of substance abuse, physical and psychological pain, and all the other stressors in the Jamisons' lives could have led them to consider desperate options and exit strategies.

But the moving-container-as-temporary-home and the moving-container-as-meth-lab aren't mutually exclusive scenarios. They could have had multiple reasons for buying land on the mountain and bringing their moving container. Bobby, the monster and the genius, may have wanted to hide his family from someone who was making threats; Sherilyn may have wanted to flee their home and its malevolent spirits. They may have both been preparing for the End Days.

It's also possible they got lost and died from hypothermia. It happens every day. One part of this scenario depicted by Brett really stayed with me, when he described the Jamisons burying themselves in leaves to try and stay warm: their eyes peering meekly through the dark foliage, the pupils dilated with fear and darting around, lost in beams of white moonlight and tufts of frozen air.

I wondered if they knew they were going to die, or if they went to sleep expecting to wake from the nightmare in the morning—if they talked to Madyson and comforted her until the end.

There's a sense in which this is just as horrifying as murder.

Wild Hogs

Just when I thought I'd considered all the outlandish theories in this case, I talked to Woodruff and Alonso and found myself looking up wild hog attacks.

I learned that back in 2009, feral pigs were a big problem for virtually every county in the state. An article entitled "War against wild hogs rages on across Oklahoma" said that state wildlife services had been fighting an "uphill battle" for over a decade. To keep population levels in check, agriculture officials, ranchers, farmers, and homeowners banded together with the aim of killing seventy percent of the wild hog population in any given area. They developed a feral swine eradication program and authorized shooting razorbacks from helicopters and luring them into high-tech trap nets. In 2020, officials reported a kill count of approximately 21,000 hogs.

These animals spread disease and destroy pastures and crops, but do they attack humans?

The answer, unfortunately, is yes—sometimes.

Feral hogs are territorial, aggressive, and can weigh up to 700 pounds. They've been known to charge at hikers and hunters with their sharp tusks. In recent years, Oklahoma's feral pigs started reacting more oddly and unpredictably. The director of the state's wildlife services, Scott Alls, said the animals became "spookier" as humans and dogs pursued them. The article didn't provide more detail of what the hogs were doing that was spooky, but it did note that they were getting more active at night, which creeped me out.

It's certainly within the realm of possibility that the Jamisons faced such an attack, but that still wouldn't explain how they vanished. I imagined running the idea by Tim Graham, wondering if his response would be: "Ain't no hawg did that."

What Happened to the Jamisons?

A commenter in the Websleuths forums wrote: "The Jamisons were running from something, and it found them."

As I mulled over the threads of the Jamison case, trying to make sense of it all, I returned to this line again and again. It captures an almost ineffable sense of dark inevitability that permeates the family's story.

But what was "it"? In truth, the Jamisons were running from many entities, both real and imagined—a collapsing marriage, a family at war, a home haunted by grief and malevolent spirits, and possibly more threatening physical entities in the form of drug dealers, law enforcement, and his father's enemies.

The Jamisons ran from their fears, smack dab into something far worse on the mountain. Sherilyn believed in both the law of attraction and spiritual entities such as demons. But demons, unlike ghosts, don't haunt places, colloquially speaking—they haunt people, attaching to them and following them to the ends of the Earth. The Jamisons tried to escape the chaos and oppression of their past, but they brought it with them to the mountain. And with their choices, Bobby and Sherilyn consigned Madyson to a world without order, reason, or safety.

We don't have any clear, direct evidence of foul play against the Jamisons, but we do have a preponderance of evidence that the family was having a shared psychotic break. They withdrew Madyson from public school to live in a metal storage pod in the wilderness on a mountain known to host meth labs and armed landowners. It's hard to imagine any scenario in which that was going to be a healthy or sustainable experience for a child.

When I started writing, I felt a kinship with Sherilyn. She was a hard worker with a passionate spirit who struggled with an insidious illness, one that is woefully disregarded and stigmatized. I was lucky enough to find the right treatment and meds and have a solid support system. After two decades of struggling, I found respite and peace, and it was then, almost as if on cue, that a series of personal and professional albatrosses broke my way at the right time. Had things gone differently—had the dominoes fallen another way—it might have been me appearing as the cursed protagonist of a true-crime mystery.

Sherilyn wanted to get better, but a series of tragic accidents and conflicts derailed her.

Despite the credible allegations of negligence and disturbing behavior, I have sympathy for both her and Bobby. They got dealt a series of bad hands, lost the plot, lost their way, and then lost everything—as we all will someday. Without any external cues to guide them, they panicked, and in their attempts to cede back control, they unwittingly made the situation worse.

They tried to make their own luck and manifest a different destiny, a new beginning off the grid, away from people, in the church of the wild. But the venue they chose is lawless and unforgiving. Whatever they encountered took their briefcase, money, and firearm; then it took their lives.

THE LAST TIME I spoke to Dana, she told me that the remaining members of the beleaguered Jamison clan still occasionally talk about the strange case that swallowed up their lives. They still think Bobby, Sherilyn, and Madyson were killed, and they're still plumb puzzled at how there could be no answers.

They're also puzzled by the way they were treated and portrayed. All the outrageous conspiracies and allegations made their lives hellish and obstructed the search for the truth.

"Oklahoma people are salt of the Earth," Dana said, laughing in disbelief at the accusations against her father.

One of the reasons I wanted to write about the Jamisons was the tragic irony of such a reclusive family having their lives posthumously dissected from the inside out. Between the information released by law enforcement, family members and friends, the local news press, and web sleuths, three generations of family secrets were harvested and put on blast for the world to see.

Perhaps initially drawn by the flurry of buzzards circling the case, I came along hoping to understand who the family behind this story really was, and why their disappearance resonated with so many people.

The news paraded past the public's gaze like a jazz funeral—with maudlin stories and garish conspiracy theories. But after the spectacle passed, what remained? The husk of a family, an empty home overlooking the water, and a gut feeling not unlike a nursery rhyme recalled from childhood—something distant but hauntingly familiar.

In the course of their lives, most families struggle with crises like traumatic grief, marital discord and divorce, financial anxiety, chronic pain from injury or disease, child custody disputes, mental illness, substance abuse, inheritance fights, etc. But they usually don't face them all at once. The Jamisons remind us what can happen when people are pushed to the brink, when the nuclear family in the dream house by the lake comes apart at the seams.

There are countless biographies of families that we aspire to emulate. We seek in portraits projected reflections of what we wish to be. But we gravitate to the Jamisons because they remind us of who we are—flawed and suffering, a product of our experience and environment. They remind us that we are not always in control of our destiny, even when—perhaps especially when—we think we are.

THE IMPACT OF the Jamison case on law enforcement was galling, revealing a sheriff system ill-equipped and untrained to handle a triple-homicide investigation or complex missing-persons case.

The impact on the public and media was uncanny. Certain true-crime mysteries have the power to attract legions of obsessive web sleuths and citizen journalists who spend years digging into every detail and clue. Sometimes their efforts help identify missing persons or even solve decades-old cold cases. But in their zeal for the truth, they sometimes perpetuate falsehoods, weaving uncorroborated rumors, speculation, and conspiracy theories into the narrative, flustering both the families of victims and law enforcement.

In the Jamison case, it wasn't only web sleuths and media outlets doing this—the victims' family and law enforcement them-

selves perpetuated misinformation and uncorroborated speculation. Sheriffs and investigators consistently leaked prejudicial
details and characterized the Jamisons as scammers, drug addicts,
and death-obsessed kooks—claims that were uncritically published and ratified by journalists and media members. Family and
friends floated bizarre conspiracy theories about cults and white
supremacists.

The Jamisons' story became a kind of world-building exercise,
a collective anthology of morbid fan fiction accepting submissions
by everyone from armchair detectives and occult psychics to Sasquatch enthusiasts, catfishers, and LARPers. You see it in the
shifty saboteurs who contacted and misled Niki with stories of a
hit list and a white supremacist pedophile abducting Madyson.
You can see it in Mark's compulsive desire to see invisible satanic
cultists hidden in the pixels of the security video.

You see a more good-faith version even in Niki's crusade for
the truth. Driven by the powerful conviction that her friends were
killed, her mind began to manifest patterns that revealed the murderer's identity, suspecting first Klein, then Sweat, and finally D.C.

To varying degrees, Heather, Brett, and Reade did the same
as they pieced together intricate criminal conspiracies based on
insufficient evidence and fading memories. Using the same general field of clues and leads, they followed the patterns—and the
money—to three very different conclusions, each passionately certain of his or her truth.

Sherilyn Jamison herself saw synchronicity everywhere, even
as her life was spiraling into disorder.

In each of these stories, you see humans searching for patterns
that give meaning to the chaos, connecting the dots of a mystery.
Like the evolutionary panic triggered in the woods, we're biolog-
ically wired to make narrative sense of the world. But just as we
can omit and misapprehend fragments of reality, so, too, can we
manufacture them.

There is a psychological phenomenon scientists call illusory
pattern perception, which, similar to pareidolia and confirmation
bias, is the tendency to perceive or interpret meaningful patterns

where they don't exist. Faces in the static, messages in the noise—recent studies have suggested these are more likely to occur when people feel a lack of control. We can all see shapes in the clouds, but with illusory pattern perception, the government designed the clouds and are communicating through them.

We have always searched for patterns, since the earliest nights when prehistoric humans looked to the sky and saw constellations. Now that our lives are merging with the Internet, the greatest pattern-finding tool in history, it is easier than ever to not only search for patterns, but to find them, prove them, and build communities around them. And there are engagement algorithms and echo chambers that can weaponize those patterns.

Humans crave absolute truth, but—or perhaps *because*—we're surrounded by uncertainty.

In lost-person searches, Koester told me, uncertainty abounds. Statistical profiles can't account for unpredictable variations in human behavior.

Most of the people who go missing in the wilderness are categorized within broadly sketched parameters—children who run away from home; hunters who lose their orientation; hikers who become sick or injured; people with mental illness, dementia, or Alzheimer's; people who are intoxicated or under the influence of drugs; those who are despondent and/or suicidal, etc.

But over the years, Koester saw a handful of cases in which the lost didn't fit into any of the normal buckets—cases for which the how and why can't fully be understood, because the missing individuals exhibited such anomalous behavior or bizarre psychological motivations. For these, he introduced an addendum category called "vision quest," which he said may apply to the Jamison case.

Sfumato

The polymath Leonardo da Vinci developed a technique of painting called *sfumato*, meaning "lines or borders, in the manner of smoke," which he used to soften the transition between colors and tones. He wanted to imbue mystery into his compositions by imitating the blurry, peripheral plane beyond which the human eye can focus.

Over time, the meaning of *sfumato* expanded to become a philosophical principle, which author Michael J. Gelb defined as "a willingness to embrace ambiguity, paradox, and uncertainty," to "confront the vastness of the unknown and ultimately the unknowable."

I couldn't have learned about this idea at a better time. The essence of *sfumato*—living with ambiguity, exploring reality's infinite gray areas without the need to impose black and white certainty—feels like the antidote to the cosmic and existential horror of true crime. It's particularly pertinent to unsolved crimes or any mystery in which the need for certainty and control compels people to follow illusory patterns.

It's okay to say, "I don't know."

ON THE WAY back through Eufaula, we stopped for gas. As I stood leaning on my cane waiting for the tank to fill, I saw a family in a car; in the back seat was a young woman with bleached blond hair sitting beside the family dog.

I thought of Maisy, the only living witness in the Jamison case. She would be an old girl now, but I wondered if somewhere in her mind, locked away in a deep, inaccessible chamber of canine memory, perhaps she still retains the raw synaptic impressions of her family's final moments. I wonder what she saw and heard that day.

I also thought of Madyson, who would have turned twenty-one this year. I imagined a different timeline—one in which Bobby was never in an accident, Sherilyn's sister was never stung by a bee, and the Jamisons never went to Panola Mountain. Madyson, a junior in college, goes on her first pub crawl with friends. On holidays and long weeks, she and her big brother Colton return home to enjoy the picaresque beauty and recreation of Eufaula Lake with their free-spirited parents—Sherilyn, who runs her own successful hair salon, and Bobby, who renovates houses and fixes any broken appliance worth flipping.

I can imagine the Jamisons who might have thrived in a town that might have been.

As our time in Eufaula came to an end, Laura and I stood with our arms around each other, gazing out over the lake from the small white beach near the Jamisons' home. Somewhere out there, under the surface, was the submerged ghost grave of North Fork Town and the algae-eaten relics of old Eufaula.

In the marshy tributaries buttressing the shore, turtles snoozed on cypress knees. Occasionally they slipped off and splashed into the water, sending ripples in every direction across the reservoir. Even the tiniest of them would merge with the waves and follow the current back to shore.

We took the 2 past Robbers Cave State Park and headed away from Wilburton and Latimer County. We waved goodbye to Iron-head Country, Little Dixie, and southeast Oklahoma.

Still ensconced in the triple-canopy foliage of the Sans Bois Mountains, dense wildwoods caressed the road. A streak of white in the trees caught the periphery of my eye and, for a moment, it looked like there was woman in a flowing gown.

Like Tim Graham when he thought he saw a buck rub, my eyes deceived me.

It made me think of Peggy the Realtor, the Lady on the Mountain, trekking through the wilderness in search of the missing family. I recalled the stories of her scouring the high sticks for years after the search ended, hoping at first to find the Jamisons alive but ultimately seeking their remains and a modicum of closure.

Peggy died suddenly from a brain aneurysm shortly before the discovery in Smokestack Hollow. I imagined her restless spirit still roaming the mountaintop as caretaker, unaware of the news—perhaps unaware of her own death.

The Lady drifts in a long arc that comes full circle at sunset, when a blood-red sun falls behind the ribbon of hillside containing an abandoned shack and a plot of black concrete. It's hard to see it for the seething mass of buzzards, but the foundation crumbles a little more each day.

Source Notes

Chapter 2

14   **his mind automatically goes to drugs:** Investigation Discovery, *Disappeared*, "Paradise Lost" :58.

16   **According to the CDC, hypothermia:** "Hypothermia Deaths." Centers for Disease Control and Prevention blog.

17   **full-flown fight-or-flight catecholamine dump:** Bond, Michael. "From Here to There: The Art and Science of Finding and Losing Our Way."

17   **Researcher Jan Souman ... We can't help walking in circles:** "We Can't Help Walking in Circles," *New Scientist*.

17   **over ninety percent:** "Majority of Missing Persons Cases Are Resolved," npr.org.

18   **fifty-one hours:** Koester, Robert. *Lost Person Behavior*.

19   **raft particles ... Salt Lake City:** "How Does a Dog Track a Missing Person," thecaninetrainingcenter.com.

20   **disaster search dogs:** "The Legacy of 9/11 Dogs," akc.org.

21   **cadaver dogs' accuracy:** "Scent of a Dead Woman," slate.com.

21   **during an inquiry:** "The jaw-dropping footage of sniffer dogs alerting in McCann apartment and car," 9news.com.au.

21   **death scent:** "Researchers isolate compounds and esters given off by dying humans," psy.org; "Understanding the Scent of Death," psy.org; "The smell of death—its chemical pattern could become a powerful forensic tool," psy.org.

22   **Jacobson's organ:** "What Is the Jacobson's Organ (Vomeronasal Organ) in Dogs? Anatomy and Uses," petkeen.com.

Chapter 3

25   **tracking aspect is out:** "Mud slows hunt for missing 3," *The Daily Oklahoman* (Oklahoma City, Oklahoma), Oct 24, 2009: 13.

27   **during one stretch:** author's interview with Sheriff Woodruff.

27   **too risky:** "Search continues for missing family," *The Eufaula Indian Journal*, Dec 31, 2009.

28   **won't personally stop searching:** "Jamison family still missing," *The Eufaula Indian Journal*, Nov 5, 2009: 1.

28   **everything seems possible:** "Jamison family was threatened by relative before vanishing, records show," *The Oklahoman*, Nov 27, 2013.

29   **didn't look like to me:** "OSBI: Skeletal remains of 3 people found near where family vanished in '09," Newson6.com.

Chapter 4

30   **Spotlight Crime of the Week:** "Spotlight Crime of the Week," *The Eufaula Indian Journal*, Nov 26, 2009: 2.

32   **Madyson is looking away:** Family statements about Madyson picture; Brooks statements; "Missing Jamison Family."

32   **it doesn't make sense; other quotes:** "Witchcraft, white supremacists, meth labs or a family grudge? Inside America's most bizarre unsolved murder mystery five years after husband, wife and daughter, six, vanished in remote mountains," *Daily Mail*.

34   **3 cats killed:** "Witchcraft, white supremacists, meth labs or a family grudge?" *Daily Mail*.

35   **if you have a problem:** Investigation Discovery, *Disappeared*, "Paradise Lost."

37   **one man they jointly feared:** "Witchcraft, white supremacists, meth labs or a family grudge?" *Daily Mail*.

Chapter 5

Drawn from author's interviews with Niki Shenold.

Chapter 6

Drawn from author's interviews with Colton Mangum, Niki Shenold, and Chrissie Palmore.

Chapter 7

53   **Upbeat and friendly:** Investigation Discovery, *Disappeared*: "Paradise Lost."

53   **potential motive; Beauchamp quotes on case:** "Family's fate remains a mystery," *The Daily Oklahoman*, May 2, 2010: 3.

54   **plumb puzzled . . . don't think he was involved:** "Jamison family was threatened by relative before vanishing, records show," *The Oklahoman*, Nov 27, 2013.

54   Drawn from author's interviews with Jack Jamison.

56   **meth stats:** *The Oklahoman*.

Chapter 8

67   **cults and stuff like that:** "Mother believes religious cult is responsible for Oklahoma family's disappearance," *The Oklahoman*.

Chapter 9

69   **Brett quotes:** "Missing Jamison Family," *Keep the Search Alive*.

70   **Anadarko:** "Brutal killing of an Anadarko preacher before multicounty grand jury," News9.com.

Chapter 10

77   **Misinformation by omission:** "Why We Miss the Obvious," *Psychology Today*.

Chapter 11

79   **Murder on the Grill:** "Get your tickets today, find out who 'grills' Tom," Donna Pierce, *The Eufaula Indian Journal*, August 19, 2010: 1–3.

83   **Their ticket to freedom:** Investigation Discovery, *Disappeared*, "Paradise Lost."

85   **Brooks quotes:** "Missing Jamison Family," youtube.com.

87   **Eufaula remains . . . dental wear on these individuals:** "Forensic investigators say bones found at Lake Eufaula are 200 to 2,000 years old," News9.com.

Chapter 12

94   **Madyson's favorite color:** "Mother believes religious cult is responsible for Oklahoma family's disappearance," *The Oklahoman*.

94   **Ain't no coyote:** "Skeletal remains possibly those of missing family," *McIntosh County Democrat* (Checotah, Oklahoma), Nov 21, 2013: 2.

Chapter 13

104   **need closure:** "Mother believes religious cult is responsible for Oklahoma family's disappearance," *The Oklahoman.*

Chapter 14

107   **3,000 autopsies:** "The Entire History of the Autopsy," *Popular Mechanics.*
108   **crime of the century:** "Families offer clues in Albuquerque's 'crime of the century,'" *El Paso Times.*
117   **hardest type of murder to solve:** Rossmo, Kim D. *Geographic Profiling.* CRC Press, 2000: 130.

Chapter 15

124   **two different people:** "Witchcraft, white supremacists, meth labs or a family grudge?" *Daily Mail.*
127   **it is an amalgam:** "The Cause of Depression Is Probably Not What You Think," *Quanta Magazine.*
128   **prone to agitation:** "Violence in Bipolar Disorder," *Psychiatric Times.*

Chapter 16

134   **very dangerous man:** "Jamison family was threatened by relative before vanishing, records show," *The Oklahoman,* Nov 27, 2013.

Chapter 19

154   **probably shot them:** Prairiechicken.blogspot.com.
162   **cell log began; Jamison family timeline:** Websleuths.com.
166   **12,000 unsubstantiated claims:** "What Is Satanic Panic? Debunked '80s Conspiracy Theory Is Making a Return," Newsweek.com.

Chapter 20

168   **built on an Indian burial ground:** "Witchcraft, white supremacists, meth labs or a family grudge?" *Daily Mail.*

Chapter 21

181   **"multi-dimensional" sensation:** "What is pain?" *Science Focus.*

Chapter 22

187 **cartels monopolized ninety-five percent:** "Mexican drug cartels move on Oklahoma," oklahoman.com.

188 **scandal-plagued sheriffs:** "Oklahoma's Scandal-Plagued Sheriffs: A Sampling," oklahoman.com.

188 **corruption in office:** "Sheriff Arrested for Corruption," kfor.com.

189 **statewide fraud conspiracy:** "Commissioner Scandal Hurt State's Image," oklahoman.com.

189 **unchecked cronyism:** "Oklahoma Gets F Grade in State Integrity Investigation," publicintegrity.org.

189 **widespread corruption was exposed:** "Lawsuit: Police Used Coercion and Hid Evidence to Wrongfully Convict 7 of Murder," thedailybeast.com.

189 **'system-wide failure' of leadership:** "Oklahoma Sheriff's Office Had System-wide Failure of Leadership and Supervision," abajournal.com.

190 **bad throughout the entire South:** "How Corrupt Is Oklahoma Government?" oklahoman.com.

190 **goes back to the founding:** "Oklahoma troubled by long line of sheriff scandals," Boston.com.

Chapter 23

200 **it was shocking . . . something unnerving about him:** "Kevin Sweat Murdered Ashley Taylor and Two Kids in Oklahoma," oxygen.com.

204 **something you can't take away:** "Kevin Sweat Attacks Lawyer With Razor Blade Before Being Sentenced to 3 Life Terms," News9.com.

Chapter 25

227 **charging fourteen people with criminal conspiracy:** "14 Charged in Drug Conspiracy," MuskogeePhoenix.com.

228 **Mules were engaged to transport the drugs:** "Eufaula Resident Sentenced in Drug Conspiracy," archives.fbi.gov.

Chapter 26

230 **somebody like Heather:** "Heather Holland Helps Families Find Their Missing Loved Ones," people.com.

231 **If it wasn't for Heather:** "Mich. woman's hobby helps solve missing person cases," usatoday.com.

Chapter 27

246   **some kind of one-off deal:** "Witchcraft, white supremacists, meth labs or a family grudge?" *Daily Mail.*

246   **the monster you are:** "Crime Watch Daily: More Questions Than Answers in Jamison Family Disappearance," youtube.com.

246   **Bobby had recently gone to police:** "Witchcraft, white supremacists, meth labs or a family grudge?" *Daily Mail.*

253   **a peculiar kind of order:** "Chaos theory explained: A deep dive into an unpredictable universe," space.com.

255   **the legend states:** "Oklahoma's Long History With Bigfoot," edmondlife andleisure.com.

256   **Bigfoot's been very good:** "Bigfoot lore lures thousands of tourists to SE Oklahoma," Newson6.com.

258   **inspection of the dives and brothels called Eufaula:** Carey, James. "The First Ironhead: Eufaula Came After the Ironhead," *Lake Eufaula Reflections*: 143.

259   **loaded with riflemen:** *Lake Eufaula Reflections*: 7.

263   **bucket of the front-loading tractor:** "OSBI finds new evidence in missing woman's case," kjrh.com.

Chapter 30

288   **the "doomsday mom":** "Doomsday mom: Lori Vallow Daybell found guilty—here's what to know about the case," cbsnews.com.

Chapter 31

291   **shared psychosis:** "Shared Psychotic Disorder," National Library of Medicine (PubMed).

294   **a family obsessed with death:** "Jamison family was threatened by relative before vanishing, records show," *The Oklahoman*, Nov 27, 2013.

295   **most common cause of family murders:** "Study: family killers are usually men and fit one of four distinct profiles," wired.co.uk.

Chapter 33

313   **animals became "spookier":** "War against wild hogs rages on across Oklahoma," oklahoman.com.

319   **a willingness to embrace ambiguity:** "Leonardo da Vinci's Sfumato Principle: Embracing Uncertainty with Ease," highexistence.com.

Acknowledgments

THIS BOOK COULDN'T HAVE BEEN written without the involvement and insight of Niki Shenold and Colton Mangum, who dredged up painful memories to help me learn more about the lives of the Jamison family—I'm incredibly appreciative. I'm also grateful to Dana Jamison, who shared a trove of personal memories to help me construct a balanced portrait of the family and its history.

Additional special thanks go out to Reade Hogan, Kellie Hurst, Brett Faulds, Heather Holland, and my editor, Michaela Hamilton, and the great team at Kensington. As always, my eternal love and thanks go to my family and the amazing puppy dog Bella, a Shar-pei mix with the heart of a Pit.

My greatest thanks go to the love of my life Laura, who fills my heart with purpose and who I hope will marry me.

Discussion Group Questions

1. How do you feel about Sherilyn and Bobby Jamison? Do they remind you of people you know? Do you sympathize with the hardships they experienced? Do you believe they could have made better decisions? If so, how?

2. Both Colton and Niki experienced severed relationships with Sherilyn before her disappearance. Do you think their behavior after her disappearance was affected by those ruptures? Do you think each of them did their best to solve the mystery of the Jamisons' deaths?

3. Have you experienced the disappearance of a friend or family member? How does the Jamison case compare to others you have experienced or read about or viewed?

4. Do you feel the authorities did the best they could in their search for the Jamison family and investigation? If not, what else do you think could have been done?

5. Sheriff Beauchamp was convinced foul play was involved because of what was missing from the Jamisons' truck and the area where their remains were found. Do you agree with his belief? How would you explain the missing items?

6. How did mental illness affect the Jamisons, particularly Sherilyn? How did the stigma placed on it by the media and law enforcement affect the investigation? How does the author's portrayal of mental illness change over the course of the book? Do you think the concept of a "family delusion" applies to the Jamisons?

7. Do you think murder/suicide is a possible explanation in this case? If so, how do you think the events played out? Who was responsible?

8. Would you say Bobby and Sherilyn were good or bad parents? Were the Jamison adults negligent in taking Madyson to the wilderness? What do you think they were doing on the mountain?